Romance of Waterfalls

Northwest Oregon and Southwest Washington

by
Barbara L. Bloom
&
Garry W. Cohen

Illustrated by
Barbara L. Bloom

Outdoor Romance Publishing
Portland, Oregon

Romance of Waterfalls
Northwest Oregon and Southwest Washington

Copyright ©1998 Outdoor Romance Publishing
Portland, Oregon

Printed in the United States

Cover Art:
Front: South Falls at Silver Falls, oil painting on canvas, Barbara L. Bloom
Back: North Falls at Silver Falls, oil painting on canvas, Barbara L. Bloom
Spine: Computer modification of a portion of the North Falls painting

Library of Congress Catalog-In-Publication Data

Bloom, Barbara L., 1936-
    Romance of Waterfalls : Northwest Oregon and Southwest Washington
    by Barbara L. Bloom & Garry W. Cohen
        p.   cm.
    Includes Index.
    ISBN 0-9662756-0-8
    1. Waterfalls--Oregon--Guidebooks.   2. Waterfalls--Washington
    (State)--Guidebooks.   I. Cohen, Garry W., 1941- . II. Title.
    GB1425.07B56   1998
    551.48'4'09795--dc21
                                                                    98-11992
                                                                        CIP

Introduction

We began visiting and enjoying waterfalls many years ago. We quickly discovered several things: that they were fun and romantic, that we were inspired by them (to take photos, draw, write poems, etc.), that we were less aware of the exertion required to reach such delightful goals, and that few acquaintances were aware of any but a few of the falls. We became advocates for the unknown falls, taking friends and relatives with us and telling everyone about them. We became our own "Waterfall Advocacy Center". Eventually, we decided that a book was the best way to introduce the falls to everyone and to inspire them to see for themselves. This inspiration became *Romance of Waterfalls*.

Along the way, we discovered that lots of other people were inspired like us. Wow! We weren't the first to wonder at them and write poetically about them.

Meriwether Lewis wrote on April 9, 1806: "On our way we passed several beautiful cascades which fell from a great height over the 'stupendious' [sic] rocks. The most remarkable of these cascades falls about 300 feet perpendicularly over a solid rock into a narrow bottom of the river on the south side".

One hundred and ten years later, in 1916, Samuel C. Lancaster, designer of the Columbia River Highway, wrote: "God...fashioned the Gorge of the Columbia, fixed the course of the broad river, and caused the crystal streams both small and great to leap down from the crags and sing their never ending songs of joy."

If two such practical individuals as an army officer and an engineer could be so inspired and write so eloquently about waterfalls that we can see for ourselves today, then all of us—residents and visitors—should give the falls the opportunity to "sing their never ending songs of joy" to us. If you do, you'll never be the same.

Acknowledgments

A great number of people and organizations provided invaluable assistance during our years working on this book. It is impossible to thank everyone who helped us. A few, however, deserve special mention. They are in alphabetic order because we couldn't choose who should go before whom.

Pete Bond of the Oregon Parks & Recreation Department

Tina Chubbs & Regina Thomas of The Library of Congress

Sarah Cohen of SLC Design

Chuck Davis of Independent Living Resources

Charles "Chuck" R. Frayer of the U.S. Forest Service

Elaine Friedman of Portland Possibilities, Inc.

Donald J. Haines of Nature of the Northwest Information Center

John Knowles of the NW Wheelchair Athletic Association

Lewis A. McArthur, an expert on history, geography, and nature

Katherine McCanna of Far West Book Service

Maureen R. Michaelson of New Sage Press

John Osaki of the NW Interpretive Association

Jim Peterson of TRIPS, Inc.

William Sullivan of Navillus

Elizabeth Winroth of Oregon Historical Society

Clyde Zeller of the Oregon Department of Forestry

Garry's Family: Margot, Sarah, and Vivian

Barbara's Family: Allison, Erick, Troy, Tyler, Matthew, Angie, Tonya

Table of Contents

About Drawing by Barbara

Probably the most portable and inexpensive hobby of all is drawing. All it takes is a pencil and paper. There is so much pleasure to be found when you sketch while your hiking. It's much more flexible than the camera. You can leave out things (that branch is right in front of the falls), move things (that tree is to far to the left), combine things (I want the bridge and the falls). When you stop and draw what you are looking at, you see more, observe more details, and if, like me, you find shapes in clouds, you'll find shapes and faces in the water falling over the rocks.

I don't think I've ever met a child that didn't draw pictures. I don't know when or why adults stop drawing. They seem to develop a fear and say things like, "I can't draw a straight line with a ruler." No one can, and no one needs to. You don't have to be perfect. You're not trying to create something of professional quality, just have fun. Drawing isn't hard. Writing is a form of drawing. Just think of the underlying basic shape of the object, and don't be distracted by its texture. Add the texture last. Everything is built of combinations and variations of four basic shapes: the cone, cube, cylinder and sphere. Find those in what you want to draw and you will do just fine.

About Poetry by Garry

I do not know what it takes to be a poet. I do know that writing something down that expresses how you feel—that plays with ideas, emotions, and words—is very rewarding. It is especially enjoyable when faced with an event or experience that strongly affects you. Like drawing, it takes only a pad and pencil to write a poem. Try it. You'll like it.

Poems need to be read out loud. We hope that when you visit a waterfall, you will read the associated poem to your loved one. You'll like some of them and hate some of them. Some you'll understand and some won't make sense. Hopefully, you'll say "I can do better than that" and you will. Create your very own Book of Romance, filled with pictures, poems, descriptions, and memories to share, to save, to remember.

About the Maps

All maps are based upon official maps of various government agencies, including various counties and special districts, the State of Oregon, the State of Washington, U.S. Forest Service, the U.S. Bureau of Land Management, and the U.S. Geological Survey. The topographic maps are digitally enhanced portions of U.S.G.S "Quad" maps.

How to Use this Book

If you are relatively new at hiking

Before planning your visit, read the following sections:
How to Visit Waterfalls and Hike
Clothing
Shoes
Take-along
Dangers

For particular needs, read the following as appropriate:
Children
Pets
Accessibility
Food & Water

If you are new to Oregon and its rainforest

Before planning your visit, read the following sections:
Weather
Seasons
Dangers
Trail Etiquette
Care of the Environment

Next:

Look through the Trip Planner to select an area within an acceptable distance and find a waterfall with a suitable difficulty and time frame.

Then:

Use the section on the falls selected, follow the directions to its parking area, to the trail to the falls, and those to the falls itself.

Waterfall Types

Each waterfall has usually been described with its own terms rather than with a universal nomenclature. We have been unable to find a comprehensive descriptive system. We have, therefore, developed our own universal system of waterfall terminology:

Plunge: Falls on its own power with little or no effect of the cliff.
   Curtain Plunge: Falls straight down in wide curtain from straight top edge.
   Free Plunge: Falls through space without touching cliff or rocks.
   Arch Plunge: The force of the water carries it through the air in an arc.
   Contact Plunge: Touches cliff while falling (although virtually unaffected by it).
Slide: Slides over rock surface while falling. Differs from a contact plunge in that the surface has an effect upon it (e.g.: deflecting it).
   Steep Slide: Slides at a near vertical angle.
   Angle Slide: A slide which is at a noticeable angle from vertical.
   Arch Slide: The water follows a convex path.
   Concave Slide: A slide falls in which the surface gets less steep in a curved shape.
Tumble: A falls in which the water bounces over a row of blocks or descends a surface made like a stack of blocks, bouncing off different ones in turn.
Cascade: A falls which resembles a very steep stream bouncing over rocks.
Dimensional Terms: The following terms are applied to further define the types above.
   Narrow: Narrow in width compared to its height.
   Wide: Wide compared to its height.
   Very Wide: Much wider than its height, often resembling Niagara Falls.
   Square: Width and height seem similar in dimension.
   Spread: The width of the waterfall increases as it falls.
   Narrowing: The width decreases from top to bottom.
   Hourglass: The falls noticeably diminishes to a "waist', then increases to the base.

Individual falls often require combinations such as "Narrowing Free Plunge". Multiple tiers are described tier by tier from the top (eg: "Wide Free Plunge, Arch Plunge, Cascade".

How to Visit Waterfalls and Hike

A visit to a waterfall is an adventure filled with fun, romance, education, beauty, music, engineering, architecture, and art in an intricate and sophisticated system. It's good for your physical and mental health. It's an inspirational—even religious—experience.

When you visit any of the waterfalls in the book, your enjoyment will be enhanced if you follow a few basic guidelines. These are not hard and fast "rules" but suggestions.

1. Hike uphill at first rather than taking "reverse hikes". This way, you work hard to get to your goal and coast back. You can trick yourself into reaching your goal.
2. Take your time! A steady, continuous pace with time to enjoy everything around you is more enjoyable and healthful than dashing about like you're in the city.
3. See it all! As you exercise your powers of observation, you'll discover far more than you have been aware. This can increase your enjoyment of life outside the woods!
4. Stay together, it isn't a race! This is a group experience. There are delights to share!
5. Get wet, it's ok. It rains and waterfalls will spray you. Relax and enjoy it. Be a kid.
6. Slowly peel as you warm up, cover up as you cool. Wear layers of clothing which allow you to vary your warmth when warm up as you hike and cool off when you rest. Women shouldn't wear heavy pullover sweaters with little or nothing underneath.
7. Take every opportunity to hold hands, hug, kiss, and enjoy being together! Whether it's your lover, grandchild, or grandmother, make the most of your relationships.
8. Don't go anywhere or do anything if it scares you! Be realistic about any situation you encounter. Don't be frightened by insignificant threats, but if it seems scary, it is! Work together and stay together. If anyone thinks it's too dangerous, do not do it!
9. Look for your "second wind". At the beginning of a hike, you'll begin to feel pain, get short of breath, feel your heart beating faster, and feel you can't go on! Instead of giving up, take very small steps but keep going. Soon you'll notice you're still out of breath but it hasn't gotten worse! Eventually, it seems to get easier and you have forgotten your discomfort. Stay "warmed up" rather than letting your body cool down. Go slowly and you'll be amazed how far you can go on your "tank of gas"!
10. Take deep breaths, stretch, and loosen your joints as you maintain a steady pace You will noticeably improve general conditioning and range of motion, improve cardiac efficiency, strengthen bones (lessening effects of osteoporosis), reduce weight, change fat in undesirable places to muscle in desirable ones, increase energy and stamina, and improve overall health. You will stay mentally and physically young!
11. Match the hiking times in this book. There's no prize for getting there first. The prize is all around you!

Clothing

Hikers wear everything imaginable. There is no reason to purchase special clothing except perhaps for hiking boots. However, attention to a few guidelines can make your trip far more enjoyable, especially when you misjudge conditions to be encountered.

At all times, wear clothing which covers the arms and legs — no shorts, skirts, or short-sleeves. You can roll up long sleeves but it's hard to make short sleeves longer. Wear layered clothing — Shirt, sweater, jacket — allows varying protection and warmth. Shirts or blouses should button up rather than being "pull-over" to allow for further variation in temperature and protection. A heavy pull-over sweater becomes unbearably hot after exertion but embarrassing for women to remove. Gloves and scarves are a must in Winter.

Everyone should wear a water repellent jacket with a hood and lots of pockets on all but the hottest days. Most people are amazed that healthy adults can die of hypothermia in 50° weather. Just get wet and have no protection from the wind for a long enough time.

Always wear socks that protect your feet from blisters and your ankles from anything that can get between your shoe and your pants. Wool or wool blend socks are best because they continue to work even when wet. Your feet can get wet from sweat as well as water.

During Summer, a bathing suit under "hiking clothes" may be convenient for a cool plunge.

Shoes

Expect a long walk on uneven ground with sharp stones, wet and muddy conditions, the possibility of falling or stubbing your toes, and attack by thorns, poisonous plants, bugs, and miscellaneous debris.

Your shoes should protect feet from sharp stones, sticks, thorns, etc., keep them dry from external and internal moisture, provide good traction on loose and slippery materials, support your foot and ankle, and be light enough to avoid fatigue.

Generally speaking, a good hiking boot is the best choice. Make certain you have worn new ones enough so they won't act like "new shoes" with all the associated pain.

Never go hiking wearing dress shoes or high heels, which are too slippery, offer little protection for the foot, and invite ruining a good pair of shoes—no fashion statements!

You should also wear heavy, well padded socks which reach well above the ankle.

Take Along

Although one can visit virtually any of the waterfalls in this book without anything, a few items can improve your enjoyment and provide help in unforeseen circumstances.

A small backpack, like a school book bag, can be left in a closet or the car trunk with many items already loaded and can be carried without discomfort. "Fanny packs" can also be used for small items. Jackets with deep pockets can carry some of the load. Serious hikers use a different approach which is not the focus of this book.

Essentials:
1. A 2 litre plastic soft drink bottle filled with cold lemonade or fruit juice.
2. A change of sox for each hiker.
3. One or more damp wash cloths each in a zip-lock sandwich bag.
4. A large plastic garbage bag for each hiker — can act as rainwear or shelter.
5. A small towel.
6. Extra handkerchiefs.
7. A pocket knife.
8. Waterproof wooden matches.
9. Quartered oranges or other fruit in a zip-lock bag.

Valuable Additional items:
1. A small compass.
2. A U.S. Forest Service "quad" map of the area.
3. Cellular phone — for emergencies.
4. Small first aid kit containing bandages, disinfectant, tape, etc.
5. Camera
6. Binoculars
7. This book!
8. Bird book
9. Wildflower book
10. Length of rope (such as a woven clothes line)
11. Dry snacks such as granola, crackers, cookies, etc. in zip-lock bags.
12. A small picnic lunch.

For babies, very young children, and other special needs:
1. Diapers in zip-lock bags — they will stay dry and can be carried out in them.
2. A roll of toilet paper in a zip lock bag (with additional bags for carrying out).
3. Kleenex in zip-lock bags (with additional bags for carrying out).
4. Medications in tight bottles in zip-lock bags.
5. Folding drinking cup.
6. Walking stick — especially if the expected terrain is particularly rough for you.

Children

Visiting waterfalls can be an enriching and enjoyable experience for children and the adults who share the adventure. It fosters close interaction between generations, the fun of discovery, mutual respect, shared appreciation of beauty and nature, and it creates patterns of self reliance and cooperation. The absence of the distractions of modern life can, in itself, offer new perceptions of self worth, enjoyment, and achievement.

In addition to the basic needs of adult hikers, children have some special needs:
1. **You Are Most Important** — Your planning, preparedness, and behavior is the key. Be gentle, matter of fact about difficulties, encouraging, thrilled at achievements and discoveries, and one who guides so invisibly that everyone feels like the leader.
2. **Test or Practice Hike** — Take a "trial run" to discover some of the likely problems. If handled properly, kids will be anxious to go with you next time.
3. **Proper Clothing** — Children need clothing which protects them from extremes of weather and temperature, and which acts as a barrier against physical assault by poison oak and blackberries. Always be prepared for the inevitable unexpected.
4. **Proper Shoes** — Kids' feet deserve equal concern and equal quality shoes as adults. Kids also need good socks to avoid blisters and protect their ankles.
5. **Safety lessons** — Teach kids the rules of the trail: expressing fears, no unnecessary risks, no showing off, holding hands, staying together, staying in sight, and "stop, don't move!" Note: Using this warning for control dilutes it—perhaps with tragic results.
6. **Keep together** — Hiking together as a group and sharing experiences and discoveries is not only safer, it's lots more fun for the kids and for you.
7. **Tailor the hike to everyone's abilities** — Plan trips that challenge but not overwhelm.
8. **Take Along Appropriate Essentials** — Carry helpful and fun items for the kids.
9. **Take Along Activity Creators** — Camera, sketch pad and crayons, nature books, magnifying glass, maps, binoculars, etc.
10. **Leadership not Sympathy** — Use positive statements such as: "We're going hiking and you'll have a lot of fun." "You're doing great." "We're almost there."

Pets

Pets are allowed except when special closures are posted. You must observe restrictions, respect others, and use good sense. Assistance dogs are not pets or subject to pet rules.

The rules of hiking with pets (some legal, some just polite):
1. Pets must never be allowed off their leash.
2. Leashes must never be more than 6 feet long.
3. Pets must always be under your control.
4. Pets must not menace, frighten, or annoy others.
5. Pets may not be left alone for more than a short time, it's inconsiderate.
6. Pets should not be left alone in a vehicle.
7. Pets must be licensed and inoculated and should wear an identification tag.
8. All buildings on park grounds are off limits to all pets.
9. Any mess caused by your pet must immediately be cleaned up.
10. Pets should be kept on the trails like their owners to protect them and the park.
11. Anyone failing to control their pet, allowing it to be a nuisance or create a disturbance may be asked to leave the park. Please be considerate of others!

If you still want to take your pet, add these to the above list:
1. Go on several short hikes in a variety of situations first. Make sure he will be ok.
2. Always walk your pet (have him go to the john) before you start the hike.
3. Do not let your pet drink the water, play with dead animals, or mess with wildlife.
4. Remember, poison oak exudes a liquid which effects the skin and mucous membrane of both dogs and people. It can wait on your pet's fur or on clothes for you to touch!
5. Take water for your pet but not food unless its impossible for him to wait.

Food & Water

Humans can exist without eating for several days but require water much sooner. Water is especially important during exertion. Its lack can make you feel tired, dizzy, and faint.

1. In real emergencies, all of the hikes in this book put you in very close proximity to water. To save a life, the risk of infection is worth taking.
2. High energy emergency rations is worth carrying.
3. For the most part, carrying food and water is only a convenience. A healthy adult can take even the longest hikes in this book without any food or water and not be harmed. However, all hikes of over an hour are more enjoyable with a drink or snack.
4. A 2 litre soft drink container filled with lemon aid is sufficient for 4 people's needs.
5. Do not carry heavy, bulky, unnecessary junk. This may make the hike miserable for one or more of the participants. Keep it simple and light.

Weather

Temperature: Cool & Damp in Winter, Warm & Dry in Summer

Snow: Rare near sea level, likely in Winter at higher elevations.

Rain: Oregon's famous "liquid sunshine" rarely limits outdoor activities, especially hiking. A continuous light drizzle or mist is typical of a rainy day.

Hiking weather: Virtually any day of the year. Many waterfall enthusiasts find the rainy Winter season with more robust falls and fewer tourists to be the best.

Note: Getting wet or cold does not give you a cold or flu! So...give yourself and your kids a break. Have fun, don't worry, and if you get cold and wet, warm up and dry off.

Seasons

Avid hikers and waterfall lovers (and lovers, for that matter) have favorite seasons in which to follow their pursuits. The best season to visit waterfalls is:

Winter: When flow is greatest and the falls are their most beautiful; when the mosses and ferns make forest green; when lack of leaves reveal many falls; when poison oak can be ignored; when seasonal falls are added to the inventory; when solitude is greatest.

Spring: When the awakening of life makes your heart soar; when flowers burst forth; when flows are large and waterfalls beautiful; when every week brings changes.

Summer: When weather is warm and rain unlikely; when the sun makes rainbows in the falls; when berries and Summer flowers abound; when birds are teaching their young.

Fall: When temperatures moderate; when Fall berries are ripe; when birds are migrating; when leaves are turning and covering the trails with color; when solitude returns.

Seasons change with elevation, going back a week per 1000 feet. Regardless, every day is the most beautiful and uplifting day at a waterfall. There are no bad times to visit one.

Dangers

Enjoying the wonders of waterfalls is a healthy and safe activity. However, one must be careful. Indeed, every year a few people are injured or even die in the wilderness. All of life has risks. One can be struck by a meteor sitting in the living room. You should be aware, however, of both the real and imagined hazards on the trail and protect yourself.

If something looks dangerous, it probably is, even without a sign or fence. Four year olds to grand mothers hike safely. Most who get hurt are young, strong, healthy, and foolish!

Real Hazards:

1. **Stupidity** — In many cases of people getting lost or hurt in the wilderness, they make a simple, obvious mistake! Stupidity can be contagious. Sometimes an entire group agrees to do something totally, obviously nuts! Stupidity kills!
2. **Over-confidence** — Young, intelligent, healthy, athletic individuals often misjudge their capabilities. Many hikes in this book include life and death decisions: "Is my balance good enough?" or "How close to the edge should I go?" or "Are those rocks too slippery?", etc. etc., etc. Over-confidence is stupidity's best disguise!
3. **Getting too close to the edge** — Keep a safe distance from streams and slopes!
4. **Shortcuts** — Little ones destroy vegetation, dislodge rocks, create erosion, and cause shortcutters to get hurt. Big shortcuts are a major cause of lost hikers.
5. **Swimming** — Avoid drowning, suffering hypothermia from near freezing water, slipping on wet rocks, falling or diving on hidden rocks, or being swept off your feet or over a waterfall. 6 inch deep fast flowing water can knock you over.

6. **Drinking the water** — Avoid drinking from streams except to save life. Giardia is a water-borne protozoan parasite contracted by drinking infected water. Although uncommon, it results in months of nausea and diarrhea. Carry your own water!
7. **Athletics** — Climbing trees, doing cart wheels at the top of cliffs, racing down trails, and other ways of showing off are likely to cause injury to the miscreant and others.
8. **Car break-ins** — Always lock your car and don't bring or display "thief bait".
9. **Falling rocks, trees, etc.** — On the trails, you are surrounded by changing terrain caused by falling rocks and trees, earthquake, volcanos, landslide, and flood. One should be careful not to do anything which might dislodge rocks or cause trees to fall. Avoid places where and times when slides and falling rocks are most likely.
10. **Attack by bears, cougars, etc.** — Seeing a predatory mammal is very unlikely, but, if you do, move quietly and slowly away from it. They aren't from Disney!
11. **Catching a disease** — Although unlikely, there are four diseases which you could contract in the woods. The hanta virus is spread by rodents and is usually contracted by people handling live or dead rodents. Rocky Mountain Spotted Fever and Lime Disease are contracted by being bitten by an infected tick. Check yourself for ticks. Don't forget giardia could be waiting for you to drink from that stream!
12. **Getting lost** — If you stay on the designated trails, don't get separated (especially children), and don't go long distances through areas with which you are unfamiliar, this is very unlikely. If you feel lost, carefully retrace your steps, find a trail and follow it downhill until you find a road or people. Even if you go the wrong way, if you are on a trail, you will eventually find a road from which you'll find people and help.
13. **Hypothermia** — Possible if you get wet and cold for a protracted period of time. Wear proper clothing, take a towel along, and don't get lost!
14. **Poison Oak** — All parts of this plant exude a poison which causes itching and rash to any part of the body. Sensitivity varies between individuals. Wear long sleeves and pants and do not get the poison on you from your clothing. If you touch it, immediate washing, even with plain water, will usually eliminate the poison and its effects.

Emergencies

Even in the wilderness, a network of professionals stands ready to deal with emergencies of all kinds. Of paramount importance, however, is to save the victim from the immediate emergency and to notify appropriate emergency services that you need them.

1. First, secure the safety of the injured person if this is possible and practical without endangering others or running the risk of making things worse.
2. If help is needed, carefully determine where you are.
3. Use cellular phone and dial "911" or send someone to find help. Carefully discuss what they are to do and where they will go and what they will do if they can't find anyone. If desirable, write a note for them to give rescuers.
4. If the emergency is a lost member of your party, leave someone at the point where the person is most likely to find you. Avoid leaving the area.
5. Use other hikers, flag down passing vehicles, knock on someone's door or anything else you can do to immediately contact the very able and ready rescue services.
6. Consult the listing of emergency facilities listed in the back of this book.

Trail Etiquette

There are rules to which you should adhere for your own enjoyment and that of others:
1. Behavior which is rude, endangers others, or harms the environment is contagious. Walk a few steps off the trail to sniff a flower and return a year later to find that hundreds followed your footsteps leaving nothing but mud where once was beauty.
2. Be quiet. Noise carries far but the sounds you want to hear are easily drowned out.
3. Cheerfully say hello to everyone you pass on the trail.
4. Inform those you pass of any unusual hazards they will encounter on the trail ahead.
5. Ask directions if necessary but avoid inconsequential small talk.
6. Offer aid to anyone obviously having trouble.
7. Share information and supplies with anyone who may need them.
8. Stay on trails! Never take shortcuts, or go where you were not intended to go. Such behavior may result in injury to you, to others on the trail, or to the environment.
9. Never throw anything—not rocks, sticks, or trash.
10. Do not litter. Carry away everything you bring with you.
11. Remove nothing from its natural state and hurt nothing. Our only exception is something which has fallen on the trail and will be destroyed. Be careful not to set a bad example, however. Note that there are specific restrictions in certain sensitive areas. Never dig plants, pick flowers, step on slugs, turn over rocks in streams, etc.
12. No running. It's a great way to hurt yourself and others and frighten wild life.

13. These excursions can be wonderful for kids and pets but the same rules apply to them as to you. You are responsible for their behavior.
14. Warn others against serious hazards, give directions to the lost, scold the seriously thoughtless, and help the injured but leave others to nature's peace and quiet.

Care of the Environment

The pleasure of everyone visiting waterfalls depends upon the behavior of all visitors. Nature causes many changes but man can make the most glorious Eden into a miserable dump with graffiti, vandalism, trash, shortcuts, and other thoughtless acts. Please leave no mark on the environment (unless it's to repair or remove someone else's misdeed).

Garbage — Whatever you take into the woods, leave nothing behind. Pack out all wrappers, cans, tissues, banana peels, etc. Zip-lock bags make excellent garbage holders.

Excretion — Unless absolutely necessary, only use proper restrooms. In the event of an emergency, go well away from trails or streams and bury all excretion products.

Walking off trails — When you step off the trail, you are standing on plants and animals which may not survive, you are compacting soil which should be loose or disrupting soil which will slide, threatening the safety of others with rocks that may fall, jeopardizing your own safety, and, most important of all, altering the environment of this wonderful, natural setting in ways which may not be immediately apparent.

Picking or digging plants — Perhaps long ago your mother told you something like: "If everybody did that, there wouldn't be any left!" Sadly, this very event has occurred for many plants and animals in the wilderness. Some of the most magnificent flowers are now rare because of the misguided "love" of visitors.

Grabbing off leaves as you walk — This behavior is unsightly and robs everyone of the natural beauty. If you insist on doing this, eventually you'll grab devils club, brambles, poison oak, or stinging nettle. They may convince you otherwise!

Chopping trees — Green (fresh) wood makes terrible firewood, chopping down trees is hard work, disturbing anything like this is illegal in these parks, open fires are restricted, and this is a really dumb and destructive thing to do.

Turning over rocks — Aside from the possibility of starting a slide or causing other obvious harm, rocks support an entire community of plants and animals which need not be disturbed by us.

Graffiti — What can we say? If you write, paint, or carve anything out here, you are creating an obvious obnoxious eyesores.

Vandalism — Construction of conveniences in the wild is difficult and expensive—trail, bridge, restroom, guard rail, sign—but easy to destroy. Please resist such stupidity!

Civic Responsibility — It is your duty as a citizen and a lover of nature to correct problems you encounter (pick up garbage, move downed limbs, etc.), to act to stop or prevent inconsiderate acts of others (often by something as simple as just saying: "Hi, can I help you?"), and to report dangerous and destructive behavior to proper authorities. Remember: "Evil exists where good people are silent."

Accessibility

We have very rarely seen anyone in a wheelchair visiting a waterfall. We cannot fully appreciate the needs and concerns of those with physical limitations different from ours. Nevertheless, we believe that lack of information and the verbal "barriers" erected by those who see limitations rather than challenges discourage the physically challenged.

It dawned on us one day that only a percentage of the hikes we describe have absolute barriers such as stairs or too narrow passages except for the physical exertion that is required of anyone. Therefore, among the headings for each falls, we list "Accessibility" under which we tell whether the falls can be viewed from the road or parking area and whether there are real barriers which would absolutely prevent a wheelchair from reaching the points described. Difficulties, hazards, and challenges are described as best as we can.

We hope that, in the future, stairs can be eliminated, trails will be widened, slopes mitigated, and other barriers diminished for the advantage of us all.

Accessible Falls

Falls which are visible from roads are trails which are reasonably accessible to those in wheelchairs, who are physical challenged in comparable ways, or just want to sightsee.

#	Falls Name	Accessibility
1	Latourell Falls	Visible from road and accessible trail
3	Sheppards Dell	Visible from paved bridge
6	Mist Falls	Visible from road
7	Wahkeena Falls	Visible from paved parking and marginally accessible trail
9	Multnomah Falls	Visible from paved viewpoint and marginally accessible trail
15	Horsetail Falls	Visible from paved parking and accessible viewpoint
21	Munra Falls	Visible from wide, level gravel trail
36	Starvation Creek Falls	Visible from accessible paved trail
37	Cabin Creek Falls	Visible from accessible trail
38	Hole in the Wall Falls	Visible from marginally accessible trail
39	Lancaster Falls	Visible from freeway
40	Wah Gwin Gwin Falls	Visible from SR 14 across Columbia and at top of falls
41	Punchbowl Falls	Visible from reasonable accessible dirt trail
42	Dead Point Creek Falls	Visible from reasonable accessible dirt trail
43	Salmon Falls	Visible from paved bridge
44	Dougan Falls	Visible from paved bridge
45	Steep Creek Falls	Visible from roadside parking
51	Curly Creek Falls	Visible from accessible trail and viewing platform
52	Miller Falls	Visible from accessible trail and viewing platform
53	Big Creek Falls	Visible from accessible trail.
54	Lower Lewis River Falls	Visible from accessible trail and viewpoint.
58	Twin Falls	Visible from campground viewpoint
59	Big Spring Creek Falls	Visible from road and parking area.
60	Dog Creek Falls	Visible from roadside parking area
64	Fishhawk Falls	Visible from parking lot and road
65	Youngs River Falls	Visible from roadside viewpoint
66	Lee Falls	Visible from gravel trail
67	University Falls	Visible (poorly) from road
68	Fern Rock Creek Falls	Visible for road and parking area
69	Bridge Creek Falls	Visible from roadside parking viewpoint
71	Falls City Falls	Visible from cliffside fence in small grassy park near street.
72	Willamette Falls	Visible from paved bridge and roadside viewpoints
74	Sahale Falls	Visible from paved bridge and from highway
79	Sullivan Creek Falls	Visible from roadside viewpoint
80	Whispering Falls	Visible from campground viewpoint
81	North Falls	Visible from parking viewpoint on road.
82	Upper North Falls	Visible from accessible paved trail.
89	South Falls	Visible from accessible paved viewpoint.
95	Majestic Falls	Visible from accessible viewing platform
97	Sahalie Falls	Visible from accessible trail and viewing platform.
98	Koosah Falls	Visible from accessible trail and viewing platform.
99	Salt Creek Falls	Visible from accessible viewing platform

Waterfall Trip Planner
3 Hour Excursions

The following waterfalls represent an abbreviated, less than a half day total outing from Portland, including driving time, walking to the falls, a short stay, and trip home.

#	Falls Name	Section	Description
1	Latourell Falls	I. W. Oregon Gorge	Short walk to two viewpoints
2	Upper Latourell Falls	I. W. Oregon Gorge	Medium uphill hike at Latourell
3	Sheppards Dell	I. W. Oregon Gorge	Beside road with short walk
4	Bridal Veil Falls	I. W. Oregon Gorge	Short reverse hike
5	Coopey Falls	I. W. Oregon Gorge	Medium uphill hike
6	Mist Falls	I. W. Oregon Gorge	Beside road and/or short hike
7	Wahkeena Falls	I. W. Oregon Gorge	Beside road and short walk
9	Multnomah Falls	I. W. Oregon Gorge	Steep uphill hike
10	Little Multnomah Falls	I. W. Oregon Gorge	At top of Multnomah (uphill)
14	Oneonta Falls	I. W. Oregon Gorge	Walk through water
15	Horsetail Falls	I. W. Oregon Gorge	Beside road
16	Ponytail Falls	I. W. Oregon Gorge	Medium uphill hike; walk behind!
17	Upper Oneonta Falls	I. W. Oregon Gorge	Past Ponytail, medium hike
19	Elowah Falls	I. W. Oregon Gorge	Steep uphill and downhill hike
20	Upper McCord Creek Falls	I. W. Oregon Gorge	Steep uphill hike with Elowah
21	Munra Falls	I. W. Oregon Gorge	Level short walk
22	Wahclella Falls	I. W. Oregon Gorge	Medium hike (beyond Munra)
23	Metlako Falls	II. Eagle Creek	Medium hike
29	Ruckel Creek Falls	II. Eagle Creek	Short hike
35	Gorton Creek Falls	III. E. Oregon Gorge	Miserable, short scramble
36	Starvation Creek Falls	III. E. Oregon Gorge	Short walk next to rest area
37	Cabin Creek Falls	III. E. Oregon Gorge	Short walk near Starvation
38	Hole in the Wall Falls	III. E. Oregon Gorge	Short hike past Cabin
39	Lancaster Falls	III. E. Oregon Gorge	Medium hike past Hole in Wall
40	Wah Gwin Gwin Falls	III. E. Oregon Gorge	Short walk in hotel parking lot
41	Punchbowl Falls	III. E. Oregon Gorge	Short walk
42	Dead Point Creek Falls	III. E. Oregon Gorge	Short walk past Punchbowl
43	Salmon Falls	IV. W. Washngtn Gorge	Seen from bridge — fish!
44	Dougan Falls	IV. W. Washngtn Gorge	Seen from bridge and walk
45	Steep Creek Falls	IV. W. Washngtn Gorge	Seen from bridge
48	Sweeney Falls	IV. W. Washngtn Gorge	Short steep walk
49	Panther Creek Falls	V. Wind/White Salmon	Short steep reverse hike
60	Dog Creek Falls	V. Wind/White Salmon	Short walk next to road
64	Fishhawk Falls	VI. Oregon Coast Rng.	Short walk
67	University Falls	VI. Oregon Coast Rng.	Short reverse hike
68	Fern Rock Creek Falls	VI. Oregon Coast Rng.	Next to roadside parking
69	Bridge Creek Falls	VI. Oregon Coast Rng.	Short walk from roadside
71	Falls City Falls	VI. Oregon Coast Rng.	Short walk
72	Willamette Falls	VII. N. Valley/Cascades	Several roadside viewpoints

4 Hour Excursions

The following waterfalls represent a somewhat longer, less than a half day total outing from Portland, including driving time, walking to the falls, a short stay, and trip home.

#	Falls Name	Section	Description
8	Fairy Falls	I. W. Oregon Gorge	Medium steep uphill hike
11	Dutchman Falls	I. W. Oregon Gorge	Beyond long, steep uphill hike
18	Triple Falls	I. W. Oregon Gorge	Beyond Upper Oneonta
24	Punch Bowl Falls	II. Eagle Creek	Beyond Metlako
30	Dry Creek Falls	III. E. Oregon Gorge	Medium long hike
46	Hardy Falls	IV. W. Washngtn Gorge	Medium steep hike
47	Rodney Falls	IV. W. Washngtn Gorge	Medium steep hike (past Hardy)
51	Curly Creek Falls	V. Wind/White Salmon	Short walk
52	Miller Creek Falls	V. Wind/White Salmon	Short walk
53	Big Creek Falls	V. Wind/White Salmon	Short walk
54	:lower Lewis River Falls	V. Wind/White Salmon	Short hike
65	Youngs River Falls	VI. Oregon Coast Rng.	Roadside view and/or short hike
66	Lee Falls	VI. Oregon Coast Rng.	Long, easy hike
70	Munson Creek Falls	VI. Oregon Coast Rng.	Short hike
73	Ramona Falls	VII. N. Valley/Cascades	Medium/long hike
74	Sahale Falls	VII. N. Valley/Cascades	Roadside viewpoint
75	Umbrella Falls	VII. N. Valley/Cascades	Short hike
77	Salmon Falls	VII. N. Valley/Cascades	Short hike
78	Henline Falls	VII. N. Valley/Cascades	Medium hike
79	Sullivan Creek Falls	VII. N. Valley/Cascades	Roadside viewpoint
80	Whispering Falls	VII. N. Valley/Cascades	Views from campground
81	North Falls	VIII. Silver Falls St. Pk.	Roadside view or steep hike
82	Upper North Falls	VIII. Silver Falls St. Pk.	Short hike
88	Winter Falls	VIII. Silver Falls St. Pk.	Roadside view or steep hike
89	South Falls	VIII. Silver Falls St. Pk.	Short walk or steep hike
90	Frenchie Falls	VIII. Silver Falls St. Pk.	Short hike on way to South Falls
92	Lower McDowell Creek Fall	IX. Mid Valley/Cascades	Short hike
93	Royal Terrace Falls	IX. Mid Valley/Cascades	Short hike
94	Crystal Pool	IX. Mid Valley/Cascades	Medium hike
95	Majestic Falls	IX. Mid Valley/Cascades	Medium hike

5 Hour Excursions

The following waterfalls represent a even longer, more than a half day total outing from Portland, including driving time, walking to the falls, a short stay, and trip home.

#	Falls Name	Section	Description
12	Weisendanger Falls	I. W. Oregon Gorge	Uphill hike beyond Multnomah
13	Hidden Falls	I. W. Oregon Gorge	Beyond Weisendanger
32	Falls Creek Falls	I. W. Oregon Gorge	Medium/long hike
55	Copper Creek Falls	V. Wind/White Salmon	Short hike
56	Middle Lewis River Falls	V. Wind/White Salmon	Short hike
57	Taitnapum Falls	V. Wind/White Salmon	Medium hike
58	Twin Falls	V. Wind/White Salmon	View from campground
59	Big Spring Creek Falls	V. Wind/White Salmon	View from roadside parking
61	Little Goose Creek Falls	V. Wind/White Salmon	Medium Hike
62	Langfield Falls	V. Wind/White Salmon	Short hike
63	Outlet Falls	V. Wind/White Salmon	Short walk

Waterfall Trip Planner

83	Twin Falls	VIII. Silver Falls St. Pk.	Medium hike past North
84	Middle North Falls	VIII. Silver Falls St. Pk.	Medium hike past Twin
91	Lower South Falls	VIII. Silver Falls St. Pk.	Medium hike past South
96	Lower Soda Falls	IX. Mid Valley/Cascades	Medium/Long hike
97	Sahalie Falls	IX. Mid Valley/Cascades	Short walk
98	Koosah Falls	IX. Mid Valley/Cascades	Short walk

6 Hour Excursions

The following waterfalls represent a still longer, more than a half day total outing from Portland, including driving time, walking to the falls, a short stay, and trip home.

#	Falls Name	Section	Description
25	Loowit Falls	II. Eagle Creek	Medium/long past Punch Bowl
31	Pacific Crest Falls	III. E. Oregon Gorge	Medium/long hike past Dry
33	Camp Creek Falls	III. E. Oregon Gorge	Medium long hike on HermanCrk
50	Falls Creek Falls	V. Wind/White Salmon	Medium/long hike
76	Tamanawas Falls	VII. N. Valley/Cascades	Medium/long hike
85	Drake Falls	VIII. Silver Falls St. Pk.	Medium/long past Middle North
86	Double Falls	VIII. Silver Falls St. Pk.	Medium/long past Drake
87	Lower North Falls	VIII. Silver Falls St. Pk.	Medium/long past Double

7 Hour Excursion

The following waterfall represents a long, nearly a full day total outing from Portland, including driving time, walking to the falls, a short stay, and trip home.

#	Falls Name	Section	Description
99	Salt Creek Falls	IX. Mid Valley/Cascades	Short walk

8 Hour Excursion

The following waterfalls represent a full day total outing from Portland, including driving time, walking to the falls, a short stay, and trip home.

#	Falls Name	Section	Description
26	Skoonichuk Falls	II. Eagle Creek	Long hike beyond Loowit
100	Diamond Creek Falls	IX. Mid Valley/Cascades	Medium hike

9 Hour Excursion

The following waterfall represents a fuller day total outing from Portland, including driving time, walking to the falls, a short stay, and trip home.

#	Falls Name	Section	Description
34	Slide Creek Falls	III. E. Oregon Gorge	Long hike past Camp Creek

10 – 12 Hour Excursion

The following waterfalls represent a very full day total outing from Portland, including driving time, walking to the fall, a short stay, and trip home.

#	Falls Name	Section	Description
27	Tunnel Falls	II. Eagle Creek	Very long hike past Skoonichuk
28	Eagle Creek Falls	II. Eagle Creek	Very long hike, past Tunnel

Northwest Oregon & Southwest Washington

Thanks to the combination of geologic and weather conditions, an amazing number of truly beautiful waterfalls can be found in this region.

In this book there are 40 falls on the Oregon side of the Columbia River Gorge (#1–#40), 20 falls on the Washington side near the gorge and up to the upper Lewis River, (#43–#62), 11 falls at Silver Falls State Park near Salem at Silverton (#83–#93). The remainder are distributed from Astoria to southeast of Eugene, from the coast to the crest of the Cascades. All are within what we have proven to be a day trip from Portland. Most would also be a day trip from other cities within the region, such as Eugene, The Dalles, Olympia, or Yakima. Of course, a weekend trip with an overnight stay in a motel or campground extends the possibilities to those from Seattle, Boise, or perhaps even Tokyo, and London!

Native Americans revered the waterfalls for their beauty and spiritual qualities. Many of these falls were discovered and described by early explorers such as Lewis and Clark as well as by settlers. During the late nineteenth and early twentieth century, great numbers of people took waterfall viewing and hiking excursions by train and steamer from Portland to Bridal Veil and several landing in the gorge including Oneonta and Bonneville. After the turn of the century, civic leaders, especially in Oregon, became interested in preserving and displaying natural wonders, including the waterfalls.

One unique expression of such concern for the environment and public access to it is the tale of the first and only state park ever located in another state! Early in the century, civic

Osprey

leaders such as Sam Hill and Simon Benson became especially interested in the Columbia Gorge. Their efforts resulted in the great manmade wonder of the world The Columbia River Scenic Highway, which opened on July 6, 1915. Meanwhile, Beacon Rock, an 800 foot high monolith on the Washington side of the Columbia first seen and named by Lewis and Clark in 1806, was purchased by Henry J. Biddle, who built a 4,500 foot long stairway to the top. In 1931, Biddle's heirs offered it to the governor of Washington as a park to avoid its being sold to the Corps of Engineers to be quarried for construction rock. The governor refused! The potential destruction of so important a landmark enraged Oregonians. At the suggestion of the Oregon Parks Department, it was purchased by J.C. Ainsworth of Portland and donated to the State of Oregon who accepted it as an Oregon State Park—the

---

Trip to the Falls

Reading directions and peering at maps,
We stalk the wild waterfall.
Watching for landmarks and counting the miles,
Our goal is nearly in sight.

Walking together and spending the day,
We stroll the trail to the falls.
Laughing and loving, enjoying the time,
Discovering our love and our souls.

---

first and only state park in the world to be located in a different state! Ultimately, widespread publicity was so embarrassing to the State of Washington and its elected officials that Beacon Rock (Oregon) State Park was finally accepted as a Washington State Park. Bickering between the two states over the environment and particularly the Columbia River Gorge continue to this day!

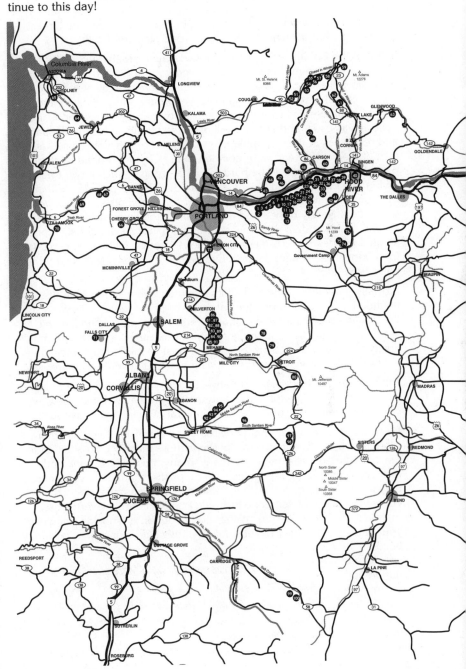

I. West Columbia Gorge of Oregon

The Columbia River Gorge is one of the great natural wonders of the world. On the Oregon side, a narrow strip of land little more than a mile wide by 40 to 50 miles long contains 77 recognized waterfalls. Unfortunately, a third or so of them cannot be reached for one reason or another. Those which are described in this book offer you the largest number and assortment of waterfalls in one place on Earth.

In 1916, the Columbia River Highway was built largely by the city of Portland, in large measure to provide access to the waterfalls. The men who raised the money, donated the land, designed, engineered, and constructed this remarkable highway were much more dedicated to the beauty of nature and to social responsibility than one has been lead to believe was usual at that time. All of the waterfalls, hiking trails, parks, and rest areas in the Columbia River Gorge were privately owned at the turn of the century and were donated to the City of Portland by their owners. In fact, it would be hard to find a group of such fervent nature loving and civic minded businessmen in our present decade. Without their unselfish attitude, every waterfall, beach, and other natural wonder would be privately owned and might well be totally unavailable to the public. One wonders what this area might be today without such public spirited forebears—turnstiles, curio shops, motels, billboards, neon, fast food franchises, condominiums, hydroelectric power plants run by the falls? Who knows?

Virtually the entire gorge and all its many attractions are within the boundaries of one or more special reserves or preserves. Please respect the remarkable beauty and unique diversity of geologic and biologic features. Driving through the gorge, you will witness evidence of man's ability to destroy and to preserve. Your goal should be to appreciate everything but to leave everything as if you had never been there.

Although there are similarities between falls, you will find each to have its own unique character and beauty. After you have visited a few, you will discover that you have declared several of them "your favorite"!

By the way, as you visit the gorge, don't be surprised if you see many more falls than described here (perhaps more than 77). In addition to the "recognized" falls, there are many, many more which apparently lack some criteria for recognition. Perhaps they don't flow year round, they're too small, their flow is too low, they're manmade, they change course too often, or someone just didn't notice them! Nevertheless, their lack of respect by the "Waterfall Hall of Fame" shouldn't diminish your enjoyment of their beauty. Many of these unappreciated falls may become spectacular during periods of high stream flows, made picturesque by snow, or transformed

> ## The Benefits of Waterfalls
> You'll find a benefit at every falls.
> Some go there for the exercise and some for natural science.
> Perhaps you'll see the face of God or learn to love more fully.
> No matter what your goal,
> An open mind and heart will have much more to find.

into amazing ice sculptures by rarely occurring freezing temperatures.

The historic Columbia River Scenic Highway was promoted by a great number of people of both high and low status. Samuel C. Lancaster, its designer, traveled extensively in Europe studying their roads. His experience inspired him to pattern the road after those he saw in Germany and Switzerland, unobtrusively curving its way through the landscape and closely approaching the scenic wonders with turnouts for attractions, arched rock railings, tunnels, and graceful bridges. It was for many years the only paved road in Oregon and the first scenic highway in the United States.

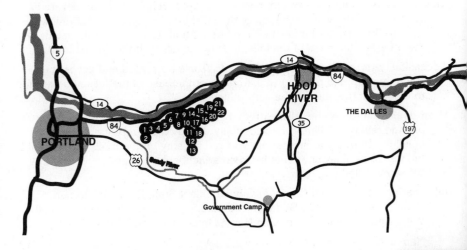

West Columbia Gorge of Oregon

1 Latourell Falls

A Stately Plunge in a Grand Bowl with Great Views Close By

Height: 249'   **Difficulty:** 4 to top; 1 to base   **Romance:** 7

Type: Narrow Free Plunge.

Description: Latourell Falls is a magnificent plunge from an overhanging lip of the cliff. The water plunges into a rocky pool in a beautiful deep canyon, creating billows of spray which frequently drenches the trail and the scenic bridge which spans the creek just downstream. Visitors often pick their way along a rocky ad hoc trail to a spot somewhat behind the falls to enjoy a soaking (and a romantic kissing spot).

Distance/Time From Portland: 32 miles, 35 minutes via I-84 and Scenic Highway.

Directions to Parking/Trailhead: I-84 east to exit 28 (Bridal Veil) (east bound only, with entrance west bound only). Westbound visitors (as from Hood River), go west to Rooster Rock State Park exit, re-enter freeway Eastbound. From exit 28, proceed to Scenic Highway, then go right, west, for 3.5 miles until Latourell sign seen on left. At milepost 13.8 of the Scenic Highway. The large, paved parking lot is beside the road.

Distance/Time From Parking: Top of falls: 10 minutes; bridge at base of falls: 5 minutes or less.

Distance/Time From Other Landmark: 2 miles drive from Sheppards Dell (#3).

Directions From Parking: Paved trail to base of falls leads directly from west end of parking lot; paved trail to elevated viewpoint ascends steeply from near the southwest corner of parking lot; unpaved trail to top of falls begins at elevated viewpoint. Trail to base of falls continues across bridge to park and picnic area northwest of falls area.

Elevation Change: To top: 225 feet; To base: 50 feet.

Restroom: In Latourell Picnic area on north side of road on west side of bridge, seasonal; 3 mile east at Bridal Veil Park; year round, modern.

Picnic Area: Excellent, large picnic area in Latourell Park near parking.

View & Kissing Spots: From the road as you approach the falls; at elevated viewpoint on the way to the top of the falls; from virtually the entire lower trail (to the base of the falls) and the upper trail (to the top of the falls); on the bridge at the base of the falls; next to the falls (off the official trail).

Accessibility to the Physically Challenged: Visible from road and accessible (though steep and narrow) to the bridge at the base of the falls and perhaps to the top of the falls for the very athletic.

Hazards: At the top of the falls, extremely dangerous unauthorized viewpoints provide real possibilities of accidentally diving off the top of a 25 story building. Unless you are certain you can fly, stay on the trail! On the trail to the top of the falls, shortcuts between switchbacks can endanger those below by dislodging rocks.

Information: On Latourell Creek, in Guy W. Talbot State Park, Multnomah County, Oregon, USGS Bridal Veil Quadrangle; Green Trails Maps: Bridal Veil, listed in USGS Geographic Names Information System.

Named for Joseph Latourell, an early settler of the area and postmaster in

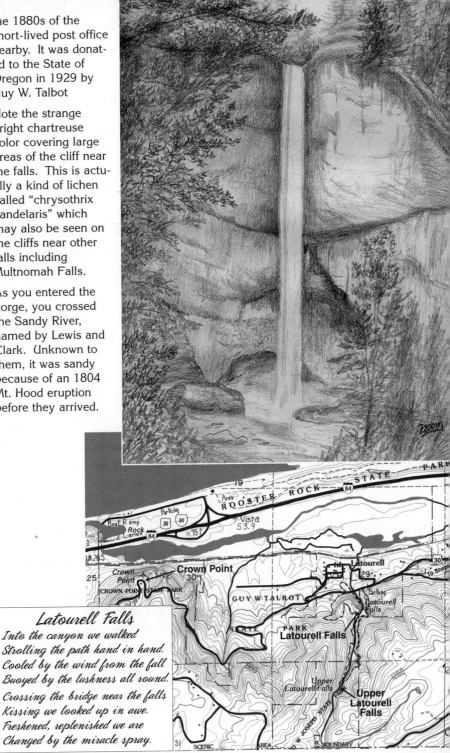

the 1880s of the short-lived post office nearby. It was donated to the State of Oregon in 1929 by Guy W. Talbot

Note the strange bright chartreuse color covering large areas of the cliff near the falls. This is actually a kind of lichen called "chrysothrix candelaris" which may also be seen on the cliffs near other falls including Multnomah Falls.

As you entered the gorge, you crossed the Sandy River, named by Lewis and Clark. Unknown to them, it was sandy because of an 1804 Mt. Hood eruption before they arrived.

Latourell Falls

Into the canyon we walked
Strolling the path hand in hand.
Cooled by the wind from the fall
Buoyed by the lushness all round.
Crossing the bridge near the falls
Kissing we looked up in awe.
Freshened, replenished we are
Changed by the miracle spray.

2   Upper Latourell Falls

A Striking Double Falls with a "Twist" Reward Your Climb and Hike

Height: 100'   **Difficulty: 4**   **Romance: 7**

Type: Wide Steep Slide, Spread Arch Plunge.

Description: A powerful but narrow block of water falls over the edge of a cliff, drops behind a tall wall of rock, lands on a concealed spot about a third of the way down, then turns about 60° to the left and shoots like a fire hose from a crack between the cliff and the rock, flinging itself in a glorious arcing plume to the pool below.

Distance/Time From Portland: 32 miles, 35 minutes via I-84 and Scenic Highway.

Directions to Parking/Trailhead: Follow directions to Latourell Falls (#1).

Distance/Time From Parking: 30 minutes to bridge at base of falls.

Distance/Time From Other Landmark: 20 minutes from Latourell Falls (#1).

Directions From Parking: Follow directions to upper viewpoint and top of Latourell Falls, then follow trail upstream. Note that there is a trail on each side of the creek. For a romantic loop with two bridge crossings, either go directly upstream on the east (left) side of the creek, cross the bridge at the falls, return on the west (right side), and cross the bridge at the top of Latourell Falls, or do it the other way around.

Elevation Change: 420 feet.

Restroom: In Latourell Picnic area on north side of road on west side of bridge, seasonal; 3 mile east at Bridal Veil Park; year round, modern.

Picnic Area: Excellent, large picnic area in Latourell Park near parking.

View & Kissing Spots: Various views are available from both the east side and west side trails and from the bridge which crosses the stream near the base of the falls. Several romantic bridges, including one at the base of Upper Latourell Falls, are very romantic kissing spots.

Accessibility to the Physically Challenged: Probably inaccessible beyond the top of Latourell Falls.

Hazards: Extreme danger around top of Latourell Falls! Stay on trails! Both the east side and west side trails are subject to slides and washouts. Trails are sometimes muddy.

Information: On Latourell Creek, in George W. Joseph State Park, Multnomah County, Oregon, USGS Bridal Veil Quadrangle, Green Trails Maps: Bridal Veil; listed in USGS Geographic Names Information System.

Like the creek and the lower falls, this feature was also named for Joseph Latourell. The land was donated to the state of Oregon by the heirs of George W. Joseph.

Look for red huckleberries and a remarkable array of wildflowers along the trail from early Spring through late Summer.

The Columbia Gorge of Oregon boasts over 200 miles of trails most of which were carved out before 1920. The trail that takes you to Upper Latourell Falls is one thread of this vast web which continues to be maintained largely by the volunteer efforts of public spirited and nature loving individuals much like those who created them in the first place.

An alternative route to the Scenic Highway is by way of the town of Corbett and Crown Point. While driving east from Portland, either exit at the Sandy River (exit #18) and follow the river and its road or exit at Corbett (exit #23) and drive up the hill to the old highway above. Incidentally, the historic "Chinook Inn" at the Corbett exit has great atmosphere and first class food! High on the gorge rim east of "Upper" Corbett, is Chanticleer Point, also called the Women's Forum State Park, the traditional spot from which to view the gorge. It's been in many movies, including *Short Circuits.*

Just beyond it, the road drops to Crown Point, an amazing edifice, and thence to the river level west of Latourell Falls (#1).

See detailed map at falls #1, Latourell Falls.

Upper Latourell Falls

We climbed so far to reach the top
Then paused a moment on the bridge
We gazed at water tumbling past
And kissed to share our feelings.

Tho walking briskly on we went
Along the trail beside the stream
We tried to see each splash and bud
While moving swiftly toward our goal.

We heard the falls before its view
Just when we were near tired
At last the plunge was in our sight
Enchanting beauty just for us.

We saw the falls from every view
Along the trails on east and west
Beside the creek and by the pool
And from the spray lashed bridge.

Its wide white block behind the wall
The sharp left turn it takes
The firehose force its mighty plunge
Restricted blasts from out of sight.

We kissed and hugged on bridge and rocks
We spent a moment by the fall
Then bathed in all its mighty spray
Absorbing love through pores and eyes.

3   Sheppards Dell

Fairyland Surround-You Falls in Romantic Grotto

Height: 125'   **Difficulty:** 1   **Romance:** 10

Type: Narrow Plunge, Cascade, Hourglass Steep Slide.

Description: A real fairyland, Sheppards Dell has to be experienced to be believed! The entire attraction takes place in a kind of amphitheater crossed by a scenic arched bridge on the old highway. Within it, the water falls from out of sight, turns toward you, tumbles to your feet, plunges magnificently in an hourglass shaped slide, turns again, squeezes through cracks and heads under the bridge toward its terminus at the river. Most incredibly, you are virtually surrounded by falling water. Within the deep coolness of Sheppards Dell, no one can fail to be moved.

Distance/Time From Portland: 30 miles, 30 minutes via I-84 and Scenic Highway.

Directions to Parking/Trailhead: I-84 east to exit 28 (Bridal Veil) (east bound only, with entrance west bound only). Westbound visitors (as from Hood River), go west to Rooster Rock State Park exit, re-enter freeway Eastbound. From exit 28, proceed to Scenic Highway, then go right, west, for two miles to near milepost 15 of the Scenic Highway. Look for the " Sheppards Dell" sign seen on the left just before you cross a concrete bridge. A small, unmarked parking areas can be found on both sides of road immediately before the bridge.

Distance/Time From Parking: Immediate.

Distance/Time From Other Landmark: 2 miles from Latourell Falls (#1); 1 mile drive to Bridal Veil Park (#4).

Directions From Parking: Follow stone steps and wall from east end of bridge to the falls.

Elevation Change: 30 feet.

Restroom: 1 mile east at Bridal Veil Park; year round, modern.

Picnic Area: None here; at Bridal Veil Park or at Latourell Falls.

View & Kissing Spots: You are presented by a great variety of beautiful changing views in every direction throughout the entire short walk from the bridge to the base of the falls.

Accessibility to the Physically Challenged: Visible from road and accessible views of falls from bridge but trail is inaccessible because of stairs and steep, narrow, rough trail conditions.

Hazards: Poison oak near parking, especially on slopes which the adventurous might try to climb for a better view; occasional slippery paved trail unless one is extremely unwary and goes outside the designated areas (which then offers the opportunity to test ones mortality).

Information: On Young Creek, Multnomah County, Oregon, USGS Bridal Veil Quadrangle, Green Trails Maps: Bridal Veil.

Sheppards Dell was opened to the public by George Sheppard as a tribute to his wife in 1915 as one of the many wonders of the Columbia River Highway. It is still one of the treasures of Oregon and the World!

The magnificent 100 foot arched concrete bridge over Sheppards Dell can be seen from the freeway. It is the product of an inspired engineer, an unheralded civil servant who designed a great many truly beautiful bridges to be found all over Oregon—bridges that were cost effective and efficient, yet works of art that continue to inspire us long after his life and work is over.

As you drove east through the gorge, you passed the massive 725 foot rock cliffs of crown point with its lighted circular drive and Vista House. In Winter, a falls slides down its north side to join the river nearby.

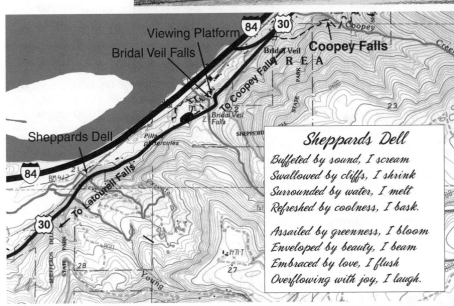

Sheppards Dell

Buffeted by sound, I scream
Swallowed by cliffs, I shrink
Surrounded by water, I melt
Refreshed by coolness, I bask.

Assailed by greenness, I bloom
Enveloped by beauty, I beam
Embraced by love, I flush
Overflowing with joy, I laugh.

West Columbia Gorge of Oregon

4   Bridal Veil Falls
Two Grand, Large Block Falls, One Flowing into the Other

Height: 160'　　　　　　　　Difficulty: 3　　　　　　　　Romance: 5

Type: Wide Free Plunge, Wide Steep Slide.

Description: From under a quaint bridge, a wide white wall of water drops to a pool then roars down another black rock wall to a second pool.

Distance/Time From Portland: 29 miles, 30 minutes.

Directions to Parking/Trailhead: I-84 east to exit 28 (Bridal Veil) (east bound only, with entrance west bound only). Westbound visitors (as from Hood River), go west to Rooster Rock State Park exit, re-enter freeway Eastbound. From exit 28, proceed to Scenic Highway, then go right, west, for one mile until Bridal Veil Park sign seen on right. There is a large paved parking lot within Bridal Veil Park.

Distance/Time From Parking: To viewing platform: 11 minutes.

Distance/Time From Other Landmark: About 1 mile drive from Sheppards Dell (#3); 1 mile to parking for Coopey Falls (#5).

Directions From Parking: Follow trail from parking lot toward restrooms, pass to the right of the restroom building and continue on this trail into the shallow Bridal Veil Creek Canyon to the raised wooden platform from which you get an awesome view of both parts of the falls.

Elevation Change: 200 feet.

Restroom: At Parking; Year Round; Modern.

Picnic Area: Excellent picnic areas, trails, and viewpoints within Bridal Veil Park.

View & Kissing Spots: A perfect view is afforded from the specially constructed raised viewing platform; can be seen from I-84. Because the falls is only a few feet from the bridge on the old highway, you can see it from the road. Be careful of traffic and don't cross the guard rail to the very dangerous areas beyond! Kiss on the platform, along pool and by huge rocks near base of falls.

Accessibility to the Physically Challenged: Although the lower half of the falls can be seen from Interstate 5 and the upper half from a spot on the scenic highway, the falls viewpoint isn't accessible at this time because the trails are too steep and narrow and there is are stairs to the viewpoint. The park does have other accessible trails, viewpoints, picnic areas, parking, and restrooms.

Hazards: A "reverse hike", the trail leads you down hill most of the way to the falls with return up hill. Lots of poison oak on sunnier, more open areas; deceptively steep and dangerous slopes off trail near falls.

Information: On Bridal Veil Creek, Multnomah County, Oregon, USGS Bridal Veil Quadrangle, Green Trails Maps: Bridal Veil; listed in USGS Geographic Names Information System.

Bridal Veil Falls, its creek, and the nearby town of Bridal Veil have shared their names since early pioneer days. Until quite recently, Bridal Veil Creek and its waterfall was a source of water for the town and waterpower for the sawmill. Thankfully, it has been restored to us as a work of natural art with little evidence of its former career. Unfortunately, most of the town of Bridal

Veil is becoming a ghost town said to be due to a dispute between the town's largest landowner and the county over payment for fire protection.

A charming, large, rustic log structure blanketed with moss faces the parking lot from across the road. It was once an inn on the historic highway, then a ranger station, and now a bed and breakfast. Please respect their privacy.

In addition to the falls trail, other paths lead to unique scenic viewpoints from the tops of the remarkable ice-age rocks carved into the 'Pillars of Hercules".

West of the Bridal Veil exit to the freeway is Rooster Rock standing like a narrow sentinel next to the river in Rooster Rock State Park (exit #25). This landmark was named by Lewis and Clark because of its shape which must have had a beak two hundred years ago. Even now, if you imagine a beak on it, you can easily see the resemblance. Incidentally, this park boasts a boat launching area and a mile long sand beach for swimming in the Columbia. This is a fine place for a picnic.

See detailed map at falls #3, Sheppards Dell.

Cormorant

Bridal Bloom

5   **Coopey Falls**
A Beautiful Plume Secluded Behind a Scenic Monastery

Height: 175'   **Difficulty:** 5   **Romance:** 4

Type: Narrow Contact Plunge.

Description: A tall, narrow plunge down a sheer rock cliff in a picturesque setting just behind an impressive Mediterranean style building in a wooded and richly landscaped estate.

Distance/Time From Portland: 28 miles, 30 minutes via I-84 and Scenic Highway.

Directions to Parking/Trailhead: I-84 east to exit 28 (Bridal Veil) (east bound only, with entrance west bound only). Westbound visitors (as from Hood River), go west to Rooster Rock State Park exit, re-enter freeway Eastbound. From exit 28, proceed to Scenic Highway intersection. Although visible from the road behind an historic monastery on private property, most people hike to it from the trailhead at the unpaved parking area at the intersection of the Scenic Highway and the short road from the Bridal Veil freeway exit.

Distance/Time From Parking: For view from above on trail to Angels Rest, .4 miles, 17 minutes.

Distance/Time From Other Landmark: About 1 mile from Bridal Veil Park (#4); 2-3 minutes to Upper Coopey Falls viewpoint.

Directions From Parking: Trail (Angels Rest Trail #415) begins at edge of Scenic Highway next to parking.

Elevation Change: 250 feet.

Restroom: 1 mile west at Bridal Veil Park; year round, modern.

Picnic Area: None here; at Bridal Veil Park.

View & Kissing Spots: Through the trees from the road (with difficulty except in Winter) and from a picturesque viewpoint on the trail above the falls. From this vantage point, you have a wonderful view of the Columbia, the monastery below the falls and the falls itself. Kiss at the overlook viewpoint.

Accessibility to the Physically Challenged: Barely visible from the scenic highway but the trail is not accessible. Although there are no stairs or other manmade structures, the trail is very narrow and rocky.

Hazards: Much of the trail crosses rock slides which leave the trail surface made up largely of angled and somewhat sharp pointed rocks which are hazards for any but the best, thick soled hiking boots; all viewpoints have no railing, a very long drop, and very questionable edges which may give way under the unwary—use your head! Very warm conditions are likely on hot sunny days because the rock slide areas have little shade and seem to attract heat.

Information: On Coopey Creek, Multnomah County, Oregon, USGS Bridal Veil Quadrangle, Green Trails Maps: Bridal Veil; listed in USGS Geographic Names Information System.

Named for the land's original owner, Charles Coopey, a successful Portland tailor who was originally from England. Coopey Falls is behind what was originally a monastery. You may be able to see the falls from the Scenic Highway through the trees. Look for the Mediterranean style monastery a short distance east of the Bridal Veil exit, Scenic Highway intersection. Respect the residents of this private property.

Look for trillium, delphinium, bleeding hearts, corydalis, currants, elderberry, vanilla leaf, colts foot, false lily of the valley, tiger lily, fairy bells, solomon's seal, snowberry, and stone crop. Note non-native plant invaders: dandelions, alyssum, deadly nightshade, vetch, money plant, and more. Look also for picas on the rock slides.

Walk a few minutes further up the trail Upper Coopey Falls viewpoint and a few minutes more to the bridge at the top of the falls. Continue to Angels Rest (a 2500 foot high promontory) and to Wahkeena Falls for a long loop hike.

If you hike to Angels Rest, try to glimpse a very narrow unnamed falls that drops over a hundred feet from a crotch between the east side of Angels Rest and the cliff. It can only be seen from this vantage point. After seeing it, we began to believe we were imagining it. Finally we ran into someone who, upon hearing about our book, sheepishly asked us if we had ever seen it, saying everyone said he was crazy. If you find it, let us know!

Fairy Bells

See detailed map at falls #10, Little Multnomah Falls.

Coopey Falls
A private place of meditation
With God and peace and contemplation.
A cloister for religious practice
In nature's own cathedral.
We walk along the cliff above
Idyllic scenery far below
With gardens, trees, and waterfall,
And glimpse there immortality.

6   Mist Falls

So High Its Mist Often Blows Away. It Deserves Far More Respect!

Height: 500'   Difficulty: 0 to roadside viewpoint   Romance: 3

Type: Narrow Contact Plunge, Narrow Plunge, Cascade.

Description: High above the gorge, a small stream drops over the edge of an awesome cliff and falls to a bowl of its own making, thence to a second landing space, then steeply tumbles to the Scenic Highway. Because Mist Falls is on the face of the gorge rather than being in a canyon like other nearby falls, its meager flow is exposed to the full force of the winds in the gorge—sometimes virtually blowing it away entirely. Unheralded and unappreciated, without even a sign to mark its name, Mist Falls bravely flows in all seasons and weather.

Distance/Time From Portland: 31 miles, 30 minutes via I-84 and Scenic Highway.

Directions to Parking/Trailhead: I-84 east to exit 28 (Bridal Veil) (east bound only, with entrance west bound only). Westbound visitors (as from Hood River), go west to Rooster Rock State Park exit, re-enter freeway Eastbound. From exit 28, proceed to Scenic Highway, then go left for about 2.5 miles (near mile marker 19). Informal parking (at best) is along roadside.

Distance/Time From Parking: Immediate (.2 miles and 15 minutes to clamber up the creek to the base of the falls).

Distance/Time From Other Landmark: Less than 1 mile to Wahkeena Falls (#7).

Directions From Parking: Its stream crosses the Scenic Highway. There is no formal trail or viewpoint.

Elevation Change: 0 to roadside viewing area; 100 feet to base of falls.

Restroom: 1 mile east at Multnomah Falls Lodge; Year Round; Modern.

Picnic Area: None here; at Wahkeena Falls or at Bridal Veil Park.

View & Kissing Spots: Along roadside, from freeway and from Washington side of the river. If you hike to the base of the falls, a kiss is definitely in order!

Accessibility to the Physically Challenged: No accessible trails but visible from the Scenic Highway, Interstate 84, and the Washington side of the Columbia.

Hazards: No legitimate parking places; no real trail to falls; slipping on rocks; falling rocks.

Information: On Mist Creek, Multnomah County, Oregon, USGS Bridal Veil Quadrangle, Green Trails Maps: Bridal Veil; listed in USGS Geographic Names Information System.

Significant and continual disputes rage over whether Mist Falls is significant enough to be considered a "real" falls and what should be considered its height. Ira A. Williams, writer of the first detailed scientific description of the gorge, *Geologic History of the Columbia River Gorge.* (which was both ultimate authority and guide book for over half a century), stated "Mist Falls springs from the cliff high up, a mere filament of water, so slender that before half its sheer drop of nearly a thousand feet is made, it is none else than a spray of mist—hence its name." Although not named by them, Mist Falls was quite clearly described by Lewis and Clark in their epic trip.

The stone chimney and other remnants of Mist Falls Lodge can still be seen near the road below the falls. It was described in 1916 as "a delightful hostelry, where visitors find both cheer and the fullest satisfaction of ordinary physical needs".

The day this drawing was made, there were still patches of snow and ice around the falls and along the scenic highway from an unusually "wintery" Winter storm.

See detailed map at falls #10, Little Multnomah Falls.

Oregon Fawn Lily

Mist Falls

Nymph of the Columbia
Caught between rock and air
Mist in its form and name

A scarf, a veil floating from a bride
A ghost hanging by one finger from cliff's edge
Floating, ever changing, appearing then vanishing

Fairy princess of the gorge
Making ice or greening moss
Perpetual mistress of the air.

West Columbia Gorge of Oregon

7   Wahkeena Falls

A Powerful Double with a Kissing Bridge Right in the Middle

Height: 242'   **Difficulty:** 2 to bridge; 5 to top   **Romance:** 7

Type: Narrow Contact Plunge, Spread Plunge, Cascade.

Description: From the rim of the gorge, Wahkeena Creek plunges into a narrow crack in the rock, runs toward you a short distance then falls again in a foamy slide which ends almost at your feet when on the trail's bridge, then cascades downhill to the parking lot. Each section seems set at an angle to the one before, creating a pleasing zigzag visual effect.

Distance/Time From Portland: 31 miles, 30 minutes via I-84 and Scenic Highway.

Directions to Parking/Trailhead: I-84 east to exit 28 (Bridal Veil) (east bound only, with entrance west bound only). Westbound visitors (as from Hood River), go west to Rooster Rock State Park exit, re-enter freeway Eastbound. From exit 28, proceed to Scenic Highway, then go left for about 3 miles to the large, paved Wahkeena Falls parking area.

Distance/Time From Parking: To parking lot view point: immediate; to bridge next to falls: .1 miles, 10 minutes and .2 miles; 38 minutes from bridge to Gorge viewpoint above falls. Total hike to top of falls: less than 45 minutes.

Distance/Time From Other Landmark: 1 mile from Mist Falls (#6); .8 miles, 45 minutes to Necktie Falls; 1.1 miles, 71 minutes to Fairy Falls; .5 miles drive to Multnomah Falls.

Directions From Parking: The falls is right in front of you in the parking lot. Trails lead a short way along the left (east) side of the cascade from the footbridge at the edge of the parking lot. The main trail to the arched stone bridge at the middle of the falls begins at the right (west) end of the paved parking area.

Elevation Change: 60 feet to bridge, 350 to top of falls.

Restroom: In park across the road from the falls, seasonal; 1 mile east at Multnomah Falls Lodge; Year Round; Modern.

Picnic Area: At parking lot and in park across the road from the falls.

View & Kissing Spots: From parking; from wooden footbridge and from arched stone bridge. A kiss in the spray at the stone bridge is a must!

Accessibility to the Physically Challenged: Falls are fully visible from road and parking; accessible to the footbridge at the middle of the falls (possibly too steep for some); may be too steep and narrow from bridge to top of falls.

Hazards: Slides and washouts. Perdition Trail from just above Wahkeena to just above Multnomah Falls once had a long set of wooden stairs to negotiate a steep section. After years of rebuilding the stairs, a really excellent one was destroyed by the forest fire of 1991. After more years of effort, a permanent solution, a concrete and steel staircase built into the cliffs was finally completed by the Winter of 1995-96, just in time for floods and slides to totally destroy it before it was opened! Two other trails to Multnomah are higher up.

Information: On Wahkeena Creek, Multnomah County, Oregon, USGS Bridal Veil Quadrangle, Green Trails Maps: Bridal Veil; listed in USGS Geographic

Names Information System.

Wahkeena is a Yakima word meaning "most beautiful". Until 1915, the falls was known as Gordon Falls for E.F. Gordon, a local landowner.

Rock walls, trails, bridges, and other works near the falls date from early in the century and before. At the turn of the century, Wahkeena was considered the most beautiful falls in the gorge. In 1915, Wahkeena's park boasted a "public comfort station" and a "station of the motorcycle highway police patrol service".

See detailed map at falls #10, Little Multnomah Falls.

Monkey Flower

Wahkeena Falls

Are there ferns in Oklahoma
To carpet forest floors?
Are there trees in Pennsylvania
That reach up to the sky?

Do the woods stay cool in Kansas
On hottest Summer days?
Is it always green in Utah
Throughout the entire year?

Can the streams in Indiana
Run fast and cold and white?
Is a waterfall in Texas
A quarter of this height?

Are there waterfalls in heaven
To shimmer in the light?
Then I'll stay here at Wahkeena
Where falls are heavenly.

West Columbia Gorge of Oregon

8   Fairy Falls

Just One of the Most Delightful Falls by which You'll Ever Get Wet

Height: 30'   **Difficulty:** 6   **Romance:** 8

Type: Spreading tumble

Description: Water pours over the lip of a low cliff made of giant cubes of rock irregularly set. The water pours over the rocks and splashes on each one. The trail crosses at the bottom of the falls.

Distance/Time From Portland: 31 miles, 30 minutes via I-84 and Scenic Highway.

Directions to Parking/Trailhead: Follow directions as for Wahkeena Falls (#7).

Distance/Time From Parking: 1.1 miles, 68 minutes from Wahkeena parking.

Distance/Time From Other Landmark: 1 mile, 61 minutes from bridge at middle of Wahkeena Falls (#7); .3 miles, 23 minutes from Necktie Falls; 1.7 miles to Multnomah Creek above Hidden Falls (#13) for a wonderful loop trail with views of 5 more falls!

Directions From Parking: Follow the trail to the bridge at the middle of Wahkeena Falls then continue uphill, crossing two footbridges, until you reach the base of Fairy Falls. You may turn east just past Fairy on a trail to Multnomah Creek or continue upstream to Wahkeena Spring picnic area from which you can go west to Angel's Rest and Bridal Veil.

Elevation Change: 600 feet.

Restroom: In park across the road from the falls, seasonal; 1 mile east at Multnomah Falls Lodge; Year Round; Modern.

Picnic Area: At parking lot and in park across the road from the Wahkeena Falls; a possibility at the gorge viewpoint; a large, pleasant, rustic rough hewn bench just below Fairy Falls can become a delightful and friendly lunch spot just out of the mist.

View & Kissing Spots: From the trail approaching the falls and as close as you want. In fact, if you don't get wet (and kiss), you're probably doing it wrong!.

Accessibility to the Physically Challenged: A rough climb with the possibility that slides and washouts can make the trail narrow and/or very rough. However, there may be no actual barrier to the very athletic wheelchair jockey.

Hazards: Trail beyond bridge at falls is subject to slides and washouts.

Information: On an unnamed tributary of Wahkeena Creek, Multnomah County, Oregon, USGS Multnomah Falls Quadrangle, Green Trails Maps: Bridal Veil.

Just above the top of Wahkeena Falls, look for Necktie Falls on the creek. A faint and dangerous trail angles toward it from the main trail. It's not the most scenic or convenient waterfall available.

To hike further, as mentioned above, if you follow the trail upstream, you will soon pass another small falls above Fairy on the same creek then reach a fork in the trail about 5 minutes beyond Fairy Falls. The left fork is Vista Point Trail #419 and "Wahkeena Trail 1 mile" (whatever that means) and will take you to Multnomah Creek just above Upper Multnomah Falls. The right fork is Wahkeena Trail and #400 to Angel"s Rest and Wahkeena Spring. The sign at the fork says "1.2 miles [downstream] to Columbia River Highway". 20 minutes further upstream, you reach another fork in the trail. You can go left to Multnomah Creek and Larch Mountain or right to Wahkeena Springs, Angel"s Rest, and the highway at Bridal Veil (4.8 miles). This spot is 1.6 miles from the Wahkeena parking lot. The Angel's Rest and Bridal Veil loop is a great hike with fabulous views and a visit to Coopey Falls—a 9 mile loop with nearly 2000 feet of elevation gain

About a minute's walk from the last fork, is the charming and very rustic picnic area at Wahkeena Springs where Wahkeena Creek flows full size out of the side of a gentle slope!

We are convinced that Fairy Falls was named for the faces of short, fat gnomes (or fairies?) that can be seen crouching and grimacing as the water lands on their heads. If you find faces in the clouds, you'll see them too!

See detailed map at falls #10, Little Multnomah Falls.

Fairy Falls

A pile of giant children's blocks
Mischievous youngsters left them here
In mythic times so long ago
Presented now for us to share.

These rocks in perfect size and shape
Their cubic shapes of gleaming black
With edges sharp and sides all square
Forgotten toys not put away.

Is that a gnome hunched down to hide
Pretending that he's just a rock
Discomfort causing him to squint
From water splashing on his head

The water laughs and bounces down
Upon each block and edge and side
Let's join it now, become a rock
We'll laugh and hug get splashed get wet.

9   Multnomah Falls

Everyone Must Visit the Mother of Falls

Height: 620'   **Difficulty:** 1 to viewpoint:; 2 to bridge:; 7 to top   **Romance:** 10

Type: Narrow Free Plunge, Wide Free Plunge.

Description: Multnomah Creek drops over the lip of a nearly 600 foot tall sheer cliff and plunges to a huge pool at the bottom, from which a second short plunge drops to form a comparatively placid stream. In a real engineering feat, an arched bridge crosses the stream high above the smaller plunge, giving a fabulous view of the fourth tallest recognized year round waterfall in North America.

Distance/Time From Portland: 31 miles, 30 minutes via I-84 and Scenic Highway.

Directions to Parking/Trailhead: I-84 east to exit 28 (Bridal Veil) (east bound only, with entrance west bound only). Westbound visitors (as from Hood River), go west to Rooster Rock State Park exit, re-enter freeway Eastbound. From exit 28, proceed to Scenic Highway, then go left for about 3.5 miles to Multnomah Falls Parking Area. For those in a hurry, exit 31 provides parking in the middle of Interstate 84 and access to the Multnomah Falls area by a convenient, paved walkway. There is a very large paved parking area on the old highway and another large one in the center of Interstate 84.

Distance/Time From Parking: 2 minutes to viewpoint; .2 miles, 8 minutes to bridge at base of falls; 1.1 miles, 50 minutes to the viewpoint at the top of falls.

Distance/Time From Other Landmark: Less than .5 mile from Wahkeena Falls (#7); 1.1 miles to Little Multnomah Falls (#10).

Directions From Parking: Walk south past the left side of the lodge to the viewpoint; continue to the right from the viewpoint on the trail to the bridge; continue to the top of the falls; take the right fork at the top of the hill to the top of the falls viewpoint.

Elevation Change: Viewpoint; 25 feet; Bridge: 100 feet; Top of falls: 675 feet.

Restroom: In Lodge at Parking; Year Round; Modern.

Picnic Area: At various points in activities complex.

View & Kissing Spots: From parking on freeway and on old road; at raised viewpoint; below viewpoint at base of lower falls; on the bridge; at views along trail to top of falls; at viewing platform at top of falls; also visible from I-84 and Washington side of the river.

Accessibility to the Physically Challenged: Fully accessible to viewpoint in front of bridge and to pool below lower falls (except when closed due to washouts). Though somewhat steep and very narrow, the paved trail to the bridge could be accessible. The trail to the top of the falls is also paved but is narrow, steep, and dangerous.

Hazards: Crowds; possibility of falling rocks. Although negotiated by thousands every year, there are great heights with very, very steep slopes adjoining trails which could be lethal for the foolish or unwary. Recently, a monster rock weighing hundreds of tons broke off the face of the cliff and fell to the bottom of the falls, showering everyone nearby with rocks and water. A basketball-size rock hit a woman on the trail. A new fence protects the trail to the bridge.

formation: On Multnomah Creek, Multnomah County, Oregon, USGS Multnomah Falls Quadrangle, Green Trails Maps: Bridal Veil.

Most visited attraction in Oregon with over two million visitors yearly. Fourth highest waterfall in North America.

Look for spawning salmon at certain times of year in Multnomah Creek below lower falls.

The historic stone lodge, built by Portland in 1929, contains displays and info, gift shop, espresso and snack bars,  cocktail lounge, meeting and banquet rooms, and a restaurant with excellent food, fireplaces, and panoramic views of the river and the falls.

See detailed map at falls #10, Little Multnomah Falls.

Multnomah Falls

Like pilgrims by hundreds they come
All cultures and colors and tongues

To gaze at the glorious sight.
With rapture and awe and delight.

The look on each face is the same.
They kiss and they stare and they pose.

Multnomah the mother of falls
Streams down as from heaven above.

Violet Green Swallow

10   Little Multnomah Falls
A Charming Backdrop to the Mighty View

Height: 15'   **Difficulty:** 7 from parking   **Romance:** 5

Type: Square Contact Plunge.

Description: Just upstream from the lip of Multnomah Falls and the viewing platform, the creek traverses a flat shelf then tumbles to the level of the top of the main falls. Thus, Little Multnomah Falls provides a picturesque backdrop for the top of the falls viewpoint.

Distance/Time From Portland: 31 miles, 30 minutes via I-84 and Scenic Highway.

Directions to Parking/Trailhead: Follow directions to Multnomah Falls (#9).

Distance/Time From Parking: 1.1 miles, 50 minutes.

Distance/Time From Other Landmark: 1.1 miles from the base of Multnomah Falls (#9); .2 miles, 8 minutes to Dutchman Falls (#11).

Directions From Parking: Walk south past the left side of the lodge to the viewpoint, continue to the right from the viewpoint on the trail to the bridge, continue to the top of the falls, take the right fork to the viewpoint. Little Multnomah Falls is no more than 50 feet upstream from the top of its much bigger neighbor.

Elevation Change: 675 feet.

Restroom: In Lodge at Parking; Year Round; Modern.

Picnic Area: At lodge.

View & Kissing Spots: At the viewing platform at the top of Multnomah Falls.

Accessibility to the Physically Challenged: Very unlikely due to steep, narrow, unpaved trail.

Hazards: This falls sings its siren song tempting the foolish to play in its outflow, in its powerful current and on its slippery rocks a few feet from the terminal 60 story plunge of its big sister. Be careful!

Information: On Multnomah Creek, Multnomah County, Oregon, USGS Multnomah Falls Quadrangle, Green Trails Maps: Bridal Veil.

Red Currant

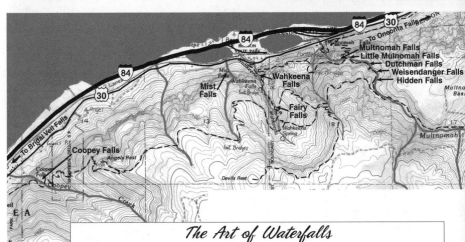

The Art of Waterfalls

There is beauty in the world
Mozart and Dizzy,
Vermeer and Picasso,
Shakespeare and Ferlinghetti,
Palaces and skyscrapers,
Women and babies.

But when you visit waterfalls
You see and feel much more
Moss and trees, birds and flowers,
Plunges and sprays, peace and love.

It's art created for itself
At which we peek in reverence
As if we're children once again
Discovering Christmas in the morn
With presents and surprises
Once secret now revealed.

West Columbia Gorge of Oregon

11   Dutchman Falls

A Sizzling Series of White Foam Falls on Black Lava

Height: 50'   **Difficulty:** 7 from parking   **Romance:** 3

Type: Multiple Square Arch Slides.

Description: Multnomah Creek traverses a thick layer of black lava in such a way that it forms a series of rounded stair steps over which the water sizzles its foamy white way.

Distance/Time From Portland: 31 miles, 30 minutes via I-84 and Scenic Highway.

Directions to Parking/Trailhead: Follow directions to Multnomah Falls (#9).

Distance/Time From Parking: 1.2 miles, 57 minutes from Multnomah Falls Lodge parking lot.

Distance/Time From Other Landmark: .2 miles, 8 minutes from viewing platform at top of Multnomah Falls near Little Multnomah Falls (#10); .2 miles, 3 minutes to the Dutchman Tunnel viewpoint for Weisendanger Falls (#12).

Directions From Parking: Follow directions to Little Multnomah Falls, but take the left fork at the top of the hill; cross the footbridge over Multnomah Creek, then the left fork of the trail upstream toward Larch Mountain.

Elevation Change: 750 feet.

Restroom: In Lodge at Parking; Year Round; Modern.

Picnic Area: At lodge.

View & Kissing Spots: Various spots along the streamside trail.

Accessibility to the Physically Challenged: If you've made it to the top of the falls, perhaps this is possible too. However, the trail is unpaved, narrow, and very uneven.

Hazards: Sharp rocks under foot on trail.

Information: On Multnomah Creek, Multnomah County, Oregon, USGS Multnomah Falls Quadrangle, Green Trails Maps: Bridal Veil.

The accompanying illustration is the largest of the three similar tiers which together comprise Dutchman Falls.

See detailed map at falls #10, Little Multnomah Falls.

Bushtit

Western Larch

Together

We walked together hand in hand
Through sounds of water, singing birds
In lush green woods so cool and deep
With sweetly smelling earth and plants.

We saw the flowers, ferns, and trees
And felt the waterfalls mystique
We found such peace in natures realm
And touched and kissed as in a dream.

West Columbia Gorge of Oregon

12   Weisendanger Falls
A Wide Plunge of Great Beauty and Power

Height: 90'   **Difficulty:** 8 from parking   **Romance:** 7

Type: Curtain Plunge.

Description: A flat shelf of very hard rock allows Multnomah Creek to flow near-ly level then plunge straight over the edge of the broken shelf in a perfectly symmetrical wall of water and land in a deep bowl flanked by cliffs. It can be seen as you approach from downstream and as the trail climbs slowly to an elevation higher than the top of the falls. It is possible to reach the pool at the bottom of this falls via a scramble down the hillside from the trail.

Distance/Time From Portland: 31 miles, 30 minutes via I-84 and Scenic Highway.

Directions to Parking/Trailhead: Follow directions to Multnomah Falls (#9).

Distance/Time From Parking: 1.4 miles, 60 minutes from Multnomah Falls Lodge parking lot to Dutchman's Tunnel viewpoint of Weisendanger Falls.

Distance/Time From Other Landmark: .2 miles, 3 minutes from Dutchman Falls (#11); .2 miles, 10 minutes to Hidden Falls (#13).

Directions From Parking: Follow Directions to Dutchman Falls then continue upstream toward Larch Mountain.

Elevation Change: 950 feet.

Restroom: In Lodge at Parking; Year Round; Modern.

Picnic Area: At lodge.

View & Kissing Spots: Dutchman Tunnel (especially in Winter), from trailside spots; and at the base of the falls (if you don't mind the scramble to it).

Accessibility to the Physically Challenged: Steep, narrow, rocky, and with soft earth make this portion of the trail highly unlikely to be accessible to the physically challenged.

Hazards: Sharp rocks under foot on trail; treacherous steep trailside slopes; slides.

Information: On Multnomah Creek, Multnomah County, Oregon, USGS Multnomah Falls Quadrangle, Green Trails Maps: Bridal Veil; listed in USGS Geographic Names Information System.

Weisendanger Falls has only recently become the official name of this falls. It is named after a great advocate for the Columbia River and its falls, who worked for the U.S. Forest Service in the area.. Previously, it has been called "Upper Multnomah Falls" and once it was lumped with its upstream twin, which we call "Hidden Falls" for obvious reasons, as if they were actu-ally one falls and listed as "Double Falls"! Even after the official name was applied to the falls, the name, "Twanklaskie", was used for this falls in another book. The dispute over its name may never end!

Watch and listen carefully all along this trail for signs and sounds of wildlife, especially birds such as Wrens (musically singing and bravely hopping among trailside brush), the Dipper (ubiquitous on streams throughout the region), Swainson's Thrush (invisibly practicing rising flute-like scales that would make Mozart jealous), invisible flocks of gregarious Bushtits flitting through the brush while keeping in audible touch with each other, and Douglas Squirrels scolding you from trees and brush and leaving piles of fragmented fir cones as evidence of their presence and their voracious appetites.

See detailed map at falls #10, Little Multnomah Falls.

Weisendanger Falls
Silently standing beneath the rocks
Sheltering us from the rain.
Hugging we stand in awe of the falls
Plunging, a curtain for our delight.

Dripping we stand in the tunnel
Carved by nature's watery course
Reluctant to face the wintery damp
Pledging our love and wringing our hair.

Wild Bleeding Heart

13   Hidden Falls

Carefully Peak at Weisendanger's Twin from Above

Height: 80'   **Difficulty:** 8 from parking   **Romance:** 5

Type: Curtain Plunge.

Description: This beautiful falls is almost identical in description to its twin, Weisendanger Falls, a very short distance downstream. This falls cannot be seen at the same time as its downstream sister. It can only be viewed from almost directly above its plunge. Its base, intermediate between the two falls, cannot safely be reached by normal mortals.

Distance/Time From Portland: 31 miles, 30 minutes via I-84 and Scenic Highway.

Directions to Parking/Trailhead: Follow directions to Multnomah Falls (#9).

Distance/Time From Parking: 1.6 miles, 70 minutes from Multnomah Falls Lodge parking lot to viewpoint above Hidden Falls.

Distance/Time From Other Landmark: .2 miles, 10 minutes from the Dutchman Tunnel viewpoint of Weisendanger Falls (#12); .2 miles, 10 minutes to Upper Multnomah Falls, a rather insignificant falls which is often barely noticeable under logjams, seen just before the upper trail to Wahkeena (#7), a 3 mile hike. Note that going straight upstream on the trail, rather than turning off for Wahkeena Falls, will take you to Sherrard Point on Larch Mountain, a rather long (5.2 miles from here) but easier and more satisfying hike than you would expect.

Directions From Parking: Follow directions to Weisendanger Falls then continue upstream toward Larch Mountain.

Elevation Change: 1050 feet.

Restroom: In Lodge at Parking; Year Round; Modern.

Picnic Area: At lodge.

View & Kissing Spots: From trailside spots near top of the falls.

Accessibility to the Physically Challenged: Inaccessible due to trail conditions.

Hazards: Sharp rocks under foot on trail; treacherous steep trailside slopes; slides. Do not try so hard to get a perfect view of this falls. This could truly be deadly!

Information: On Multnomah Creek, Multnomah County, Oregon, USGS Multnomah Falls Quadrangle, Green Trails Maps: Bridal Veil.

Weisendanger Falls has only recently become the official name of the near-by (downstream) twin of this falls. This falls has no official name (although it does have several unofficial and highly inappropriate ones, including "Ecola Falls" most recently. We have named it "Hidden Falls" for reasons that will be obvious when you visit it! "Hidden Falls" will do until someone officially makes up their mind.

We have chosen not to include Upper Multnomah Falls, a few minutes upstream from Hidden Falls, in the book. It's an artistic judgement. Take a look anyway, and decide if we did the right thing.

The trail on which you are hiking was built before 1900. In fact, the first bridge spanning the lower part of Multnomah Falls was a rickety looking wooden one built in the 1890s over which crowds of day trippers from Portland began their climb past the falls of Multnomah Creek and on up to 4,055 foot Sherrard Point on Larch Mountain just as thousands do today. Each step you take links you to the romance and appreciation for these natural wonders of Native Americans and pioneers alike. The view of Mount Saint Helens, Mount Adams, Mount Hood, and Mount Jefferson from Sherrard Point makes it well worth the 5 mile hike from here!. If you want less struggle, you can use the two car method—leave one at Multnomah Falls Lodge and take the other to the parking lot at Larch

Mountain—and hike downhill all the way.

See detailed map at falls #10, Little Multnomah Falls.

Every Time I See You

Every time I see you, you are new.
A wider flow, a rock has moved.
A log has fallen, you've turned aside.
Familiar face, smiling through the spray.

Glacier Lily

West Columbia Gorge of Oregon

14   **Oneonta Falls**

A Wonderful Falls Anywhere, a Reward and Delight in a Special Place

Height: 100' **Difficulty:** 10 if you don't like to get wet, 3 otherwise **Romance:** 10

Type: Narrow Contact Plunge.

Description: At the end of the Oneonta Gorge, a deep, narrow crack in the ground, a beautiful contact plunge falls descends the black basalt cliff. Although you can see to the end of the gorge from the road, the falls coyly conceals herself just to the right of your line of sight. To see the falls, you must brave the cold water which in places occupies the entire gorge from wall to wall to a depth of 4 feet or more. To reach the falls and play in its white spray as it plunges into its deep clear pool, is a real rite of passage—enjoy!

Distance/Time From Portland: 37 miles, 40 minutes via I-84.

Directions to Parking/Trailhead: I-84 east to exit 35 (Dodson); from intersection with Scenic Highway, go west 3 miles to Oneonta Gorge. At milepost 22 of the Scenic Highway. Park on the widened roadside east and west of Oneonta and on the bridge over the creek.

Distance/Time From Parking: About .25 miles, time varies from 10 to 60 minutes depending on your prowess and eagerness and foot traffic.

Distance/Time From Other Landmark: .5 miles drive to Horsetail Falls (#15).

Directions From Parking: Steps lead to streamside from both ends of the old bridge. To reach the falls you must tightrope along logs, teeter on rocks, edge along cliff sides, and probably just get quite wet no matter what you do to traverse the .5 mile upstream to the falls.

Elevation Change: 0.

Restroom: 2 miles west at Multnomah Falls Lodge; Year Round; Modern.

Picnic Area: No picnic tables but logs and rocks make great spots for lunch.

View & Kissing Spots: Everywhere within the Oneonta Gorge is scenic and romantic, especially near the falls and swimming in its pool.

Accessibility to the Physically Challenged: Excellent view into the Oneonta Gorge from the scenic highway, but the falls cannot be seen except from the end of the gorge. Stairs, rocks, logs, and deep water prevents access.

Hazards: Getting soaked with ice cold water; slipping on rocks or logs; having too much fun! Wear shoes that protect your feet, provide good traction climbing on rocks and logs, but can get soaked without being ruined. We suggest old Nikes, hiking sandals, and rubber "socks" used by wind surfers and skin divers—bare feet is not a good choice!

Information: On Oneonta Creek, Multnomah County, Oregon, USGS Multnomah Falls Quadrangle, Green Trails Maps: Bridal Veil; listed in USGS Geographic Names Information System.

Historical conjecture has it that the name "Oneonta", which is from a town in New York, was applied to the gorge, creek, and falls because of an incident with a Columbia River steamboat of that name which plied the river in the 1860s and 70s.

The depth and narrowness of Oneonta Gorge and its cold water, "air condition" it even on the hottest days!

Don't expect to stay dry walking to the falls! You will have to swim or wade. If you're unsure about it, go as far into the gorge as you want.

Folks climb 10 feet and dive with the falls into the pool. It looks like fun! Be careful!

At the entrance to Oneonta, there's an old bridge and a newer one. Originally, the railroad ran where the highway does now and the road crossed the old bridge then straight east through a tunnel (now filled) in the cliff. Look for evidence!

See detailed map at falls #15, Horsetail Falls.

Oneonta Falls

When Summer heat has finally come
To cool moist western Oregon,
Our mossy backs begin to dry
And natives long for misty rain.

An air conditioned place exists
To sooth and cool our mind and bodies
In just an hour from Portland's heat
A world apart is Oneonta.

We walk into the narrowing crack
Between its towering cliffs
Tightroping logs, tiptoeing stones
As walls reach edge of stream.

And now we choose to wade chest deep
Or edge along on toehold ledge
We yearn to reach the promised end
Perhaps instead we now turn back.

At last we've passed the deepest part
Where walls meet water deep and cold.
It widens to reveal a splendor
The falls named Oneonta.

The falls are there, a whitened plume
Which streams and sprays from high above.
And slides down gloriously
Into this space we share.

Its icy water beckons us to just get wet and
wild
To swim beneath its pounding spray
Leave heat and inhibitions
Somewhere in other worlds outside.

15   Horsetail Falls

Wow, What a Picture, You Just Can't Help Loving It

Height: 176'   **Difficulty:** 0 to base of falls, 6 to top   **Romance:** 7

Type: Hourglass Contact Plunge.

Description: A beautiful plume of water drops over the edge of a cliff, slides down the black rock face, seems to cross over itself halfway down to form an hourglass shape, then plunges into a large, clear, blue pool at the bottom. A truly magnificent site!

Distance/Time From Portland: 37 miles, 40 minutes via I-84.

Directions to Parking/Trailhead: I-84 east to exit 35 (Dodson); from intersection with Scenic Highway, go west 2 miles to Horsetail Falls Park. At milepost 22.2 of the Scenic Highway. There is a good, large, paved parking area.

Distance/Time From Parking: 0 to base of falls; .3 miles, 20 minutes of steep switchbacks to top of falls.

Distance/Time From Other Landmark: 20 minutes from base of Horsetail Falls to Ponytail Falls (#16); a half mile east of the Oneonta Gorge (#14).

Directions From Parking: Viewing and picnic area around base of falls. Trail to top of falls and to Ponytail Falls begins just to the left of the base of the falls.

Elevation Change: 0 to base of falls; 200 feet to top of falls.

Restroom: 2.5 miles west at Multnomah Falls Lodge; Year Round; Modern.

Picnic Area: Limited picnic area near base of falls.

View & Kissing Spots: From road and parking lot; from I-84 and the Washington side of the river. Kiss anywhere within sight of the falls.

Accessibility to the Physically Challenged: Falls are fully visible from freeway, road, and park at base of falls.

Hazards: People walking while looking at the falls instead of watching traffic, being run over by drivers gawking at the falls instead of watching the road and the pedestrians.

Information: On Horsetail Creek, Multnomah County, Oregon, USGS Multnomah Falls Quadrangle, Green Trails Maps: Bridal Veil; listed in USGS Geographic Names Information System.

Supposedly, the waterfall is named for its resemblance to a horse's tail hanging over the wall. It does!

In 1916, when the Columbia River Highway was built, Horsetail was listed as 208 feet tall rather than its present listing of 176 feet. We haven't a clue what caused the change (or error).

People find great pleasure swimming in Horsetail's deep, cold pool (and under the falls themselves) during hot Summer weather. Note that the water is extremely cold year round and the bottom is rocky. Don't die of exposure or drown!

The damp, shady, and cool environment near Horsetail Falls is perfect for a wide variety of mosses, ferns, and wildflowers of the forest floor. The climb to the top of the falls offers a remarkable assortment of fauna.

We've seen elk in the marshy woods and meadows north of the falls, between the scenic highway and the freeway. See the sketch and related story on page 252 (the last page of the book, after the Index) for a personal example (or anecdote) of elk experience in this area. Keep your eyes peeled!

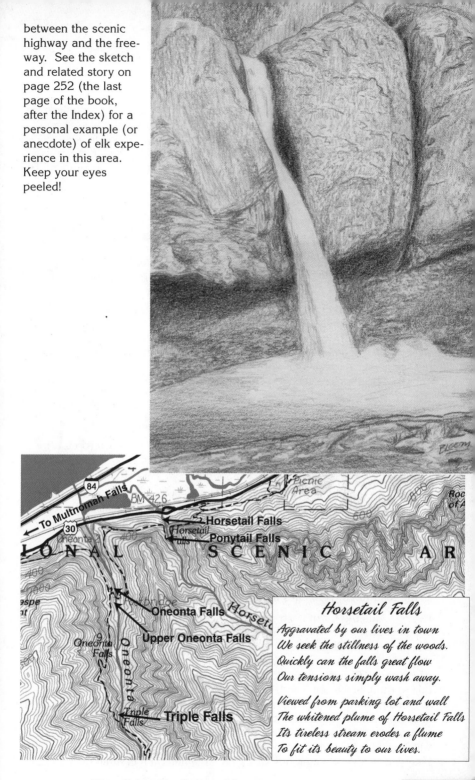

Horsetail Falls
Ponytail Falls
Oneonta Falls
Upper Oneonta Falls
Triple Falls
To Multnomah Falls

Horsetail Falls

Aggravated by our lives in town
We seek the stillness of the woods.
Quickly can the falls great flow
Our tensions simply wash away.

Viewed from parking lot and wall
The whitened plume of Horsetail Falls
Its tireless stream erodes a flume
To fit its beauty to our lives.

West Columbia Gorge of Oregon

16   Ponytail Falls

Take Your Kids, Lover, Mother and Kiss Them Behind the Falls

Height: 125'   **Difficulty:** 6   **Romance:** 10

Type: Narrow Steep Slide to Arch Plunge.

Description: A "Walk-Behind" Falls! Horsetail Creek drops a short distance from the top of the cliff into a crack worn by the creek, then blasts almost horizontally out of the crack over a cliff into a pool below. Although the top layer of the cliff is hard enough to resist the wear of the water, beneath is a softer layer which has crumbled away, forming a grotto behind the falls. The trail goes through this space, right behind the falls.

Distance/Time From Portland: 37 miles, 40 minutes via I-84.

Directions to Parking/Trailhead: Follow directions to Horsetail Falls (#15) or park at the unpaved roadside parking area at the west end of the trail.

Distance/Time From Parking: .3 miles, 20 minutes to behind falls.

Distance/Time From Other Landmark: 20 minutes from base of Horsetail Falls (#15); 27 minutes to Upper Oneonta Falls (#17).

Directions From Parking: Trail leads upward immediately to the left of the Horsetail Falls picnic area to the east of the falls. Its .4 mile to this falls. The trail ends (or begins) on the Scenic Highway a short distance to the west of the Oneonta Gorge. This can provide a 2.7 mile loop hike without retracing your steps.

Elevation Change: 200 feet.

Restroom: 2.5 miles west at Multnomah Falls Lodge; Year Round; Modern.

Picnic Area: Limited picnic area near base of Horsetail Falls.

View & Kissing Spots: Can be seen from the top of Horsetail Falls (on trail); from the trail approaching the falls from east and west; also visible from Interstate 84 and the Washington side of the river. Kiss behind the falls!

Accessibility to the Physically Challenged: The steep, narrow, gravel trail of switchbacks would be too difficult and dangerous to be considered accessible.

Hazards: A little poison oak; minor possibility of falling rocks or slides.

Information: On Horsetail Creek, Multnomah County, Oregon, USGS Multnomah Falls Quadrangle, Green Trails Maps: Bridal Veil.

Some refer to Ponytail Falls as Upper Horsetail Falls.

Here's a side trip for the extremely adventurous, very trail-wise, and physically fit. Just beyond the point when you reach the first view of Ponytail Falls from the trail, look for a faint path on your left, angling upward from the trail. You may see a wooden sign nailed to a tree higher up the slope which says "Trail not Maintained". This trail is slippery year round, either due to mud, loose soil, sand, wet leaves, etc. In addition, as the sign says, it is unmaintained. It also approaches extremely dangerous cliffs. Follow it at your own risk, be extremely careful, and don't blame us! This is not for kids or amateurs! Nevertheless, the trail will take you to a fork, the right part of which will lead you to the top of Ponytail Falls. The left fork will ultimately take you to a very dangerous view of a large natural rock arch high on the cliffs and to views of Rock of Ages and St. Peters Dome, two huge castle-like rock formations visible from the freeway, from Rock of Ages Ridge. Those who tackle this hike do so "because it"s there", not for the views. Several other, less dangerous and physically demanding hikes lead to better views of the gorge!

See detailed map at falls #15, Horsetail Falls.

Ponytail Falls
*The trail goes right behind the fall
That thunders down as light streams through.
You sneak a kiss from one and all
At such a time what else to do?*

Vanilla Leaf

17   Upper Oneonta Falls
A Pretty Falls in an Unforgettable Setting

Height: 55'   Difficulty: 4   Romance: 5

Type: Narrowing Steep Slide.

Description: Viewed from the bridge on the trail above the Oneonta Gorge, Oneonta Creek runs across a broad, flat shelf of rock then meets a steep vertical drop set at an angle to the stream such that the creek slides down in several stripes along a long space. At the bottom of the falls, the water forms a clear pool and squeezes through a narrow, curving trough till it reaches the upstream edge of the gorge into which it disappears (to form Oneonta Falls unseen below).

Distance/Time From Portland: 37 miles, 40 minutes via I-84.

Directions to Parking/Trailhead: Follow directions to Horsetail Falls (#15) or park at the unpaved roadside parking area at the west end of the trail west of the Oneonta Gorge.

Distance/Time From Parking: 1.2 miles, 47 minutes from Horsetail Falls parking.

Distance/Time From Other Landmark: .8 miles, 27 minutes from Ponytail Falls (#16); .1 mile further to intersection with Oneonta Trail #424 to Triple Falls (#18) (1 mile, 44 minutes).

Directions From Parking: Trail leads upward immediately to the left of the Horsetail Falls picnic area to the east of the falls. It is .8 mile from Ponytail Falls, 1.2 miles from the Horsetail Falls parking area. The trail ends (or begins) on the Scenic Highway a short distance to the west of the Oneonta Gorge. This can provide a 2.7 mile loop hike without retracing your steps.

Elevation Change: 320 feet.

Restroom: 2.5 miles west at Multnomah Falls Lodge; Year Round; Modern.

Picnic Area: At Horsetail Falls.

View & Kissing Spots: Beautiful views of the Columbia River Gorge along the trail from Ponytail Falls. During the Winter, with care, one can see Oneonta Falls from the trail. Listen for it first. The view of the Oneonta Gorge from just above the Upper Oneonta Falls is wonderful. You can clearly see from one end of this amazing crack in the ground to the other, and often hear the excited squeals of the visitors below. The best view of Upper Oneonta Falls is from the trail at the west end of the bridge, from which spot one can see the falls and the cascades of the creek behind it. This is a very romantic trek.

Accessibility to the Physically Challenged: None.

Hazards: Stinging nettle, poison oak, and various thorny things are conveniently located for those masochistic souls who insist upon exposing skin to nature or grabbing trailside plants. The trail can be steep and muddy in spots. Find poison oak in sunny spots, Attempts to get a better view can be a lure to unanticipated but brief flying lessons! There is thick brush and steep slopes bordering the long drops into the Oneonta Gorge and the Columbia River Gorge, along the lip of which you travel en route. Note the cliffside memorial marker for one who was careless. Stay on the trail!

formation: On Oneonta Creek, Multnomah County, Oregon, USGS Multnomah Falls Quadrangle, Green Trails Maps: Bridal Veil.

This falls is sometimes ignored, sometimes treated as part of Oneonta Falls, and sometimes called Oneonta Falls (calling the "real" Oneonta Falls "Lower Oneonta Falls"). We think this set of names is the right one!

The illustration is of a very pretty view of the falls looking upstream from the footbridge across the creek. The entire watershed is really beautiful.

See detailed map at falls #15, Horsetail Falls.

Columbine

Everyone Loves the Falls

When native peoples saw the gorge
And all its waterfalls
They surely felt the hand of God
Had made this special place.

Today you'll see a crowd of cars
At every park and trail
With faces of a thousand lands
And every tongue on Earth.

Millennia have come and gone
Since man first saw this place
But nothing's changed in heart or head
All people love these falls.

18   Triple Falls

After a Long Hike, It's Unique, Fun, and Lovely

Height: 135'   Difficulty: 8   Romance: 8

Type: Triplet: Narrow Contact Plunges.

Description: A wide, tumbling creek courses toward you on the trail, then splits into three equal size streams just as it reaches the lip of a sheer vertical cliff and plunges like three ponytails past dark rocks and lush greenery to a common pool at the bottom. A rustic footbridge above the falls also offers romantic views. A magic and beautiful place.

Distance/Time From Portland: 37 miles, 40 minutes via I-84.

Directions to Parking/Trailhead: Follow directions to Horsetail Falls (#15) or park at the unpaved roadside parking area at the west end of the trail west of the Oneonta Gorge.

Distance/Time From Parking: 2.2 miles, 91 minutes from Horsetail Falls parking area. 20 minutes to Ponytail Falls, 27 minutes to Upper Oneonta, 5 minutes to Triple Falls Trail fork, and 39 minutes to Triple Falls.

Distance/Time From Other Landmark: 44 minutes to Upper Oneonta Falls (#17); about 5.5 miles to Larch Mountain upstream from Triple Falls on the Oneonta Trail.

Directions From Parking: Trail leads upward immediately to the left of the Horsetail Falls picnic area to the east of the falls. The trail ends (or begins) on the Scenic Highway a short distance to the west of the Oneonta Gorge. This can provide a 2.7 mile loop hike (plus the side trip to Triple Falls) without retracing your steps. In either case, a fork in the trail west of Upper Oneonta Falls offers a middle (south) fork to Triple Falls, a 1.8 mile round trip.

Elevation Change: 600 feet.

Restroom: 2.5 miles west at Multnomah Falls Lodge; Year Round; Modern.

Picnic Area: There is a lovely area to have a picnic above the falls.

View & Kissing Spots: On trail approaching falls, especially the main one only 100 feet directly in front and slightly above the falls—a perfect view and kissing spot! The top of the falls is fun and romantic too!

Accessibility to the Physically Challenged: None.

Hazards: Poison Oak in sunnier spots; some narrow spots with steep, eroding slopes; foolishness at top of falls.

Information: On Oneonta Creek, Multnomah County, Oregon, USGS Multnomah Falls Quadrangle, Green Trails Maps: Bridal Veil.

Lots of berries along the trail. It's amazing how they can slake your thirst.

The trail climbs continuously through lush forest with views of the spectacular mixed forest and of the creek far below.

The flat bedrock immediately above the falls provides pools and shallow portions of the creek for a refreshing dip in Summer heat. Be careful, however!

Upstream from Triple Falls, the trail along Oneonta Creek becomes a cool, moist forest under-story carpeted with oxalis, corydalis, bleeding heart, false lily of the valley, trillium, and many kinds of fern. A picturesque unnamed falls with too little water except in Winter and Spring can be seen across the creek about 5 minutes beyond the bridge above the falls.

Following the trail upstream from Triple Falls leads ultimately to Sherrard Point on Larch Mountain in a little over 6 miles, passing intersections with trails to Nesmith Point, Franklin Ridge, Multnomah Falls, and Bell Creek.

See detailed map at falls #15, Horsetail Falls.

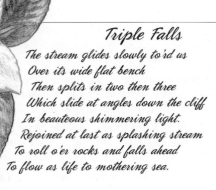

Trillium

Triple Falls

The stream glides slowly to'rd us
Over its wide flat bench
Then splits in two then three
Which slide at angles down the cliff
In beauteous shimmering light.
Rejoined at last as splashing stream
To roll o'er rocks and falls ahead
To flow as life to mothering sea.

19   **Elowah Falls**

A Plunge Bigger, Taller, and Much More Secluded than Latourell

Height: 289'   **Difficulty:** 7   **Romance:** 8

Type: Narrow Free Plunge.

Description: A magnificent plunge from the lip of a great cliff to thunder into a pool at the bottom. Although quite close to the freeway (as the crow flies), when within Elowah's canyon, you feel a deep sense of seclusion. Even on Summer weekends, you will usually be totally alone when you stand on the bridge at the bottom of the falls.

Distance/Time From Portland: 37 miles, 40 minutes via I-84.

Directions to Parking/Trailhead: I-84 east to exit 35 (Dodson); go east 2 miles to large parking area just before the road swings back onto the freeway. From the east, exit 37 leads to an underpass to the south side of the freeway, from which you can go east to the good, very large unpaved parking lot.

Distance/Time From Parking: 24 minutes total to view of falls; 11 minutes to Upper McCord Creek Falls trail fork; 13 minutes from there to falls.

Distance/Time From Other Landmark: 37 minutes to Upper McCord Creek Falls; 24 minutes from fork to Upper McCord Creek Falls (#20).

Directions From Parking: Trail begins at southwest corner of parking lot, passing giant old wooden municipal drinking water tank and shortly intersects the trail to Nesmith Point. Bear left (unless you are a glutton for punishment) and stroll up hill through the forest for .4 mile to the trail fork for Elowah Falls (go left). It's about .4 mile downhill to the base of Elowah Falls from the fork.

Elevation Change: 250 feet.

Restroom: 7 miles west at Multnomah Falls; 3 miles east at Bonneville Dam.

Picnic Area: No designated picnic areas here.

View & Kissing Spots: At viewpoint where the trail dips into McCord Creek canyon; on bridge below the falls; from awe inspiring points on the Upper McCord Creek Falls trail; and from I-84 if you really look quick.

Accessibility to the Physically Challenged: Must be considered inaccessible.

Hazards: A partial "reverse hike" with a substantial downhill portion with a rather long, steep, uphill return. Although it takes you further uphill on the way, the trail to Upper McCord Creek Falls provides striking views of Elowah from above without requiring you to return uphill when you might be tired.

Lots of poison oak along the trail in sunnier, more open areas. There are a number of steep spots which can be slippery when wet or very dry. Wear good boots! Watch out for slides and trail outages.

Information: On McCord Creek, in Yeon State Park, Multnomah County, Oregon, USGS Tanner Butte Quadrangle, Green Trails Maps: Bonneville Dam; listed in USGS Geographic Names Information System.

Given its unexplained Native American name in 1915 by the Mazamas. It is the second highest (or third if you include Mist Falls) waterfall in the gorge.

At the beginning of the hike, look for wildflowers and plants which like the forest floor with the dappled sunlight of mixed woods, such as bleeding heart and trillium. This gives way to young Douglas firs, then alternating shady moist areas (with fir trees, sword ferns, and many wildflowers), sunny dry areas (with garry oaks, poison oak, and roses), and rock slides (with pica and parsley ferns). The canyon's conditions encourages slugs, moss, liverworts, lichens, wildflowers such as monkey flowers, and salmonberries. Watch for Osprey which often nest on large fir trees near the mouth of the canyon.

Don't forget, despite apparent seclusion, the bottom of the falls can be seen from a great many vantage points—don't do anything you don't want in someone's home videos!

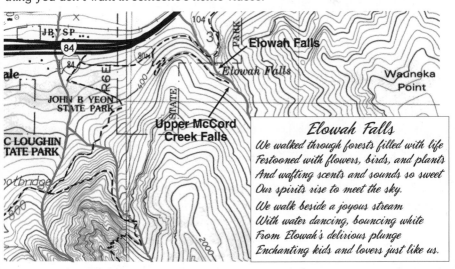

Elowah Falls

We walked through forests filled with life
Festooned with flowers, birds, and plants
And wafting scents and sounds so sweet
Our spirits rise to meet the sky.

We walk beside a joyous stream
With water dancing, bouncing white
From Elowah's delirious plunge
Enchanting kids and lovers just like us.

20   Upper McCord Creek Falls

A Crazy, Fun, Surprising, Fantastic Falls — You've Got to Experience It

Height: 100'   Difficulty: 7   Romance: 8

Type: Twin: Narrow Steep Slides.

Description: A "Fantasy Island" or "fairyland falls! From the best view on the trail, you can see a wide creek coming straight toward you through a series of stair steps, then splitting into two nearly equal streams, each falling picturesquely down a black rock wall surrounded by greenery. It reminded us of the altar in a great cathedral. It creates a feeling of reverence as if in God's own Temple. You will love this falls the first time you see it and like it better every time you see it!

Distance/Time From Portland: 37 miles, 40 minutes via I-84.

Directions to Parking/Trailhead: Follow directions for Elowah Falls (#19).

Distance/Time From Parking: 35 minutes total to top of falls; 11 minutes to fork between Elowah Falls trail and Upper McCord Creek Falls trail; 24 minutes to Upper McCord Creek Falls viewpoint.

Distance/Time From Other Landmark: 24 minutes from fork to Elowah Falls (#19).

Directions From Parking: Follow the directions to Elowah Falls until you get to the trail fork after .4 miles. Bear right for about another .4 mile uphill to Upper McCord Creek Falls.

Elevation Change: 400 feet.

Restroom: 7 miles west at Multnomah Falls; 3 miles east at Bonneville Dam visitor centers.

Picnic Area: Some nice, though undeveloped spots are at the top of the falls.

View & Kissing Spots: As you reach the highest elevations of the trail, beautiful views of the Columbia River Gorge, then the McCord Creek Gorge, then Elowah Falls (now below you), and of Upper McCord Creek Falls after you enter the woods above Elowah. Kiss at the top of the falls.

Accessibility to the Physically Challenged: Absolutely not.

Hazards: Be careful at the top of the falls, especially with pets, children, and adults! Weak downhill slopes with increasing steepness, near the falls make off-trail forays potentially very exciting. Do not try to reach bottom of the falls. Lots of poison oak along the trail in sunnier, more open areas; some devils club in brushy damp areas. Care must be taken on narrow rock cliff side trail facing Elowah. It is safely traversed by hundreds of visitors without incident. However, this portion of the trail is only about 4 feet wide with only a hand rail and your wits between you and a 300 foot sheer drop. Do not overly rely on the handrail. In the unusual times when the gorge ices up, the cliffside trail becomes covered with a heavy and treacherous coating that should discourage you from trying to cross. This is really dangerous!

Information: On McCord Creek, in Yeon State Park, Multnomah County, Oregon, USGS Tanner Butte Quadrangle, Green Trails Maps: Bonneville Dam.

Over the years, McCord Creek has had several other names, including Pierce Creek and Kelly Creek. It was named for W.R. McCord, an early pioneer in the area who built the first fish wheels near the mouth of the stream bearing his name.

Pika may be heard or seen on the wide rock slide before the fork to Elowah. Because the trail passes through so many habitats, an amazing variety of plants can be found in distinct locations along the trail. Look for: Leopard Lily, Trillium, Thimble Berry, Salal, Huckleberry, Wall Flower, Columbine, Wild Delphinium, Penstemon, Hair Bells, Stone Crop, Monkey Flower, Salmon Berry, and many, many more.

See detailed map at falls #19, Elowah Falls.

Pica

Upper McCord Creek Falls
Fantasy Island must have been here
Or Eden or Zanadu.
Straining to see it, touch it, be near
Perfection this heaven's view.

21   Munra Falls

A Wall of Sizzling Water Right at Your Fingertips — Delightful!

Height: 60'   Difficulty: 1   Romance: 8

Type: Spread Steep Slide.

Description: As you walk along the trail you are surprised by a wide but shallow flow of water sizzling down a wall of dark gray rock right beside you as you cross a wooden bridge on the trail. Why is Munra Falls so delightful, especially to children? Perhaps the reason is its "reach out and touch it" nearness, the bubbles scooting down the wall like pachinko balls, the sizzling sound of the water, its refreshing coolness, your surprise when you come upon it, how quickly and easily you reach it, or the smug feeling of discovering something so delightful that's so little known.

Distance/Time From Portland: 40 miles, 40 minutes via I-84.

Directions to Parking/Trailhead: I-84 east to exit 40 (Bonneville); go right (south) perpendicular to freeway and away from Bonneville, to the small, gravel parking area at the end of the road.

Distance/Time From Parking: 8 minutes.

Distance/Time From Other Landmark: 35 minutes to Wahclella Falls (#22).

Directions From Parking: Walk south from parking area on level trail past fish hatchery area, across bridge at Munra Falls.

Elevation Change: Perhaps 30 feet.

Restroom: At Bonneville, across freeway.

Picnic Area: Large picnic area at Bonneville Hatchery across freeway.

View & Kissing Spots: Can be seen from several spots on the trail beyond it but from the parking lot, it is virtually invisible until you are practically within arms reach of it! This is a great kissing spot!

Accessibility to the Physically Challenged: To the bridge.

Hazards: When windy or raining, the bridge can become slippery.

Information: On an unnamed tributary of Tanner Creek, Multnomah County, Oregon, Bonneville Dam Quadrangle and USGS Tanner Butte Quadrangle, Green Trails Maps: Bonneville Dam.

Munra Falls has no official, registered name. We have used the name previously used by others. "Munra", which is officially used as the name of a nearby high spot, "Munra Point", immortalizes "Grandma Munra" who once ran a railroad eating house at Bonneville.

Note that the view of the falls in our drawing is from across the creek. The charm and romance of Munra Falls is greatest when experienced from the bridge, nearly within arms reach of the water. Unfortunately, we really couldn't do justice to it from that perspective. Therefore, we waded across the creek during lower (and warmer) water in the Summer and drew it from the other side. Because the stream can be much too high and powerful, be very cautious about following our example!

Right at the parking lot and trailhead, the remnant of the original Columbia River Highway is visible in the face of an old bridge across the creek. This is officially trail #400. A hike to the west on this trail for a couple of miles

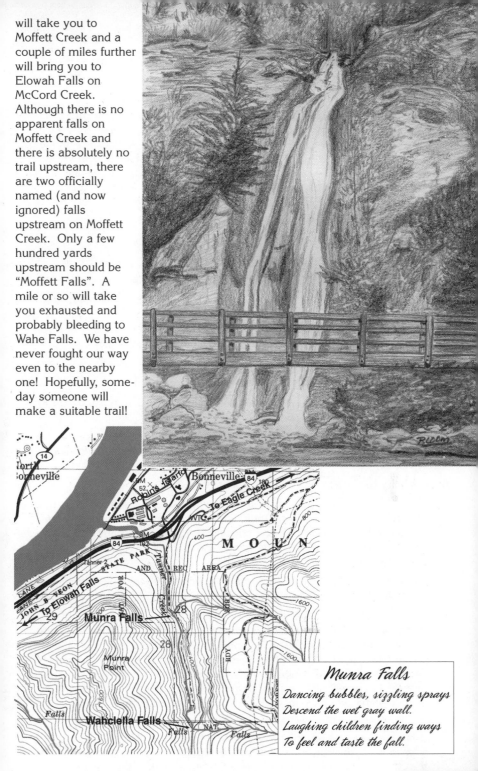

will take you to Moffett Creek and a couple of miles further will bring you to Elowah Falls on McCord Creek. Although there is no apparent falls on Moffett Creek and there is absolutely no trail upstream, there are two officially named (and now ignored) falls upstream on Moffett Creek. Only a few hundred yards upstream should be "Moffett Falls". A mile or so will take you exhausted and probably bleeding to Wahe Falls. We have never fought our way even to the nearby one! Hopefully, some-day someone will make a suitable trail!

Munra Falls

Dancing bubbles, sizzling sprays
Descend the wet gray wall.
Laughing children finding ways
To feel and taste the fall.

West Columbia Gorge of Oregon

22   Wahclella Falls

Two Plunges Join to Become One Blasting to the Pool — Wow!

Height: 125'   Difficulty: 5   Romance: 7

Type: Narrow Contact Plunge, Narrow Arch Plunge.

Description: Tanner Creek enters the head of its canyon via a powerful and beautiful falls. The main watercourse (Tanner Creek) plunges over a cliff and drops about 50 feet into a very narrow slit in the main cliff facing you. From the left, smaller East Falls plunges an equal distance down the side wall of the slot and joins it. Perhaps twenty feet from the initial plunge, the combined waters are forced through a narrow nozzle of rock and blast outward and downward with a mighty roar, falling to a clear blue pool below.

Distance/Time From Portland: 40 miles, 40 minutes via I-84.

Directions to Parking/Trailhead: Follow directions for Munra Falls (#21).

Distance/Time From Parking: .9 miles, 43 minutes.

Distance/Time From Other Landmark: 35 minutes from Munra Falls (#21).

Directions From Parking: Walk south from parking area on level trail past fish hatchery area, across bridge at Munra Falls, then follow trail upward to fork in trail. Both lead to falls, the choice depends on trail conditions and you. Assuming both are ok, they can provide a pleasant loop hike.

Elevation Change: 300 feet.

Restroom: At Bonneville, across freeway; at Cascade Locks.

Picnic Area: Many unofficial but scenic spots near falls. Large picnic area at Bonneville Hatchery across freeway.

View & Kissing Spots: Quite different and beautiful views of falls approaching from both trails. Each of the bridges along the trail are natural kissing spots, especially the one at the base of the falls.

Accessibility to the Physically Challenged: Not accessible.

Hazards: Steep, narrow spots on upper trail which sometimes slide to no trail at all. Be careful! Muddy lower trail. Slipping on rocks at tempting spots along creek or near falls. Some poison oak is found in sunny and dry spots, especially across the footbridge on the west side of the creek along the lower trail.

Information: On Tanner Creek, Multnomah County, Oregon, USGS Bonneville Dam Quadrangle and USGS Tanner Butte Quadrangle, Green Trails Maps: Bonneville Dam.

Although in 1915 the Mazamas named the falls, "Wahclella" for a nearby Native American village near Beacon Rock, its current, "official" USGS-Geographic Names Information System name is still its previous one, Tanner Creek Falls. Perhaps someday someone will go through the arduous process of changing the official name. Tanner Creek is named for J.T. Tanner who made a Donation Land Claim at its mouth in the 1850s.

The trail splits into upper and lower trails about two thirds of the way to the falls. The lower trail is often muddy and the upper trail often washes out, presenting a treacherous few feet of trail to negotiate. Take one then return by the other. Distances are not too great to double back in the event of problems. Lower trail crosses the creek on a scenic footbridge soon after the fork. The trails join at another footbridge right at the base of the falls. Wahclella is particularly spectacular in Winter and Spring when flows are highest.

Notice the sensuously curved rocks sculpted as modern works of art by nature's watery hand.

The varying environments of this trail— from creekside dampness, to deep forest, to dappled shade, to sunny slopes, to dry sunbaked rock slides, to waterfall spray— provide a wonderful microcosm of the many ecosystems of the gorge.

Look for particularly friendly and noisily cheerful dippers in the creek.

While you're near the Bonneville Dam, make sure to stop at the hatchery with its pools of giant sturgeons, salmon, and trout and to view the migrating fish at the visitor center upstream from the dam itself (which is also something interesting to tour). They have gift shops, informative displays, and restrooms!

See detailed map at falls #22, Munra Falls.

Shooting Star

Wahclella Falls

Another perfect Northwest day
With misty rain so nice and cool.
The Winter woods smell sweet and clean
So bright and green from ferns and moss.

Wahclella roared as white as foam.
The falls were full from Winter rain.
Creating mist to shower us
As on the bridge we hugged and kissed.

II. Eagle Creek Area

The Eagle Creek area in the Columbia River Gorge just east of Bonneville Dam is a wonderfully scenic one with a great many wonderful waterfalls. It is frequented by large numbers of hardy souls enjoying the seclusion, the beauty, and the many wondrous sights.

Eagle Creek cuts a deep, narrow groove in the layers of lava for many miles. If you continue hiking upstream beyond Eagle Creek Falls, you will eventually reach Wahtum Lake, a popular high mountain wilderness lake for fishing and camping. Of course, if you continue far enough, who knows? California, Mexico?

Along the Eagle Creek trail, there are several spots called camps. These are basically wide spots where there is room for a few sleeping bags or tents. There are no amenities such as restroom (except the woods), water (except the creek), fireplaces (except rocks you gather), campsites (except places you choose). If there's a sign saying "Camp", it's a lot. This is a wilderness experience.

Thanks to the availability of fish in the river and at the fish hatchery, both bald eagles and osprey are often seen near the Eagle Creek Hatchery and nearby Bonneville Dam. The bald eagles are more likely to feed on dead salmon and lamprey hurt by the dam or which have died after spawning. The osprey, on the other hand, are much more likely to be seen diving into the water to catch a fish in their talons. Keep you eyes peeled while you're driving to and from the trailhead. Incidentally, a large number of bald eagles can be found roosting on Sauvie Island downstream from Portland, especially during the Winter. During that season, they feed on the huge flocks of ducks, geese, and swans that winter there.

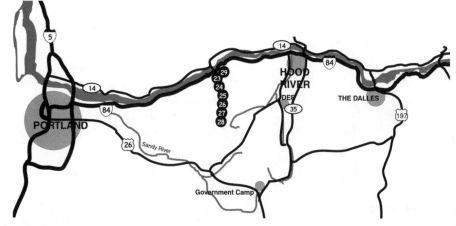

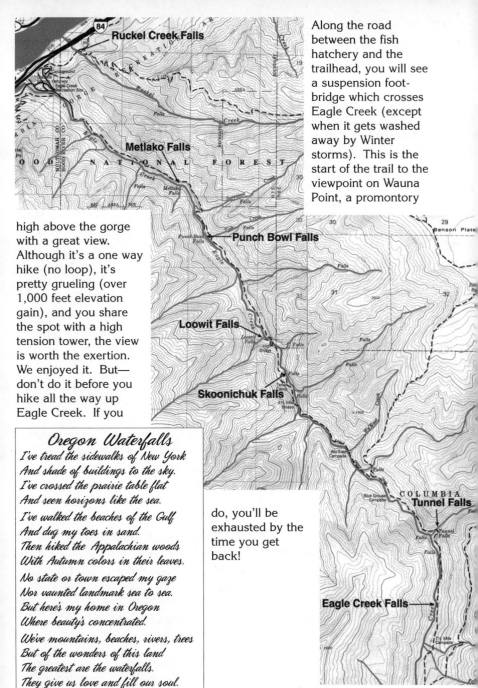

Along the road between the fish hatchery and the trailhead, you will see a suspension foot-bridge which crosses Eagle Creek (except when it gets washed away by Winter storms). This is the start of the trail to the viewpoint on Wauna Point, a promontory high above the gorge with a great view. Although it's a one way hike (no loop), it's pretty grueling (over 1,000 feet elevation gain), and you share the spot with a high tension tower, the view is worth the exertion. We enjoyed it. But—don't do it before you hike all the way up Eagle Creek. If you do, you'll be exhausted by the time you get back!

Oregon Waterfalls

I've tread the sidewalks of New York
And shade of buildings to the sky.
I've crossed the prairie table flat
And seen horizons like the sea.

I've walked the beaches of the Gulf
And dug my toes in sand.
Then hiked the Appalachian woods
With Autumn colors in their leaves.

No state or town escaped my gaze
Nor vaunted landmark sea to sea.
But here's my home in Oregon
Where beauty's concentrated.

We've mountains, beaches, rivers, trees
But of the wonders of this land
The greatest are the waterfalls.
They give us love and fill our soul.

So come and visit waterfalls
You'll find yourself inside their world.
Somehow they strike a primal chord
Connecting us through time and space.

23   Metlako Falls

A Fire-hose Plunge from the Rim of the Canyon to the Creek Below

Height: 108'   **Difficulty:** 4   **Romance:** 6

Type: Narrow Arch Plunge.

Description: As if from nowhere, a mighty plunge of water arches from a small space set back from the sheer cliff facing the Eagle Creek Trail and roars into Eagle Creek itself.

Distance/Time From Portland: 41 miles, 41 minutes via I-84.

Directions to Parking/Trailhead: Drive east on Interstate 84 to the Eagle Creek Recreation Area exit #41, next exit past the one for Bonneville Dam. If you are coming from the east (such as from Hood River), you must exit at Bonneville then reenter eastbound to reach the Eagle Creek exit. From the exit, drive past the fish hatchery to as far upstream (south) as you can go and park along the road. Because of the popularity of this area, you may have to park a long way from the end of the road trailhead.

Distance/Time From Parking: 1.5 miles, 50 minutes.

Distance/Time From Other Landmark: .4 miles to Lower Punch Bowl Falls trail.

Directions From Parking: From the trailhead, hike upstream past two scary cliff edge sections for 1.5 miles, 50 minutes to Metlako Falls viewpoint on the right.

Elevation Change: 350 feet.

Restroom: Modern, year round next to parking lot near hatchery and a primitive one near the trailhead; at Bonneville 1 mile west, or Cascade Locks 4 miles east. There are no restrooms along the Eagle Creek Trail.

Picnic Area: At Eagle Creek Campground and at campgrounds and picnic areas along the trail, including an informal space at the Metlako Falls Viewpoint.

View & Kissing Spots: At the main viewpoint and at a more dangerous (no railing) informal area just down the trail from the main one.

Accessibility to the Physically Challenged: Not accessible due to narrow and steep trail.

Hazards: High cliffs with narrow trail carved from the cliff with no railing, only a cable hand hold; poison oak; very dangerous clifftop viewpoints.

Information: On Metlako Creek (tributary of Eagle Creek), Hood River County, Oregon, USGS Bonneville Dam Quadrangle, Green Trails Maps: Bonneville Dam; listed in USGS Geographic Names Information System.

Metlako was named for a Native American goddess of approximately the same name. We're not sure from which people she arose.

The Eagle Creek area is quite famous for its unique geologic strata and its fossils. Look for petrified trees, seams of coal-like material, and alternating layers of lava and rounded rocks and other sedimentary material.

On the trail, look for Wauna Falls sliding down the opposite cliff of the Eagle Creek Gorge .4 miles, 13 minutes from Metlako Falls. Unfortunately, it is nearly hidden by trees. Were it more visible, it might be a significant attraction. It might even be worth being in our book!

Further upstream from the Metlako viewpoint but before the trail for Lower Punch Bowl Falls, you will cross Sorenson Creek as it tumbles its way downhill. This stream has a significant waterfall Sorenson Falls, as it nears Eagle Creek. Unfortunately, if it is visible at all, it is only from the other side of Eagle Creek or other places inaccessible to normal humans.

See detailed map at the section head, II, Eagle Creek Area.

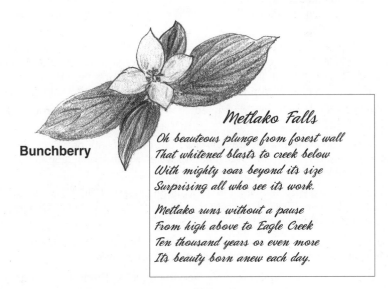

Bunchberry

Metlako Falls

Oh beauteous plunge from forest wall
That whitened blasts to creek below
With mighty roar beyond its size
Surprising all who see its work.

Metlako runs without a pause
From high above to Eagle Creek
Ten thousand years or even more
Its beauty born anew each day.

24   Punch Bowl Falls

So Beautiful — One of the Most Widely Used Images Anywhere

Height: 50'   **Difficulty:** 6 to viewpoint; 7 to streamside   **Romance:** 10

Type: Hourglass Contact Plunge.

Description: An enormous round bowl of sheer vertical cliffs encloses a deep pool of clear blue water formed by a truly magnificent vase-shaped flow of very clear water which flows out of an artistically rounded gap in the bowl to land picturesquely in its icy lake.

Distance/Time From Portland: 41 miles, 41 minutes via I-84.

Directions to Parking/Trailhead: Follow directions for Metlako Falls (#23).

Distance/Time From Parking: 1.9 miles, 65 minutes to the lower falls cutoff; 2.1 miles, 73 minutes total to upper viewpoint.

Distance/Time From Other Landmark: .6 miles, 23 minutes from Metlako Falls (#23); 1.1 miles, 40 minutes to Loowit Falls (#25).

Directions From Parking: Follow directions to Metlako Falls then continue for .4 miles, 15 minutes past the nearly impossible to view Sorenson Falls on Sorenson Creek to the trail downhill to Lower Punch Bowl Falls viewpoint. Take this .1 miles, 5 minute side trip to streamside, a "swimming & diving falls", a great ice cold swim in the pool beneath Punch Bowl Falls, and/or a terrific water level view of Punch Bowl. On return to the main trail, continue south for .2 miles, 8 minutes and to a spectacular high viewpoint of the falls.

Elevation Change: 400 feet.

Restroom: Modern, year round next to parking lot near hatchery and a primitive one near the trailhead; at Bonneville 1 mile west, or Cascade Locks 4 miles east. There are no restrooms along the Eagle Creek Trail.

Picnic Area: At Eagle Creek Campground and at campgrounds and picnic areas along the trail, including wonderful informal areas at the cutoff for the lower falls viewpoint, at the Punch Bowl Falls Viewpoint, and especially at the lower falls viewpoint.

View & Kissing Spots: From lower trail (to the level of the base of the falls); from excellent designated viewpoint from level higher than the falls viewing it across its punch bowl. Kiss at viewpoints, in the water near the base of the falls (or as close as you can get), and beside the falls downstream.

Accessibility to the Physically Challenged: Not accessible due to narrow and steep trail.

Hazards: High cliffs with narrow trail carved from the cliff with no railing, only a cable hand hold; poison oak. Diving into water which looks deep enough (see note below).

Information: On Eagle Creek, Hood River County, Oregon, USGS Tanner Butte Quadrangle, Green Trails Maps: Bonneville Dam; listed in USGS Geographic Names Information System.

This falls is pictured on more posters, ads, etc. than nearly any other falls. Punch Bowl is one of the most beautiful sights anywhere.

A very popular (although potentially very dangerous) Summer swimming spot is the falls just downstream from where the lower trail meets Eagle

Creek. This may appropriately be called "Lower Punch Bowl Falls although it doesn't resemble its famous upstream neighbor. People dive off the cliff above and around the falls into the deep blue pool below. We wouldn't do this without being absolutely sure what was under the water. Keep in mind that all such streams change drastically with each storm. Often huge rocks and logs are moved great distances, changing deep pools into shallow ones or depositing rocks where there was previously safe, deep water.

If you are a good swimmer and like ice cold water, you can also swim in Punch Bowl's pool, wade the creek, and generally get wet, wild, and cold! A great adventure (and means of cooling off) on a really hot Summer day.

See detailed map at the section head, II, Eagle Creek Area.

Dutchman's Breeches

Punch Bowl Falls

You are not the tallest waterfall.
You've higher neighbors all around.
You are not the biggest of the falls.
There's more with greater flow.

You are just the perfect waterfall.
With such sweet shape and symmetry,
Of fluid carved your verdin walls
And perfect liquid transparency

25   **Loowit Falls**

A Surprising Falls Slides Down a Cliff then Bounces and Slides Again

Height: 125'   **Difficulty:** 6 to viewpoint; 8 to base of falls   **Romance:** 5

Type: Narrow Contact Plunge, Spreading Concave Slide.

Description: For an incredibly long distance, a narrow course of water forcefully slides down a slightly angled uniform layer of bare black lava rock flanked by moss and forest. Near the bottom, the rock cliff curves somewhat upward then back to its former angle—making a sort of water-park ride effect—before entering Eagle Creek.

Distance/Time From Portland: 41 miles, 41 minutes via I-84.

Directions to Parking/Trailhead: Follow directions for Metlako Falls (#23).

Distance/Time From Parking: 3.2 miles, 1 hour and 53 minutes to viewpoint; 3.6 miles, 2 hours and 43 minutes including side trip to base of the falls.

Distance/Time From Other Landmark: 1.1 miles, 40 minutes from Punch Bowl Falls (#24); .2 miles, 20 minutes to High Bridge; .4 miles, 50 minutes to base of the falls; .6 miles, 49 minutes to Skoonichuk Falls (#26).

Directions From Parking: Follow directions to Punch Bowl Falls then continue on the trail for 1.1 miles, 40 minutes until you see Loowit Falls on the opposite cliffside. It is possible, though somewhat hazardous, to hike to the falls itself by a crude path along the cliffside and creek which begins at the far side of High Bridge, further up the trail.

Elevation Change: 500 feet.

Restroom: Modern, year round next to parking lot near hatchery and a primitive one near the trailhead; at Bonneville 1 mile west, or Cascade Locks 4 miles east. There are no restrooms along the Eagle Creek Trail.

Picnic Area: At Eagle Creek Campground and at campgrounds and picnic areas along the trail.

View & Kissing Spots: From the Eagle Creek Trail directly across from the falls; from the base of the falls. A kiss under the falls is wonderful!

Accessibility to the Physically Challenged: Not accessible due to narrow and steep trail.

Hazards: High cliffs with narrow trail carved from the cliff with no railing, only a cable hand hold; poison oak, drowning (?). Be smart and careful if you attempt to go to the falls or play in the water! Do not attempt it except when it's dry and the water is low.

Information: On Loowit Creek (tributary of Eagle Creek), Hood River County, Oregon, USGS Tanner Butte Quadrangle, Green Trails Maps: Bonneville Dam; listed in USGS Geographic Names Information System.

Benson Falls, a rather insignificant falls, slides down a cleft in the cliff on the trail side of the creek near the viewpoint for Loowit Falls. Although Benson Falls is sometimes listed with other falls on Eagle Creek, we did not consider it sufficiently scenic to be included in this book.

People often hike to the bottom of Loowit where they bathe, sunbathe, and slide down its last section. If it's a hot Summer day, you just have to play in the water at the base of Loowit! Although we have made this trek and found it worth the trouble, we recommend great caution. Its side trail is a mere path at best, is poorly maintained if at all, is very steep and poorly defined, high water and slides can change or virtually eliminate the path, and its a reverse hike which requires a difficult uphill climb to return to the Eagle Creek Trail at High Bridge. Have fun but use your head, assess conditions, and be very careful.

See detailed map at the section head, II, Eagle Creek Area.

Oregon Junco

Loowit Falls

Sliding down its smooth rock flume
Loowit shows its playful face.
Swooping to the brightness from the gloom
Bouncing at the end of its wet race.

Playing in the shower at its end,
Laughing as we dance in its cold spray.
Loowit shows its sensual bend,
Giving joy and love all day.

26   Skoonichuk Falls
Short but Powerful and Picturesque.

Height: 30'   **Difficulty:** 8   **Romance:** 4

Type: Hourglass Contact Plunge, Square Slide.

Description: Skoonichuk Falls squeezes through a gap between two opposing walls of lava. The stream spills out of its placid pool, plunges downward, spreads as it slides over the underlying rock, then strikes its "anvil stone", and bounces with great force, finally spraying into the stream beyond.

Distance/Time From Portland: 41 miles, 41 minutes via I-84.

Directions to Parking/Trailhead: Follow directions for Metlako Falls (#23).

Distance/Time From Parking: 3.8 miles, 2 hours and 42 minutes.

Distance/Time From Other Landmark: .6 miles, 49 minutes from Loowit Falls (#25); .4 miles, 28 minutes from 4.5 Mile Bridge.

Directions From Parking: Follow directions to Loowit Falls then continue for about .2 miles, 20 minutes to High Bridge from which you can get a beautiful view of the area. Continue for another .4 miles, 29 minutes until you see Skoonichuk Falls on Eagle Creek to your left ahead.

Elevation Change: 600 feet.

Restroom: Modern, year round next to parking lot near hatchery and a primitive one near the trailhead; at Bonneville 1 mile west, or Cascade Locks 4 miles east. There are no restrooms along the Eagle Creek Trail.

Picnic Area: At Eagle Creek Campground and at campgrounds and picnic areas along the trail; on rocks at top of falls and at nearby camping area.

View & Kissing Spots: At trailside vantage points.

Accessibility to the Physically Challenged: Not accessible due to narrow and steep trail.

Hazards: High cliffs with narrow trail carved from the cliff with no railing, only a cable hand hold; poison oak.

Information: On Eagle Creek, Hood River County, Oregon, USGS Tanner Butte Quadrangle, Green Trails Maps: Bonneville Dam.

Upstream (before you reach Tunnel Falls), you will pass several other falls. We have not included them in the book for various reasons: some were too hard to see, some were insignificant much of the year, and some just weren't sufficiently interesting or attractive to us. One of them seems no longer to be there! Look for Benson Falls on the east wall of the canyon more or less opposite Loowit Falls, Tenas Falls also on the east side past Tenas Camp, Wy'east Falls on a tributary trail near Wy'east camp, and Blue Grouse Falls on Eagle Creek itself just before the turn for Tunnel Falls. Let us know if you find and like any of them enough for us to include them in a later addition.

The Eagle Creek canyon is a wonderland of nature. Some of the largest examples of many popular species of trees are visible along the trail. In addition, a great diversity of wildflowers grow in perfusion. A hike all the way to Eagle Creek Falls offers a constantly changing palette of colors and shapes: Chocolate Lily, Fawn Lily, Penstemon, Wild Delphinium, Hair Bell,

Dog Violet, Rhododendron, Salal, Trillium, Huckleberry, Salmonberry, Dogwood, Indian Pipe, Bunchberry, Monkey Flower, Bleeding Heart, Dutchman's Breeches, Thimbleberry, False Lily of the Valley, Fairy Bells, Solomon Seal, Pinedrops, Paintbrush—and flowers beyond name and number. This is one of the most amazing wildflower gardens you'll ever see.

See detailed map at the section head, II, Eagle Creek Area.

Corydalis

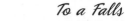

To a Falls

Are you low? Is your heart sick?
Are you sore? Do your joints ache?

Let it go. Get your face wet.
Stretch your legs. Get the kinks out.

Climb the hill. You can do it.
Look around. Here is real life.

You are small. Nature's so big.
Be at peace. You will survive.

Feel and see beauty here now.
You're at peace, young and in love.

27   Tunnel Falls

A Very Big, Tall Falls Running Down a Huge Walk-Through Column

Height: 120'   **Difficulty:** 8   **Romance:** 10

Type: Narrow Contact Plunge.

Description: A fabulous "Walk-Behind" Falls! The falls is set in a 180° amphitheater of sheer cliffs. Near the middle of this curved cliff, the rock bulges some 10 feet to form a 20 foot wide rock column set against the cliff face. The falls slides down this column from top to bottom. The trail is carved into a horizontal rock layer in the middle of the vertical expanse and, most amazing of all, it runs through a tunnel carved through the column. You can lean out of the tunnel on either side and receive a shower from the thundering falls. Wow!

Distance/Time From Portland: 41 miles, 41 minutes via I-84.

Directions to Parking/Trailhead: Follow directions for Metlako Falls (#23).

Distance/Time From Parking: 6.2 miles, 5 hours and 18 minutes.

Distance/Time From Other Landmark: 2.4 miles, 2 hours and 36 minutes from Skoonichuk Falls (#26); 2 miles, 2 hours and 8 minutes from 4.5 Mile Bridge; .2 miles, 12 minutes from Blue Grouse Falls; .3 miles, 17 minutes to Eagle Creek Falls (#28).

Directions From Parking: Follow Directions to Skoonichuk Falls (#26) then continue for 2.4 miles, 2 hours and 36 minutes to Tunnel Falls.

Elevation Change: 1,100 feet.

Restroom: Modern, year round next to parking lot near hatchery and a primitive one near the trailhead; at Bonneville 1 mile west, or Cascade Locks 4 miles east. There are no restrooms along the Eagle Creek Trail.

Picnic Area: At Eagle Creek Campground and at campgrounds and picnic areas along the trail.

View & Kissing Spots: On the trail approaching and leaving the falls basin. Kiss in the tunnel or under the spray on either side!

Accessibility to the Physically Challenged: Not accessible due to narrow and steep trail.

Hazards: Figuring out how to get here on the freeway and how to get where you are going afterward! High cliffs with narrow trail carved from the cliff with no railing, only a cable hand hold; poison oak. Do not lean on the railings around the falls. Like other railings, they are only an aid. A hiker leaned out to get a better look a few years ago. His weight was too much for the railing. It gave way. He fell. He did not survive!

Information: On the East Fork of Eagle Creek, Hood River County, Oregon, USGS Wahtum Lake Quadrangle, Green Trails Maps: Bonneville Dam; listed in USGS Geographic Names Information System.

See detailed map at the section head, II, Eagle Creek Area.

White Breasted Nuthatch

Tunnel Falls

A black stone column rises high
In perfect symmetry
Its wide curved shape so even
Its back against the cliff.

From clifftop rim to pool below
One hundred feet or more
The column wears a waterfall
That hugs it end to end

To bring its beauty to our kind
Some men worked hard and long
To carve a trail along the cliff
And tunnel through the column.

Now you and I can see it close
And feel its waters spray.
We stand and wonder at God's plan
And at the works of man.

Eagle Creek Area

28   Eagle Creek Falls
View Eagle Creek's Most Powerful Falls Up Close

Height: 110'   **Difficulty:** 9   **Romance:** 6

Type: Hourglass Slide to Arch Plunge.

Description: Eagle Creek spreads placidly over a wide, flat shelf of rock. The stream would stop at a vertical wall of water were it not for a narrow crack through which the stream pours. As the flat shelf of rock forming the bed of Eagle Creek reaches the opening in the wall, the stream has gouged a crack in the shelf so that the stream plunges down from three sides combining into a blast of water that shoots down and outward into the broader valley beyond. When first seen in the distance from the trail, Eagle Creek Falls shows its tall, white plunge down the cliff side. From the top and side, you can look into the watery mouth of hell created by the power of the confluence of the flows from all directions.

Distance/Time From Portland: 41 miles, 41 minutes via I-84.

Directions to Parking/Trailhead: Follow directions for Metlako Falls (#23).

Distance/Time From Parking: 6.8 miles, 5 hours and 29 minutes.

Distance/Time From Other Landmark: .3 miles, 17 minutes from Tunnel Falls (#27).

Directions From Parking: Follow Directions to Tunnel Falls then continue for .3 miles, 17 minutes.

Elevation Change: 1,100 feet.

Restroom: Modern, year round next to parking lot near hatchery and a primitive one near the trailhead; at Bonneville 1 mile west, or Cascade Locks 4 miles east. There are no restrooms along the Eagle Creek Trail.

Picnic Area: At Eagle Creek Campground and at campgrounds and picnic areas along the trail and near the top of the falls.

View & Kissing Spots: From the trail at least .1 mile before you reach the fall; at the top of the falls. Kiss at scenic spots and while you cool your feet in the stream above the top of the falls.

Accessibility to the Physically Challenged: Not accessible due to narrow and steep trail.

Hazards: High cliffs with narrow trail carved from the cliff with no railing, only a cable hand hold; poison oak. Be especially careful along the narrow trail next to the falls and in the water upstream. Becoming "one" with this falls is likely to be a fatal experience!

Information: On Eagle Creek, Hood River County, Oregon, USGS Wahtum Lake Quadrangle, Green Trails Maps: Bonneville Dam.

When we showed a friend this drawing, she wailed, "You mean that's what I missed by not going on past Tunnel Falls?" Actually there's another spectacular view of this falls which we decided not to use. As you approach it on the trail, you can see it spewing out and down through the trees. We just liked this view from near the top better. We should have added the two of us just upstream, soaking our feet in the stream (which we did). Barbara just couldn't draw and soak at the same time!

See detailed map at the section head, II, Eagle Creek Area.

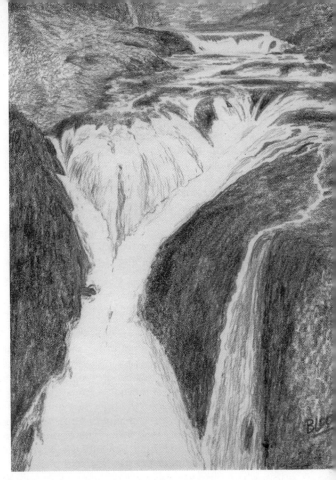

Bald Eagle

Escape

Far from traffic, noise, and fumes
Woods are lush, the water clear.
Stretching muscles, flexing joints
Hear my step, my heart, my breath.

Flowers add their sweet perfume:
Scents of berries, trees, and earth.
Sounds of nature fill the air:
Flowing water, singing birds.

29   Ruckel Creek Falls

A Scene from Long Ago in a Charming and Secluded Setting

Height: 50' **Difficulty:** 3 **Romance:** 5

Type: Narrow Steep Slide.

Description: This is a very historic and scenic falls although rather difficult to view to its best advantage. Ruckel Creek tumbles downhill through a narrow, wooded canyon. When it reaches the site of the original Historic Columbia Gorge Highway, an arching stone bridge spans the creek just at the point that the creek drops over a rock ledge to fall to a large pool below. It's secluded and romantic from the bridge and picturesque when viewed from creekside downstream.

Distance/Time From Portland: 41 miles, 41 minutes via I-84.

Directions to Parking/Trailhead: Follow directions for Metlako Falls (#23) but, from once off the freeway, drive past the fish hatchery to the large paved parking lot next to the large, quaint restroom building. Park near the woods, farthest from the creek.

Distance/Time From Parking: About .6 miles, 20 minutes.

Distance/Time From Other Landmark: 2.1 miles, 70 minutes from Metlako Falls (#23).

Directions From Parking: Take a path from the parking lot uphill through the woods; in 10 minutes or less uphill, the initial path intersects Trail #400; turn left on #400 and hike for about 5 minutes along the cliff-face, along a fence, and eventually walk down to a broad meadow on the other side of the hill; hike for 5 minutes along the right side of the meadow until it reaches a stone marker and rock/dirt remnant of a road which angles uphill along the hillside; continue on this road for 5 minutes until you reach the old highway bridge with Ruckel Creek Falls beneath. Once you see where the falls is located, you can return to the meadow and pick your way through the brush, which obscures any view of the creek or falls from the meadow, to frolic by the stream and pool at the base of the falls. Hopefully, someday there will be a trail to the base of the falls. **Alternative:** For a shorter, level hike, park in a small "driveway" next to the south side of the freeway just east of the Eagle Creek complex. There is room for 2 or 3 cars to park near a gate on the remnant of the old highway. Caution: pulling on or off the freeway can be very dangerous! Note that it's far easier to find this freeway parking spot after you've visited the falls from Eagle Creek and looked at the spot on the ground.

Elevation Change: 100 feet

Restroom: Modern, year round next to main parking lot near hatchery; at Bonneville 1 mile before Eagle Creek exit or at Cascade Locks 4 miles further east.

Picnic Area: Several excellent picnic areas all around Eagle Creek area.

View & Kissing Spots: From the charming old arched stone bridge; from various locations along Ruckel Creek below the falls. Kiss on the bridge.

Accessibility to the Physically Challenged: Not possible from Eagle Creek, but from the turn-in past Eagle Creek mentioned above, if the gate or fence can be managed, one may traverse to the bridge if the road is in repair.

Hazards: Relatively hazard free except for the brush and briars through which you may navigate to reach the creek and the base of the falls.

Information: On Ruckel Creek, Hood River County, Oregon, USGS Bonneville Dam Quadrangle, Green Trails Maps: Bonneville Dam.

Ruckel Creek was originally named Deadman Creek. Because of the unpleasant connotations, it was changed to commemorate J.S. Ruckel, the builder of the portage railroad at the Cascades (rapids) of the Columbia and founder of the Oregon Steam Navigation Company. I'm partial to Deadman Creek.

The old bridge above the falls is part of the original Columbia River Highway. Hopefully, it will eventually be restored.

When the trees are bare, you can see the falls from the freeway.

Ruckel Creek Trail to Benson Plateau (a grueling 3,700 foot climb) begins past the falls. That hike was tough for both of us but the view and the cute little spotted owl that watched us going up and coming down made it worth it.

See detailed map at the section head, II, Eagle Creek Area.

Skunk Cabbage

Masterpieces

*It's sad to know
Henry David Thoreau never saw this waterfall
And Monet never sketched it;
But maybe their deprivation led them to their art,
While we, by luck have masterpieces.*

III. East Columbia Gorge of Oregon

From Cascade Locks to Hood River, the Columbia Gorge provides a number of delightful hikes and a number of striking, though little visited, falls. Individual hikes and scenic views include: Cascade Locks to Herman Creek, Herman Creek itself, Gorton Creek, Starvation Falls to Lancaster Falls, Wah Gwin Gwin on the heights in Hood River (the town), and the two falls on the Hood River (the river) near Dee—a total of 13 falls. We are aware, incidentally, that the two falls on Hood River cannot actually qualify as being in the Columbia River Gorge. However, after much soul searching, we decided that they were more likely to fit into an excursion to falls of the east gorge than with ones near Mount Hood. On the other hand, they are also not too far from Tamanawas, Sahale, and Umbrella. Regardless, see them all!

When Lewis and Clark finally reached the Columbia River Gorge, they discovered a unique place with people and customs unlike any they had ever encountered. They saw small villages of wooden houses at the mouth of virtually every stream entering the Columbia. Beside the snug looking houses were drying racks hung with tons of salmon curing in the air. Extremely strong and light weight wooden canoes waited for their owners' use. The native people's pet dogs barked from the shore at the strangers.

The eastern end of the Columbia River Gorge on the Oregon side is like its western half, characterized by a great many small streams and a few larger

---

The Tourist

We stood before the falls and stared
Delighted by its misty spray.
The woman asked "Is this the falls?"
No answer came from anyone.
What could we say to her?
How could she miss this giant falls
Ten feet or so in front of her
Which washed the face and heart with joy?
Despite our silence, she went on...
"I saw Yosemite last week.
Now there are waterfalls!"

The crowd dispersed without response
Just knowing glances shared
Not sure what words to say
But certain none would help
'Cause waterfalls, like love,
Are not to be explained,
But savored, sought, and shared.
And when your in its glow,
Each one is best of show.

---

ones which traverse the wall of cliffs forming the gorge either by cutting through them, falling down them, or a combination of both. Most of the smaller streams arise fairly locally, whereas the larger ones usually begin on the flanks of one of the medium size mountains in the vicinity of Mount Hood such as Larch Mountain. Thus, throughout the Oregon side of the gorge, there are no significant, definable watersheds, even though many streams have multiple waterfalls (Latourell, Coopey, Wahkeena, Multnomah, Oneonta, Horsetail, McCord, Tanner, Eagle, Herman).

Pacific Rhododendron

Mule Deer (Doe)

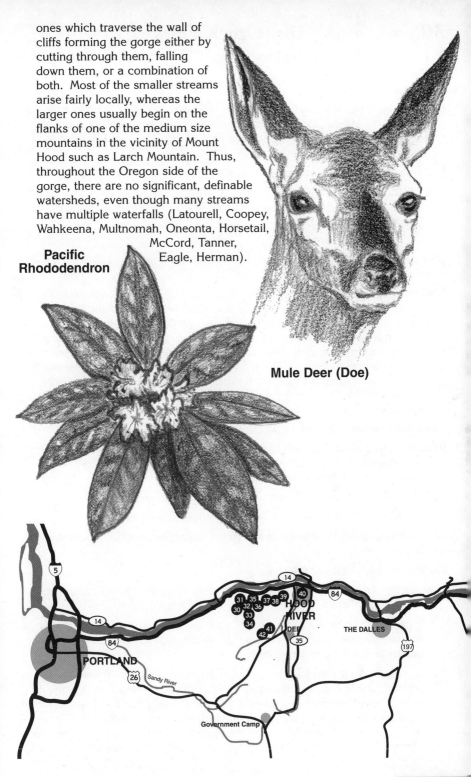

30   Dry Creek Falls

An Attractive and Interesting Falls after a Scenic Hike

Height: 70'   **Difficulty:** 6   **Romance:** 5

Type: Narrow Arch Plunge.

Description: A plume of water plunges from a point virtually out of sight to the right of the stream, lands in a deep, narrow crack between high rock walls, heads toward you and streams downward in a picturesque slide to the stream below.

Distance/Time From Portland: 45 miles, 45 minutes via I-84.

Directions to Parking/Trailhead: I-84 east to exit 44 to park near entrance of the Bridge of the Gods where you will find a large paved parking area.

Distance/Time From Parking: 2.2 miles, 73 minutes to falls from Cascade Locks trailhead.

Distance/Time From Other Landmark: 1.7 miles, 74 minutes to Pacific Crest Falls (#31).

Directions From Parking: From the park at the Bridge of the Gods (in the center of the circular ramp to the bridge), take the Pacific Crest Trail south for a short distance to cross under the freeway. At the street just after the freeway underpass, follow the Pacific Crest Trail to the left (do not take Ruckel Creek Trail to the right). After about 45 minutes, you will cross a power line road, continue for another 23 minutes to reach the footbridge crossing Dry Creek. Go upstream (right) for 5 minutes to the base of the falls. Note: you can also reach Dry Creek Falls from the Herman Creek Trail via the Pacific Crest Trail Cutoff.

Elevation Change: 800 feet.

Restroom: In park at Cascade Locks trailhead, seasonal; at restaurants and service stations in near trailhead in Cascade Locks; at Herman Creek Campground trailhead, seasonal, primitive.

Picnic Area: At park at trailhead; at Dry Creek footbridge.

View & Kissing Spots: On Dry Creek footbridge; at base of falls.

Accessibility to the Physically Challenged: Possibly accessible, though trail is dirt and uneven.

Hazards: Steep slopes next to trail.

Information: On Dry Creek, Hood River County, Oregon, USGS Carson Quadrangle, Green Trails Maps: Bonneville Dam.

Note that Dry Creek (and apparently the area at the base of the falls) is the source of drinking water for the people of Cascade Locks. Observe signs and treat this area with particular care.

You may take a long loop hike of over 10 miles (and over 6 hours) from either Cascade Locks trailhead or Herman Creek Campground trailhead to the other, visiting both Dry Creek Falls and Pacific Crest Falls, and returning via the road. The road portion between them requires about 75 minutes walking with sore feet. This hike might be a candidate for a 2-car method with which you leave a car at each end to avoid the in-return walk.

Cascade Locks was founded and named for a canal with locks which was

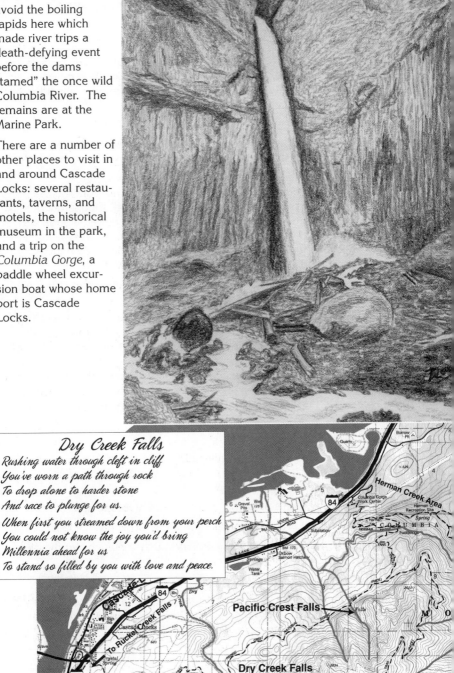

built in the 1800s to allow steamers to avoid the boiling rapids here which made river trips a death-defying event before the dams "tamed" the once wild Columbia River. The remains are at the Marine Park.

There are a number of other places to visit in and around Cascade Locks: several restaurants, taverns, and motels, the historical museum in the park, and a trip on the *Columbia Gorge*, a paddle wheel excursion boat whose home port is Cascade Locks.

Dry Creek Falls

Rushing water through cleft in cliff
You've worn a path through rock
To drop alone to harder stone
And race to plunge for us.

When first you streamed down from your perch
You could not know the joy you'd bring
Millennia ahead for us
To stand so filled by you with love and peace.

East Columbia Gorge of Oregon

31   Pacific Crest Falls

A Picturesque and Cool Falls Worth the Long Hike

Height: 40'   Difficulty: 6   Romance: 4

Type: Narrow Steep Slide.

Description: Just when you think your feet are going to fall off, you round a corner and there it is: a weak but tall flow in a deep cleft in the rock which emerges just beyond the trail, its stream crossing your path without the benefit of a bridge (to help cool your feet)!

Distance/Time From Portland: 48 miles, 45 minutes via I-84.

Directions to Parking/Trailhead: Either follow directions for Dry Creek Falls (#30) (from Bridge of the Gods) or follow directions for Falls Creek Falls (#32) (from Herman Creek Campground).

Distance/Time From Parking: 3.9 miles, 2 hours 20 minutes from Cascade Locks trailhead; 1 hour 11 minutes from Herman Creek Campground trailhead (8 minutes from Herman Creek Campground to power line road; 9 minutes to intersection of Herman Creek Trail and Pacific Crest Trail; 12 minutes on Pacific Crest Trail to Herman Creek footbridge; 25 minutes to intersection with main Pacific Crest Trail; 17 minutes to falls).

Distance/Time From Other Landmark: 1.7 miles, 74 minutes from Dry Creek Falls (#30).

Directions From Parking: From park at Bridge of the Gods, take Pacific Crest Trail south for a short distance to cross under freeway. At street just after freeway underpass, follow Pacific Crest Trail to the left (do not take Ruckel Creek Trail to the right). After about 45 minutes cross power line road, continue for another 23 minutes to reach footbridge crossing Dry Creek. To visit Dry Creek Falls, leave trail and go upstream (right) for 7 minutes to base of falls. To Pacific Crest Falls, continue across footbridge for 1 hour 7 minutes.

Elevation Change: 1,000 feet.

Restroom: In park at Cascade Locks trailhead, seasonal; at restaurants and service stations in near trailhead in Cascade Locks; at Herman Creek Campground trailhead, seasonal, primitive.

Picnic Area: No formal picnic areas but plenty of fun places to enjoy.

View & Kissing Spots: Approaching falls from the west, at base of falls.

Accessibility to the Physically Challenged: Very rough conditions for the physically challenged.

Hazards: Slippery rocks at base of falls.

Information: On an unnamed tributary of Herman Creek, Hood River County, Oregon, USGS Carson Quadrangle, Green Trails Maps: Bonneville Dam.

You may take a long loop hike of over 10 miles (and over 6 hours) from either Cascade Locks trailhead or Herman Creek Campground trailhead to the other, visiting both Dry Creek Falls and Pacific Crest Falls, and returning via the road. The road portion between them requires about 75 minutes.

While you are above the Columbia River, you should look from every viewpoint for Mount Saint Helens and Mount Adams across the river and, any time you have the opportunity, look for Mount Hood. They are beautiful, snow-capped volcanoes. All this you probably already know. What you may not have heard, is the Native American legend of the three mountains and The Bridge of the Gods at Cascade Locks. First we list the characters and set the scene: Two handsome braves, Klickitat (Mt. Adams), Wy'east (Mt. Hood), and a beautiful maiden, Loowit (Mt. St. Helens), they dwell in a beautiful land split by a huge river bridged by an amazing natural bridge (Bridge of the Gods). The two braves, who are of course from opposite sides of the river, begin quarreling over the maiden.

They grow red hot with anger, hurl burning stones at each other, roar with fury, and shake the earth so violently that the bridge is torn apart and falls into the river. The gods were so unhappy with their antics that they turned all three of them to stone and froze them white. They would stay that way forever except that sometimes, their passion would be so strong that they would briefly come to life enough to frighten everyone with the anger and power still smoldering in their rocky hearts. If geologists dismissed these tales as myth, the 1980 eruption of Mount Saint Helens certainly gave them reason to revisit such stories.

See detailed map at falls #30, Dry Creek Falls.

Heavenly Water

Falling crystal drops

Heaven's polished glowing tears

Wash my face and soul.

Falls Creek Falls

Cool off in this Big, Tall Trailside Falls

Height: 125'   Difficulty: 5   Romance: 6

Type: Spreading Contact Plunge.

Description: A spray of water drops over the edge of the sheer cliff only a few feet from the trail and sizzles down the rock face. Look for rainbows in its spray and be sure to take advantage of it to cool off, play, and refresh. Twice when we have visited this falls in the afternoon, the sun struck the water perfectly and made a rainbow in the mist near its base. As a result. we often refer to it as "Rainbow Falls"!

Distance/Time From Portland: 48 miles, 45 minutes via I-84.

Directions to Parking/Trailhead: I-84 east to exit 47 then east to Herman Creek Camp. If closed, park at roadside and hike through campground. If open (or walking), follow the paved driveway into the campground. Bear right until you reach a large, gravel parking area with a quaint little house in the center (the rustic restroom). The trail begins at the west side (opposite the entrance) and is marked by a large sign, map, etc.

Distance/Time From Parking: 2.2 miles, 1 hour 40 minutes from Herman Creek Horse Camp Trailhead.

Distance/Time From Other Landmark: 1 miles, 45 minutes to Camp Creek Falls (#33).

Directions From Parking: Follow the trail from the parking area (sign says: "Herman Creek Trail 1/4 mile; Pacific Crest Trail 1/4 mile") 13 minutes to the power line and its dirt road; cross this clearing to the trail where it re-enters the forest. Go 24 minutes to a fork to Herman Creek Bridge and Pacific Crest Trail. Bear left for 6 minutes to a clearing with 5 ways out. Go straight across and bear right on an abandoned road. 27 minutes later, you will reach a rustic campground at the more or less well marked intersection with Gorton Creek Trail #408. Go straight ahead for 5 minutes to a steep trail heading uphill to your left. This is Nick Eaton Way #447, a very long, very steep route to a ridge paralleling Herman Creek at 2000 foot elevation. Unless you're looking for a severe challenge, bear right! 16 minutes later you'll cross a creek with little flow except in Winter. If you look carefully, you may see an amazing, unnamed, multi-step falls nearly 200 feet tall. 8 minutes to another side creek without a falls. 1 minute later, you round the corner to see a glorious site, Falls Creek Falls!

Elevation Change: 880 feet.

Restroom: In center of parking area; rustic and in fair condition; sporadically locked! Try restaurants and service stations west in Cascade Locks.

Picnic Area: Very rustic and informal ones at campground and at spots on trail.

View & Kissing Spots: Approaching and leaving. Kiss in the spray of the falls.

Accessibility to the Physically Challenged: Very unlikely or impossible.

Hazards: Despite some poison oak in sunnier places and a few really dangerous drops, this hike is less dangerous as well as sunnier and hotter than most of this length, especially others near the gorge. Plan accordingly.

Information: On Falls Creek (a trailside tributary of Herman Creek), Hood River

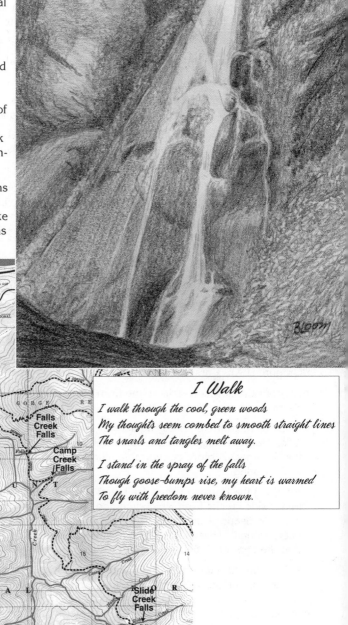

County, Oregon, USGS Carson Quadrangle, Green Trails Maps: Bonneville Dam.

Note there are several other falls and showery seeps along the trail. Enjoy them all!

Our forebears showed little imagination in geographic names. There are hundreds of Falls Creeks and dozens of Falls Creek Falls, including another in this book.

Unusual winter storms occasionally create impassible glacier-like conditions on streams crossing the trail.

I Walk

I walk through the cool, green woods
My thoughts seem combed to smooth straight lines
The snarls and tangles melt away.

I stand in the spray of the falls
Though goose-bumps rise, my heart is warmed
To fly with freedom never known.

East Columbia Gorge of Oregon

33   Camp Creek Falls
Another Beautiful and Convenient Trailside Shower

Height: 150'   **Difficulty:** 5   **Romance:** 6

Type: Narrow Contact Plunge.

Description: A big pretty falls appearing as a long, sizzling slide down its cliff no more than 30 feet from the trail allowing easy access to its cooling waters.

Distance/Time From Portland: 48 miles, 45 minutes via I-84.

Directions to Parking/Trailhead: Follow directions as to Falls Creek Falls (#32).

Distance/Time From Parking: 3.2 miles, 2 hours and 25 minutes.

Distance/Time From Other Landmark: 1 mile, 45 minutes from Falls Creek Falls (#32); 1.9 miles, 85 minutes to Slide Creek Falls #34).

Directions From Parking: Follow directions to Falls Creek Falls then continue up the trail for 1 mile, 45 minutes to Camp Creek Falls.

Elevation Change: 1,100 feet.

Restroom: In center of parking area; fair condition; open only when your not there! Try restaurants and service stations in Cascade Locks a few miles west.

Picnic Area: Several very undeveloped picnic or wilderness camping places along the trail.

View & Kissing Spots: From the trail approaching the falls from both directions. Kiss under the falls shower.

Accessibility to the Physically Challenged: Very difficult if not absolutely inaccessible.

Hazards: Poison oak; some dangerous slopes, possible ice in Winter.

Information: On Camp Creek (tributary of Herman Creek), Hood River County, Oregon, USGS Carson Quadrangle, Green Trails Maps: Bonneville Dam.

Herman Creek received its name from association with Mr. James H. Herman, an early settler in the area.

If you're hot, take a refreshing shower in the cold water of this delightful falls. Because this trail tends to be well lit by the sun, it becomes warm in the Summer. A more comfortable hike with waterfalls at full power is earlier in the Spring.

All along the Herman Creek Trail, you will find delightful mini-showers and minor side creeks from which you can cool yourself. Some of these tiny streams disappear into their streambed, under cobbles and huge boulders. Look around! These streams sometimes swell to such amazing proportions that the enormous boulders are moved.

As mentioned under Falls Creek Falls, during years with snow and cold weather in the gorge, the side streams which cross the trail can become months-long temporary glaciers, making the trail difficult or even totally impassible. When they begin to thaw, watch out for bridges of snow and ice which have been very dangerously undercut. In the Winters of 1995-96 and 1996-97, we were repeatedly prevented from reaching this falls by these huge, treacherous barriers. These frustrations occurred until late Spring!

Once when we hiked from Cascade Locks to Dry Creek Falls (#30), then to Pacific Crest Falls (#31), and on to the Herman Creek Trail to Falls Creek Falls (#32) and Camp Creek Falls, east of Pacific Crest Falls we came upon the small herd of Mule Deer shown below. At first, they froze and so did we. Gradually, they became less afraid and resumed browsing while Barbara slowly got out her pad and sketched them. They eventually worked their way over the hill and out of sight. We continued our hike touched by the wonder of the experience. May you discover similar delights!

See detailed map at falls #32, Falls Creek Falls.

> ## Camp Creek Falls
> *A veil of mist drifts softly down*
> *From heavens heights above*
> *No crowds to cheer or spread renown*
> *Just nature sharing love.*

Mule Deer

East Columbia Gorge of Oregon

34   **Slide Creek Falls**

The Furthest of Herman Creek's Trailside Falls

Height: 100'   **Difficulty:** 6   **Romance:** 5

Type: Narrow Steep Slide.

Description: Reminiscent of Falls Creek Falls, the water drops over the lip of the cliff and sizzles down th face of the cliff.

Distance/Time From Portland: 48 miles, 45 minutes via I-84.

Directions to Parking/Trailhead: Follow directions for Falls Creek Falls (#32).

Distance/Time From Parking: 5.1 miles, 3 hours and 50 minutes.

Distance/Time From Other Landmark: 1.9 miles, 85 minutes from Camp Creek Falls (#33).

Directions From Parking: Follow directions to Camp Creek Falls then continue on the trail for 45 minutes to Casey Creek Campground (a very rustic and undeveloped campground) and the intersection with the Casey Creek Trail #476; then continue 40 minutes to Slide Creek Falls, a total of 1.9 miles.

Elevation Change: 1,900 feet.

Restroom: In center of parking area; fair condition; open only when your not there! Try restaurants and service stations in Cascade Locks a few miles west.

Picnic Area: Several very undeveloped picnic or wilderness camping places along the trail.

View & Kissing Spots: Along the trail and in front of the falls or underneath it.

Accessibility to the Physically Challenged: Too difficult to be considered accessible.

Hazards: Poison oak; some dangerous slopes, possible ice in Winter, and blown down trees after Winter and Spring storms.

Information: On Slide Creek (tributary of Herman Creek), Hood River County, Oregon, USGS Carson Quadrangle, Green Trails Maps: Bonneville Dam.

This falls varies widely in flow depending upon the season and weather. Of course, it is at its best when it is hardest to get to it and vice versa!

At Casey Creek Camp, there is a thin path which heads downstream toward Herman Creek itself. If you feel energetic, this trail leads to a view of Casey Creek Falls at the point where the two streams join. This is not a developed trail and is a long, steep walk back to the trail from a falls of lesser interest.

If you attempt this hike after as severe a Winter as those in 1995-96 and 1996-97, your way may be blocked by snow and ice barriers and/or downed timber. When we finally weren't blocked by ice, we ran into a huge stretch of forest (perhaps a half mile or more) before Casey Creek Camp in which hundreds of trees had fallen across the trail. Most of these sat about waste high. We had to clamber over each one, endlessly, and exhaustingly! As a result, we call this experience "Our Marine Boot Camp Hike"! If the trail is unencumbered, your time from Camp Creek Falls to Slide Creek Falls may be much shorter than the time we listed here.

Really serious hikers take the Herman Creek Trail and others you have passed along the way to this point, for long, overnight hikes into the back country. If you continue upstream from here, you will eventually reach Wahtum Lake in about 7 more miles.

Be sure to look for Calypso Orchids (the prom orchids of the elves) in the Spring along the trail between the parking area and the power lines. They are often quite plentiful near the trail in shady areas of deep forest litter. If you see them please, please, please do not pick them or otherwise disturb them!

See detailed map at falls #32, Falls Creek Falls.

Penstemon

Triumph

Huffing and puffing and sweating we walk
Trudging the trail in the rain.
Gasping and panting for breath without talk
Trying to smile through our pain.

Onward and upward pretending we're fine
Telling our hearts to be still.
Rounding each switchback we look for a sign
Marking the top of the hill.

Suddenly Spring's in our step once again
Seeing the glorious sight.
Years disappearing once more we begin
Giggling with childish delight.

Hugging and kissing and laughing are we
Forgetting all else but this day.
Loving each creature and plant that we see.
Warmed by the chill waters spray.

35   Gorton Creek Falls
A Dangerous and Grueling Short Hike to a Beautiful Big Falls
Height: 140'   **Difficulty:** 2 to "waterworks", 10 to falls   **Romance:** 7

Type: Narrow Contact Plunge, Narrow Contact Plunge.

Description: A surprisingly beautiful falls in an intimate bowl. The falls descends nearly perpendicular to the course of the stream, resulting from it. When viewed straight on, the 40 foot upper portion of the falls can be seen descending to a shelf or pool from which the 100 foot lower portion slides down the sheer vertical cliff face to a small, cold pool.

Distance/Time From Portland: 52 miles, 52 minutes via I-84.

Directions to Parking/Trailhead: I-84 east to exit 51; drive about one half mile to Wyeth Trail at south end of Wyeth Campground, where you can park. When campground is closed, park at roadside near the park entrance.

Distance/Time From Parking: 6 minutes from the trailhead to the "waterworks" (one quarter mile), .25 miles, 20 to 40 minutes or more from the "waterworks" to the falls. Note that the lower portion of the falls can be seen through the trees from a very short distance past the "waterworks".

Distance/Time From Other Landmark: Approximately 5 miles west of Starvation Creek Falls (#36) and its wayside.

Directions From Parking: Trail leads directly away from the well marketed trailhead parking area. Note, when campground is closed, one must hike from the road through the campground following signs to trailhead. The trail parallels Gorton creek through a cool, tree-shaded glen, initially as a broad dirt road gradually narrowing to a comfortable trail. The trail crosses Trail #400 which crosses the creek on a bridge. Continuing along the creek, in little more than a quarter mile, you reach a narrow gap in a cliff through which the stream squeezes. A crude, old dam for fresh water. is visible at this point. The real hike begins here! To the falls, one must find ones own way by negotiating boulders, logs, sliding hillsides, and crisscrossing the creek. There is no trail and constantly changing hazards thanks to the annual extreme effects of water and slides.

Elevation Change: 600 feet.

Restroom: Modern restrooms at campground when open.

Picnic Area: At campground.

View & Kissing Spots: From several vantage points beginning a short distance past the "waterworks"; and at the base of the falls.

Accessibility to the Physically Challenged: Relatively accessible to near the "waterworks"; probably inaccessible to anyone even with a helicopter much of the year!

Hazards: Just before the "waterworks", the trail is very deteriorated and angled toward the creek. Be careful not to slip. From the "waterworks" to the falls one can expect dangerously swift, deep water much of the year; crumbling, sliding slopes; loose and crumbling downed logs over which one must climb; huge boulders to scale; several fords of the creek; and the need to devise your own way through the mess! If the water is too high, this could be suicidally dangerous!

Information: On Gorton Creek, Hood River County, Oregon, USGS Carson Quadrangle, Green Trails Maps: Hood River.

Gorton Creek was named in honor of Edwin Gorton who homesteaded along it around 1890.

Note: this is one of the most difficult hikes for its length in this book. It should only be undertaken under suitable weather and water conditions by those who able to handle its challenges. Save it for Summer when the water in the stream is at its lowest.

Note that probably its greatest challenge is finding a way through the barriers. When we went back and did it again the next day, it was less grueling and took far less time. However, the next year, everything had moved and we had the same situation again!

Gorton Creek Falls

It took such pain to reach you
But now we're glad we came.
Beyond the logs and wet feet
We shared your beauty and our love.

36   Starvation Creek Falls

A Powerful, Complex Falls in a Delightful and Convenient Park Setting

Height: 186'   Difficulty: 1   Romance: 7

Type: Narrow Contact Plunge, Steep Slide, Cascade.

Description: Less than 100 yards from the freeway and a busy rest stop, this delightful falls seems to originate at the top of a great rock at the head of a narrow, deep canyon, secluded and wild. After two big drops, the falls disappears behind a giant rock, lands in a pool and continues in a hard to see but very scenic way.

Distance/Time From Portland: 55 miles, 55 minutes via I-84.

Directions to Parking/Trailhead: I-84 east to Starvation Creek Rest Area/Park at milepost 55 (east bound only, with Exit east bound only). There is a huge, paved parking area.

Distance/Time From Parking: Immediate; less than 60 seconds!

Distance/Time From Other Landmark: 10 minutes from Cabin Creek Falls (#37).

Directions From Parking: From parking lot, walk east past restrooms a few yards to stream and trail heading to the right toward the falls.

Elevation Change: 0

Restroom: At Parking; Year Round; Modern.

Picnic Area: Excellent, well screened picnic sites along both sides of the creek from the falls to the freeway.

View & Kissing Spots: At end of trail near base of falls; along creek approaching falls; in hiding spots in picnic areas.

Accessibility to the Physically Challenged: Totally accessible, wide, paved trail.

Hazards: Being bitten while trying to feed the chipmunks??

Information: On Starvation Creek, Hood River County, Oregon, USGS Mt. Defiance Quadrangle, Green Trails Maps: Hood River.

Originally named "Starveout Creek in December of 1884 because of a blizzard which stalled two trains at this point. None of the stranded passengers actually starved, but their two week long visit with little or no food did not inspire poetic descriptions of the scenery. Incidentally, the only supplies reaching the trains came thanks to a few enterprising Hood River entrepreneurs who used snow shoes to pack in food which they sold at extremely inflated prices to those with the resources to pay. There is also an extant photo which was taken by a hardy newspaperman.

Every day, hundreds of people stop at this very large, busy rest stop yet only a very small percentage is even aware that one of the largest and loveliest waterfalls in the gorge is less than 100 yards away. Thanks to the over 100 foot high natural rock wall between the parking lot and the falls, you can feel as remote as if you were at the end of a long hike. Concrete work at the base of the falls is for a drinking water system.

Ira A. Williams described it in 1916 thusly: "Belying its name, this last of the spectacular waterfalls in plain view as we pass eastward along the Columbia River Highway, does nothing if not provide a gratifying even if fleeting repast of delight to every keen lover of the finest that Nature affords."

With some difficulty the determined and fit can reach the pool at the bottom of the falls (obscured from view by a huge wall-like rock). It can be a great spot to cool your feet (or even more of you) on a hot day.

Look for chipmunks and Steller's jays around the parking lot and park.

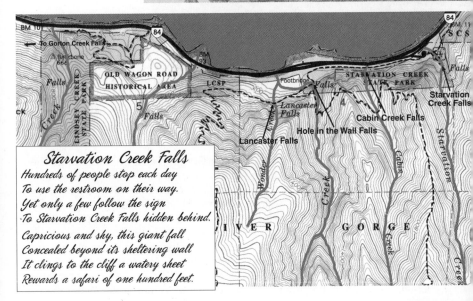

Starvation Creek Falls

Hundreds of people stop each day
To use the restroom on their way.
Yet only a few follow the sign
To Starvation Creek Falls hidden behind.

Capricious and shy, this giant fall
Concealed beyond its sheltering wall
It clings to the cliff a watery sheet
Rewards a safari of one hundred feet.

East Columbia Gorge of Oregon

37   Cabin Creek Falls

A Delightful View of One of the Old Highway's Scenic Wonders

Height: 190'   Difficulty: 1   Romance: 5

Type: Narrow Contact Plunge, Spreading Contact Plunge.

Description: Cabin Creek drops over the lip of a cliff into its own narrow crack in the rock, turns 90° and swooshes out in a second, much bigger horsetail which falls down the face of the cliff only a few feet from the trail (which is the remains of the old highway). Unfortunately, a giant rock, half the height of the falls, stands guard between the trail and the falls, partially obscuring the view.

Distance/Time From Portland: 55 miles, 55 minutes via I-84.

Directions to Parking/Trailhead: Follow directions for Starvation Creek Falls (#36).

Distance/Time From Parking: .3 miles, 10 minutes from Starvation Creek Rest Area parking lot.

Distance/Time From Other Landmark: .3 miles, 10 minutes from Starvation Creek Falls (#36); 10 minute from Hole in the Wall Falls (#38).

Directions From Parking: Go to the southwest edge of the parking lot where you will see a trail leading west along the barrier/guard rail on the south side of the parking lot entrance ramp. Walk west along this trail noticing the remnants of the original highway still visible beneath the trail's litter.

Elevation Change: 0

Restroom: At Parking; Year Round; Modern.

Picnic Area: At Starvation Creek.

View & Kissing Spots: At trailside. Because of the rock in the way and the nearness of the falls to you, you would need a helicopter for a really good view.

Accessibility to the Physically Challenged: Should be totally accessible from the parking lot to the falls.

Hazards: Falling while trying to get a better view.

Information: On Cabin Creek, Hood River County, Oregon, USGS Mt. Defiance Quadrangle, Green Trails Maps: Hood River.

Note how the remnants of the old road is slowly being absorbed into the forest by moss and higher plants. Obviously, without intervention, this road and other works of man would completely disappear within a few decades.

As you drive through the Columbia River Gorge from from Portland to The Dalles (only 83 miles), incredible changes are evident—changes in climate, temperature, moisture and rainfall, appearance of the terrain, and in the species of trees and all other flora. The west end of the gorge is obviously a temperate rainforest. Well before you reach The Dalles, you can see that you are in a desert. The change is gradual and unnoticeable in any one area but is discernible when you compare two locations. Trees change from firs to pines. The dominant plants of the forest floor transitions from Sword Fern to Oregon Grape to Grass to Sage Brush. The area around Starvation Creek Falls and its neighbors can be compared to that of the Multnomah

Falls area and to that around Punchbowl Falls and Dead Point Creek Falls to see the remarkable change in a very short span. Driving just a little east of Hood River (such as to the Governor Tom McCall Preserve at Rowena) places you in an entirely different world, one that you'll enjoy experiencing. If timed just right, a Springtime trip east of the Cascades can reveal vast fields of amazing wildflowers, whose brief lives are spent like earthbound moths: all at once they begin rapidly sprouting from the ground, shooting up to full size, aggressively blooming, then withering to nothing in the heat of the sun.

See detailed map at falls #36, Starvation Creek Falls.

Bloom

Chipmunk

Cabin Creek Falls

Through dappled light the road still shows
The highway through the gorge
Once such a feat, a wonder of the world
This road they built for falls.

Beside the road without a sign
Flows Cabin Creek's great falls
So lush with moss and fern and blooms
You'll fall in love like us.

Descending through its cliffside crack
It roars and gushes down
And coyly hides behind a rock
Its beauty for itself.

38   Hole In The Wall Falls

A Surprising and Romantic Alteration of Nature

Height: 100'   Difficulty: 2   Romance: 7

Type: Arched Plunge, Narrow Steep Slide.

Description: From a large round hole a short distance below the top of a sheer cliff, a blast of water arches to a small space between large rocks below. A few feet from the falls, a wooden footbridge provides convenience for hikers, a viewpoint of the falls, and a romantic stopping spot.

Distance/Time From Portland: 55 miles, 55 minutes via I-84.

Directions to Parking/Trailhead: Follow directions for Starvation Creek Falls (#36).

Distance/Time From Parking: .6 miles, 20 minutes from Starvation Creek Rest Area parking lot.

Distance/Time From Other Landmark: 10 minutes from Cabin Creek Falls (#37); 15 minutes from Lancaster Falls (#39).

Directions From Parking: Follow the directions to Cabin Creek Falls then continue on the trail until it turns to the left and enters a blackberry choked clearing. Follow the path south toward the cliffs until you see and hear the falls.

Elevation Change: 0

Restroom: At Parking; Year round; modern.

Picnic Area: At Starvation Creek.

View & Kissing Spots: Approaching the falls and on the bridge at base of falls.

Accessibility to the Physically Challenged: Relatively accessible to near the falls.

Hazards: Blackberries.

Information: On Warren Creek, Hood River County, Oregon, USGS Mt. Defiance Quadrangle, Green Trails Maps: Hood River.

Before about 1915, Warren Creek Falls, plunged from the sheer cliff about 50 yards east of the present Hole In The Wall Falls. Unfortunately, it often sprayed directly on the Columbia River Highway. To avoid this problem, a hole was drilled in 1938 at a westerly angle from above the original falls to an opening on the cliff, eliminating Warren Creek Falls and creating the unique Hole In The Wall Falls. You can bushwhack your way east and somewhat south for a hundred yards or so to the bowl-shaped cliff formed by the old falls. Considering how many falls were given over to public ownership, preserved, and enhanced by the far sighted creators of this highway, modifying just one of them must be viewed in perspective. Strangely, Warren Creek Falls remains the "official" USGS-Geographic Names Information System name. It was originally named for an early U.S. Forest Service ranger, Warren Cooper, not for Frank M. Warren the pioneer fish packer who went down with the Titanic and whose name is remembered in the name of the town of Warrendale near Bonneville.

From year to year and even season to season, the area near the footbridge at the base of the falls offers an ever changing testament to the power of nature. You may see a lush and tranquil scene one time then next time see a scoured and remolded one with the bridge totally destroyed.

Between Hole in the Wall Falls and Lancaster Falls, the trail intersects the trail to Mount Defiance. For those who are looking for a real test of their physical condition and a scenic view from a very high vantage point, this trail is a severe answer to your dream. There is a short, easy 1 mile hike back to near Cabin Creek Falls and the main trail to the summit of Mount Defiance, climbing 5,000 feet in a gruelingly steep 12 mile loop, returning via Starvation Ridge. This excursion is only for the very fit and/or very masochistic!

See detailed map at falls #36, Starvation Creek Falls.

Nootka Rose

Hole in the Wall Falls

The map said "Hole in the Wall Falls"
What could inspire this name?
We took the trail to get a look
Because we were so curious.

So short a walk for such reward
The mystery was revealed.
A hole there was right in the cliff
With water gushing forth.

Its origin the work of man
Who moved it for a road.
Romantic, though a little odd.
Come share its love and yours.

39   Lancaster Falls

A Close Encounter with Part of a Really Big and Obscure Falls

Height: 250'   Difficulty: 3   Romance: 6

Type: Narrow Steep Slide, Square Steep Slide, Cascade.

Description: From the trail at the base of the falls, you can only experience the final portion of the falls, an abbreviated but powerful plunge to the trail. Because the falls is close enough to the trail to get you wet and because the trail crosses Wonder Creek without a bridge or other formal method, you can experience the falls from the top down and/or from the bottom up! For a view of the whole falls in all its splendor, view it from the freeway (as we did for this drawing) or from the other side of the river.

Distance/Time From Portland: 55 miles, 55 minutes via I-84.

Directions to Parking/Trailhead: Follow directions for Starvation Creek Falls (#36).

Distance/Time From Parking: 1.3 miles, 35 minutes from Starvation Creek Rest Area parking lot.

Distance/Time From Other Landmark: 15 minutes from Hole in the Wall Falls (#38).

Directions From Parking: Follow directions to Hole In The Wall Falls. Cross the bridge at the base of the falls and follow the trail uphill until you reach Lancaster Falls for .2 miles, 15 minutes.

Elevation Change: 100 feet.

Restroom: At Parking; Year Round; Modern.

Picnic Area: At Starvation Creek.

View & Kissing Spots: From trail at base of falls (have fun getting wet seeing only the lowest part of the falls); from the freeway (to see it all and stay dry).

Accessibility to the Physically Challenged: Inaccessible due to narrow, steep, trail past Hole In The Wall Falls.

Hazards: Slipping on the rocks, falling.

Information: On Wonder Creek, Hood River County, Oregon, USGS Mt. Defiance Quadrangle, Green Trails Maps: Hood River; listed in USGS Geographic Names Information System.

This stately attraction was named for Samuel C. Lancaster, designer of the Columbia River Highway. Unfortunately, unless you can clamber around on the rocks and in the water, and find a really great view upward from the portion of the falls beside the trail to the higher, bigger ones above, you will only see the bottom 20 feet or so of the falls. To see it all, you may have to look from Interstate 84 or from the Washington side of the Columbia.

The trail to Lancaster Falls continues to the west for quite a long way. Eventually, you can reach and follow the power lines to a stair made from a notched log. If you go far enough (and are willing to make your own trail through blackberries and poison oak, you will reach two different streams, Lindsey Creek and Summit Creek, each with an attractive waterfall a short clamber upstream of your makeshift trail. We have seen photos of them and have tried to reach them many times in all seasons from every direction except by air. Despite great pain and perseverance, we haven't reached them! If you're a trail blazer, maybe you can get there! Let us know!

See detailed map at falls #36, Starvation Creek Falls.

Western Red Cedar

Lancaster Falls

Your torrent fills the creek below
And makes our trail just stepping stones.
Your powerful plunge just twenty feet
Yet close enough to make us wet.

No vantage point nearby
Affords a look at all of you.
Two hundred feet beyond our view
Of falling water paints your cliff.

Wah Gwin Gwin Falls

Picturesque from a Distance, Romantic Close Up

Height: 207'   **Difficulty:** 0   **Romance:** 7

Type: Narrow Contact Plunge.

Description: A small creek meanders across the grounds and formal gardens of the Columbia Gorge Hotel (a magnificent recreation of elegant places and times gone by) until it reaches the sheer cliff at the end of the estate passes under a lovers bridge and plunges straight down the cliffside. Please note that the hotel and its falls are private property, the owners of which have thus far allowed visits by non-paying guests. Respect their privacy and the atmosphere they have worked so hard to create. Do not take advantage of their tolerance.

Distance/Time From Portland: 61 miles, about 60 minutes.

Directions to Parking/Trailhead: Drive east on Interstate 84 to the first Hood River exit, #60; at the end of the exit ramp, turn left (north) across the freeway to the frontage road; turn left (west) and drive to the entrance of the Columbia Gorge Hotel, a fantastic, world class hostelry and restaurant. Park in their substantial parking lot if there is room.

Distance/Time From Parking: 1 minute.

Distance/Time From Other Landmark: 5 miles, 5 minutes drive from Starvation Creek Falls (#36).

Directions From Parking: Follow the creek through the hotel's magnificent gardens as it traverses the grounds from southwest to northeast where it drops over the cliff below a romantic footbridge. There is no practical way to reach the base of the falls at this time.

Elevation Change: 0

Restroom: In Hood River (do not use the hotel restroom unless you are a paying customer).

Picnic Area: None (although there is a wonderful but expensive restaurant).

View & Kissing Spots: The only view of the entire falls and its picturesque surroundings is from across the Columbia (from where our drawing was made) or from a boat. Despite the inadequacy of its view, a kiss or a wish from the bridge atop the falls is very worthwhile.

Accessibility to the Physically Challenged: Yes and visible from roadside.

Hazards: Being tempted by the elegance of the hotel and its restaurant.

Information: On Phelps Creek, Hood River County, Oregon, USGS Hood River Quadrangle, Green Trails Maps: Hood River; listed in USGS Geographic Names Information System.

Wah Gwin Gwin is Chinook for fast waters. Such names beginning with or containing the syllable "Wah", have to do with water (Wahkeena, Wahclella, Elowah, Wahtum Lake, Walla Walla, etc).

The historic Columbia Gorge Hotel has one of the finest gourmet restaurants in the Pacific Northwest. As a hotel, it is truly a place of old world charm with virtually every room uniquely decorated, even with antiques. Whether for a delectable Sunday brunch, an elegant celebration, a first or second honeymoon, or a one of a kind romantic tryst, this is definitely the place! We've even seen weddings being performed on the bridge above the falls and in their magnificent formal gardens.

While you are in the Hood River area, take the opportunity to watch the wind surfers. A marine park at the next freeway exit east offers access for the participants and viewing for visitors. Thanks to the almost continuous winds in the gorge and the wide expanse of the Columbia, this is literally the premier place in the world for the sport. It looks cold, scary, and exciting. It's fun to watch!

Hike to the Falls

My legs are aching, lungs on fire
But still I struggle on.
Whatever thoughts I had before
My focus now inside.
I cannot stop. I must go on
No matter what the pain.
I'm nearly there. I hear the roar.
And soon I'll see the falls.
When I arrive, I'll sit and smile.
I'll let the world go by.
I'll drink in all the beauty there
But all too soon go home.

41   Punchbowl Falls

Lots of Water and a Charming Shape but Dwarfed by its Setting

Height: 25"   **Difficulty:** 1   **Romance: 3**

Type: Hourglass plunge.

Description: The Hood River squeezes through a narrow rock canyon until its bedrock shelf breaks and the river falls in a striking hourglass shape into a huge pool in an enormous bowl formed by sheer basalt columns. The only negative aspect is that the bowl is so large that the waterfall is too far away.

Distance/Time From Portland: 81 miles, 90 minutes.

Directions to Parking/Trailhead: Drive east on Interstate 84 to exit #64, State Route 35; turn right (south) and drive south for about 7 miles until you see signs for Odell and Dee; turn right and drive west past the large group of fruit packing plants until you reach route 281 (about 2 miles); turn left and drive southwest for about 6 miles until you reach the right turn at the sawmill at Dee; drive across the bridge (which spans the East Fork of Hood River) and immediately turn right; in little over a mile, look for a parking area next to the road a short distance upstream from a bridge across the West Fork of Hood River. There is a small amount of parking on and along dirt roads which form the byways of this small park. **Alternative:** You can reach this attraction from Portland by taking route 26 past Government Camp to route 35, then driving north on route 35 for somewhat less than 35 miles. The loop drive gives you views of all four sides of Mount Hood and offers you a smorgasbord of waterfalls along the way.

Distance/Time From Parking: No more than .1 miles, 5 minutes from parking.

Distance/Time From Other Landmark: Dead Point Creek Falls (#42) can be seen across the canyon from virtually the same viewpoints as Punchbowl, although its better views are somewhat further downstream along the cliff. Tamanawas Falls (#76) is about 25 miles south on State Route #35.

Directions From Parking: Walk along the dirt road from the parking area and walk to the cliff edge viewing areas when obvious.

Elevation Change: 0 feet.

Restroom: None here. Try in Dee or Hood River.

Picnic Area: No formal picnic area here but many lovely, scenic spots would be ideal for picnicking on a blanket.

View & Kissing Spots: At any of the cliffside viewpoints. Caution! Don't swoon and fall off the cliff!

Accessibility to the Physically Challenged: With care, the physically challenged can find viewpoints along the dirt road and at several points which lead you closer to the cliffside.

Hazards: The undeveloped, unmarked, and unguarded clifftop viewpoints are potentially very dangerous. As with all cliffside locations, treat them with respect and give the edge an extra measure of room! It is a very long way down! Do not be tempted to swim or dive in this area!

Information: On Hood River. Hood River County, Oregon, USGS Dee Quadrangle, Green Trails Maps: Hood River; listed in USGS Geographic Names Information System.

Note that the correct name of this falls is "Punchbowl" (one word), unlike the similarly shaped falls on Eagle Creek, "Punch Bowl" (two words).

There is a crumbling wooden staircase which snakes its way down the opposite cliff to the fish ladder next to the falls. There is a locked gate at the top of the stairs to prevent unwanted and unwary guests from taking it.

See detailed map at falls #42, Dead Point Creek Falls.

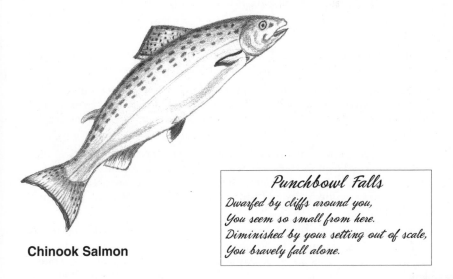

Chinook Salmon

Punchbowl Falls
Dwarfed by cliffs around you,
You seem so small from here.
Diminished by your setting out of scale,
You bravely fall alone.

42   Dead Point Creek Falls

Remarkably Shaped Falls that's the Showpiece in Another's Domain

Height: 115'   **Difficulty:** 1   **Romance:** 4

Type: Wide Contact Plunge, Narrow Contact Plunge.

Description: A truly amazing falls that is many times taller and more interesting than Punchbowl Falls, in whose back yard it resides. Dead Point Creek Falls drops over an overgrown cliff face and falls in a wide sheet to a ledge from which it condenses into a far narrower plunge which continues to its ultimate end in Hood River.

Distance/Time From Portland: 81 miles, 90 minutes.

Directions to Parking/Trailhead: Follow directions for Punchbowl Falls (#41).

Distance/Time From Parking: About .1 miles, 5 minutes from parking.

Distance/Time From Other Landmark: The best views of both Punchbowl Falls (#41) and Dead Point Creek Falls are within 100 feet of each other.

Directions From Parking: Walk along the dirt road from the parking area and walk to the cliff edge viewing areas when obvious.

Elevation Change: 0 feet.

Restroom: None here. Try in Dee, Hood River, or Government Camp.

Picnic Area: No formal picnic area here but large rocks and flat spots seem made for a scenic picnic "al fresco".

View & Kissing Spots: At cliffside viewpoints somewhat further downstream from the earlier ones which are better for Punchbowl.

Accessibility to the Physically Challenged: With care, the physically challenged can find viewpoints along the dirt road and at several paths which lead you closer to the cliffside.

Hazards: Be very careful near the high, steep, unguarded clifftop viewpoints. Because Dead Point tends to lure you to try ever more treacherous viewpoints, don't get carried away (lest there's too little left of you for the rescuers to carry away)! Poison oak can be a problem in this area. Watch out for it!

Information: On Dead Point Creek (tributary of Hood River). Hood River County, Oregon, USGS Dee Quadrangle, Green Trails Maps: Hood River.

Dead Point Creek got its name in pioneer times from the fact that it originated on a prominence (a "point") which was covered with dead trees. A nearby point covered with live trees, was the birthplace of "Green Point Creek". Get it?

For years, an old blue automobile could be seen standing vertically at the ledge half way down the falls—evocative of humorous, tragic, and suspicious speculation (at least by us). Unfortunately, it has apparently been washed away by the powerful floods of recent years or else has finally just rusted away.

The Hood River Valley, which runs south from the city of Hood River to east of Mount Hood, is famous for its apples, pears, peaches, and other fruit. In Spring when the trees are in bloom, it's like a fairyland of pink and white. In late Summer and Fall, when the crop ripens, myriad fruit stands offer delicious snacks, luscious gifts for friends, and tempting varieties to inspire you to take home enough fruit for deserts and preservation. A stop for just a couple of apples will inevitably end with big bags of fruit and promises of culinary wonders to come. Have fun!

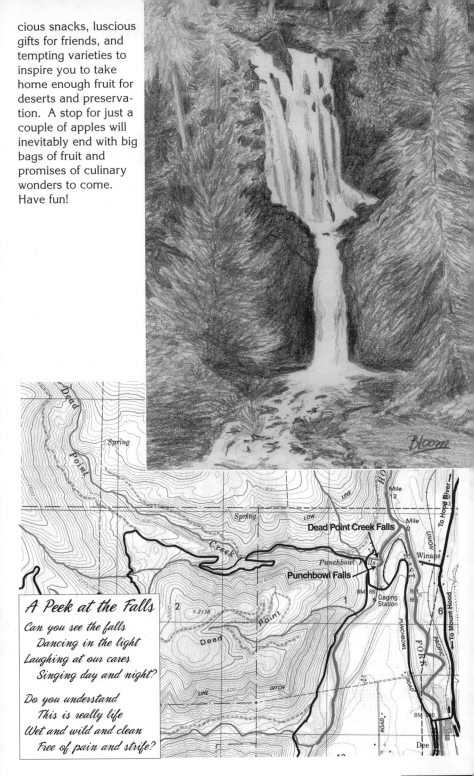

A Peek at the Falls

Can you see the falls
    Dancing in the light
Laughing at our cares
    Singing day and night?

Do you understand
    This is really life
Wet and wild and clean
    Free of pain and strife?

East Columbia Gorge of Oregon

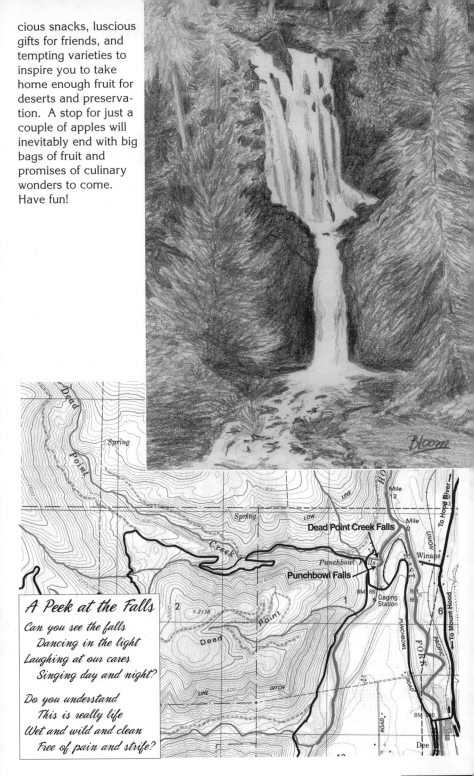

IV. West Columbia Gorge of Washington

The Washington side of the Columbia Gorge shares many of the same high cliffs below even higher mountains, it lacks the deep shade and nearby glaciated peaks. As a result, the north bank of the Columbia is warmer and drier with far fewer waterfalls. There are a number of splendid falls, many of them farther from the gorge itself, however.

Although the gorge has no towns or cities of significant size, the small towns are interesting and fun places with rich and interesting histories. Stevenson was named for George H. Stevenson in 1880.

Carson was originally called "Ash" by Lewis and Clark in 1805 after discovering ash trees there, the first they'd seen since heading west. Later it was named Carson for Carson Creek. I'm not sure how the creek got its name.

North Bonneville was named for Bonneville Dam, which was named for a pioneer town of Bonneville, which was, in turn, named for a soldier, Captain Benjamin Louis Eulalie Bonneville.

Just west of the dam between mile markers 38 and 39 is the site of Fort Rains (amazingly, it's named for Major Gabriel Rains, not for the weather) which was founded in 1855 and was the scene in 1856 of an extended battle between local Native Americans who were disgruntled over encroachment by settlers and the contingent of soldiers manning the blockhouse-type fort. The battle ended when troops arrived from The Dalles and dragoons under the command of Lt. Phil Sheridan arrived from Fort Vancouver. Phil Sheridan was later to become famous for his cavalry campaign in the Shenandoah Valley of western Virginia.

Skamania (both the town and the county) is a Native American name which is said to mean Swift River. In the more than a hundred year history of the town of Skamania, it has been called almost everything except Dead: Mendota, Marrs Landing, Fresedale, Edgewater, Butler's Landing, and Butler.

Just east of the town of Stevenson, you will find signs for Skamania Lodge, the most modern and luxurious hostelry in the gorge, and the Columbia River Gorge Interpretive Center, a unique, modern museum of gorge memorabilia and educational center which explains much of the history, ecology, and economy of the area. The two of them are no more than a short walk from SR 14 and from each other (although you'll drive, of course). Both have gift shops with souvenirs, maps, books, and information. The lodge has an excellent restaurant, bar, and complete meeting services. They were built with money provided by the Columbia Gorge Scenic Area law, perhaps as an apparently unsuccessful effort to gain enthusiasm and cooperation from the reluctant residents of the Washington side of the river. Nevertheless, you will enjoy a visit to these facilities.

Although they are not in the book, there are a number of other, interesting and enjoyable waterfalls located in this area. A particularly fun place to visit is Lacamas Park in

Camas, Washington. It is a full service urban/suburban park with a lake for fishing and boating, vast open areas for games and sun bathing, picnic and bar-beque areas,

Pacific Dogwood (bloom)

swimming areas, and several streams which flow through a steeply descending wild area forming at least four waterfalls. The water-falls are great sources of enjoyment and watery recreation. If you are looking for a non-wilderness experience, perhaps a Sunday with your extended family or friends, including lots of kids of varying ages, visit this park. We're sure you'll have a fun day!

Raccoon

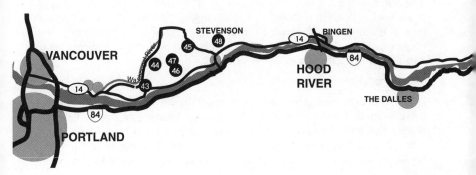

43   **Salmon Falls**
A Powerful Small Falls with Leaping Fish
Height: 30'   **Difficulty:** 0 to bridge, 3 to top of falls   **Romance:** 3

Type: Square Steep Hourglass Slide.

Description: A bridge provides an excellent viewpoint just downstream from where the Washougal River squeezes through a narrow canyon and plunges over a rock ledge next to a rustic fish ladder. During the fish migration from late August to October (and perhaps other runs), huge fish can be seen in the shallows and dramatically leaping the falls.

Distance/Time From Portland: Approximately 35 miles, 45 minutes.

Directions to Parking/Trailhead: Drive north on Interstate 5 (or Interstate 205) to SR-14; drive east past the Cape Horn viewpoint, perhaps the highest highway points in the entire gorge. Stop and see the gorge laid out below you. Continue to between mile markers #26 and #27, approximately 10 miles east of Washougal, turn left (north) onto Salmon Falls Road and go .3 miles, 5 minutes to the bridge where the road ends at Washougal River Road. Roadside parking is just south of the bridge.

Distance/Time From Parking: The falls are visible from the bridge.

Distance/Time From Other Landmark: Only about 5 miles, 10 minutes drive to Dougan Falls (#44).

Directions From Parking: View the falls from the bridge and/or visit the top of the falls and its fish ladder by walking upstream along the highway to a dirt road/driveway which leads down to the river. Be careful to respect any warning signs, prohibitions, or private property encountered.

Elevation Change: None to the bridge, 20 feet to the top of the falls.

Restroom: At Dougan Creek Campground, in Washougal, or in Stevenson.

Picnic Area: None.

View & Kissing Spots: At bridge.

Accessibility to the Physically Challenged: Good views from the bridge.

Hazards: None (except falling from bridge) at viewpoint; blackberries, slippery rocks, and being swept over the falls at the top of the falls.

Information: On the Washougal River, Skamania County, Washington, USGS Bridal Veil Quadrangle, Green Trails Maps: Bridal Veil.

The origin of the name of the Washougal River and the exact meaning of it is somewhat open to debate. It is indisputable that the Chinooks had a village at the mouth of the river from ancient times and that the "wah" syllable means water in their language. These facts support the argument that the name means "rushing waters" in Chinook.

Watch for Salmon and Steelhead in the river below the bridge too.

Note: Although we suggest you go to this falls via the Salmon Falls Road, there is another route. You can drive through Washougal to the Washougal River Road and drive upstream until you reach Salmon Falls Road and the falls. We not only find our route more scenic but if someone is going to name a road for this waterfall, doesn't it deserve to be used to get there?

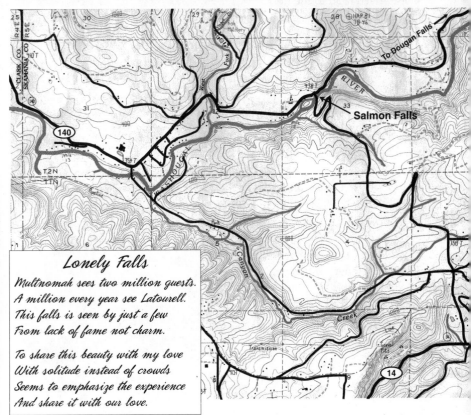

Salmon Falls

To Dougan Falls

Lonely Falls

Multnomah sees two million guests.
A million every year see Latourell.
This falls is seen by just a few
From lack of fame not charm.

To share this beauty with my love
With solitude instead of crowds
Seems to emphasize the experience
And share it with our love.

44 **Dougan Falls**

A Huge, Wide Niagara of a Falls Accessible to All

Height: 50'   **Difficulty:** 0 to bridge; 2 to base or top of falls   **Romance:** 4

Type: Very wide, low tumble.

Description: The Washougal River widens to nearly 100 yards, then plunges from a shelf of rock to a lower level just upstream from a conveniently located bridge.

Distance/Time From Portland: 40 miles; 55 minutes.

Directions to Parking/Trailhead: Follow directions to Salmon Falls (#43); turn right (east) on Washougal River Road and drive upstream; continue past the fish hatchery to the bridge over the river just before the end of the road. The falls are visible just upstream from the bridge. Lots of parking is available near the bridge and picnic area.

Distance/Time From Parking: You're there! There are short paths down to the riverside on both sides of the bridge. In addition, you can reach the top of the falls on the north side by way of paths from the north side of the river and from the road.

Distance/Time From Other Landmark: 5 miles, 10 minutes drive from Salmon Falls (#43); 16 miles and 45 minutes drive to Steep Creek Falls (#45) via unimproved road to the right.

Directions From Parking: You can't miss it!

Elevation Change: None to the bridge, 10 feet to the base of the falls.

Restroom: At picnic area across the road, primitive.

Picnic Area: Across the road from the falls.

View & Kissing Spots: At bridge and from various spots along road, from rocks beside the top of the falls, and on rocks around pool at bottom of the falls.

Accessibility to the Physically Challenged: Bridge views completely accessible.

Hazards: Only slippery rocks near stream and falls.

Information: On the Washougal River, Skamania County, Washington, USGS Bobs Mountain Quadrangle, Green Trails Maps: Bridal Veil; listed in USGS Geographic Names Information System.

At Dougan Creek Camp across the road from the falls, you can find multiple primitive restrooms, picnic tables, and limited camping facilities.

The fish hatchery which you passed on your way from Salmon Falls is open to visitors at certain times of the year. They are very friendly and helpful when they are there and not too busy.

Salal

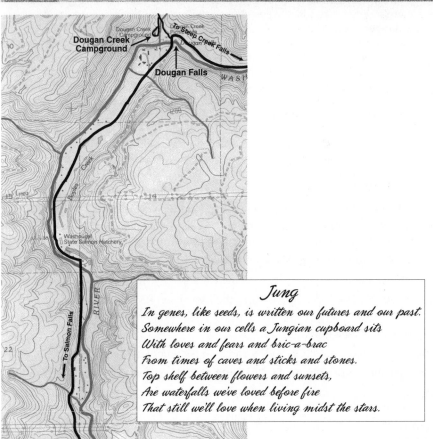

Dougan Creek
Campground

Steep Creek Falls

Dougan Falls

Jung

In genes, like seeds, is written our futures and our past.
Somewhere in our cells a Jungian cupboard sits
With loves and fears and bric-a-brac
From times of caves and sticks and stones.
Top shelf between flowers and sunsets,
Are waterfalls we've loved before fire
That still we'll love when living midst the stars.

West Columbia Gorge of Washington

45   Steep Creek Falls
A Big, Cool, Convenient, and Accessible Falls

Height: 50'   **Difficulty:** 0   **Romance:** 6

Type: Curtain Plunge.

Description: Steep Creek runs through the woods over a level rock layer. Suddenly, it reaches a small canyon into which it falls by sliding down a sheer cliff into a clear blue pool. The outlet of the pool immediately joins the larger Rock Creek as it runs under a rustic wooden bridge. A very private and charming place to visit. The cliffs on Rock Creek opposite the falls present a long row of curtain-like minor and seasonal falls—neat!

Distance/Time From Portland: Alternative #1: 56 miles, 100 minutes; **Alternative #2:** 57 miles; 75 minutes.

Directions to Parking/Trailhead: Alternative #1: During good (dry) weather, if you're already at Dougan Falls (#44), turn right on the dirt road across the Dougan Falls bridge; continue upstream along the river passing several small falls. Eventually, you cross the Pacific Crest Trail and reach the top of the ridge from which you can see far to the east and south; a sign directs you right to Beacon Rock (avoid this road unless you are in a tracked vehicle) or leftward to Stevenson (12 miles); bear left and continue along this narrow gravel road for another 6 miles. Note: when intersecting the many unmarked side roads, always choose the one that heads downhill. After a while, you will be driving along Rock Creek. You can't miss the falls. It's right in front of you and just to the right of the very noticeable Steep Creek Bridge between mileposts 5 and 6. **Alternative #2:** During rainy or snowy weather or if you are in a hurry, take SR14 to the well marked road to the Skamania Lodge and the Columbia Gorge Interpretive Center near milepost 42 (it's second street and Foster Creek Road) 1 mile west of Stevenson; turn left a short distance past the Interpretive Center onto Ryan Allen Road; after about a mile, turn left on Red Bluff Road (Ruelle Road is on the right) which quickly changes into a gravel road (CG2000); follow this road steeply uphill until you reach the wooden bridge between mileposts 5 and 6. The falls will be to your left and behind you as you cross the bridge. Parking is along the roadside on ether side of the bridge.

Distance/Time From Parking: You're there!

Distance/Time From Other Landmark: 16 miles, 45 minutes drive from Dougan Falls (#44) or 6 miles, 10 minutes from Stevenson.

Directions From Parking: You can't miss it.

Elevation Change: None (except on the road getting here, which is substantial!).

Restroom: At Dougan Falls (#44) or the Stevenson Park (often locked). Note: merchants in Stevenson are not very hospitable with their restrooms!

Picnic Area: None here.

View & Kissing Spots: On bridge and alongside pool at the base of the falls.

Accessibility to the Physically Challenged: Bridge views completely accessible.

Hazards: The pass from Dougan Falls could be dangerous or impassable. Stay on the tack-like planks and watch out for traffic on the one lane bridge!

Information: On Steep Creek (tributary of Rock Creek), Skamania County,

Washington, USGS Bonneville Dam Quadrangle, Green Trails Maps: Bonneville Dam.

Driving from Dougan Falls, you cross Stebbins Creek as it joins the river from the right just before the road and the river turn left. The creek forms a charming small falls facing a small falls on the river. It's beautiful but everything is owned by a man we met who is very anxious about tres-passers. Stay on the road!

A tale about hiking alone: A diver was inexplicably found drowned in his wet suit in the pool at the base of tiny Stebbins Creek Falls!

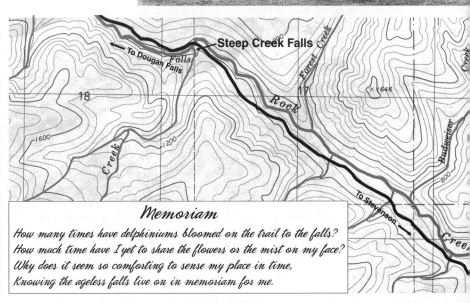

Memoriam

How many times have delphiniums bloomed on the trail to the falls?
How much time have I yet to share the flowers or the mist on my face?
Why does it seem so comforting to sense my place in time,
Knowing the ageless falls live on in memoriam for me.

46   **Hardy Falls**

A Powerful Falls with a Viewpoint from Above

Height: 120'   **Difficulty:** 6   **Romance:** 6

Type: Narrow Contact Plunge.

Description: Downstream from Rodney Falls (visible upstream), Hardy Creek flows strongly over rocks and boulders to reach a high cliff down which it roars. An excellent wooden platform has been built just above and to the right of the lip of the falls, providing an excellent view almost straight down the powerful drop. Hardy is also visible from the trail some distance before reaching the viewpoint, especially during the Winter or early Spring when leaves don't obscure the view.

Distance/Time From Portland: 43 miles, 55 minutes.

Directions to Parking/Trailhead: Go to Beacon Rock, mile post 35 on SR-14, either east from Vancouver or west from the Bridge of the Gods at Cascade Locks. The well marked road to the campground is at milepost #35, just west of the rock on the other side of the road. Take the road to the campground area and park in the large parking area near restroom and picnic tables. If the gate is closed at the road's entrance next to SR-14, you will have to park along the road or in the Beacon Rock parking area.

Distance/Time From Parking: 40 minutes total; 20 minutes from parking to fork in trail under power lines, 20 minutes from fork to Hardy Falls.

Distance/Time From Other Landmark: 5 minutes to Rodney Falls (#47).

Directions From Parking: The trail leads uphill to the right from the parking lot. Continue on trail for 20 minutes to power lines then 20 minutes more to the falls.

Elevation Change: 600 feet.

Restroom: At Parking; at Beacon Rock (not always open); if necessary, drive a few miles east to the Bonneville Dam Visitors Center.

Picnic Area: At Beacon Rock Camp Ground.

View & Kissing Spots: On the trail through the trees; at platform at top of fall.

Accessibility to the Physically Challenged: None.

Hazards: None (unless you are really stupid around viewing platform).

Information: On Hardy Creek, Skamania County, Washington, USGS Beacon Rock Quadrangle, Green Trails Maps: Bonneville Dam; listed in USGS Geographic Names Information System.

While you are in the Beacon Rock area, why not take advantage of the opportunity to walk to the top of this remarkable over 850 foot high sentinel of the gorge. The 4,000 foot long stairs which take you to the top were built near the turn of the century by Henry J. Biddle, before which the rock had remained unscaled. Although such claims are made for large rocks everywhere, Beacon Rock is said to be second only to Gibraltar in size. It was first named and described by Lewis and Clark in 1805 during their famous exploration. Until the present name was made official at the beginning of this century, it was more commonly called "Castle Rock".

There is a legion associated with the volcano "plug" called Beacon Rock.

Once upon a time, there was a beautiful princess who fell madly in love with a handsome young brave. They married and had a son. Unfortunately, an ugly old chief wanted her for his own. The old chief sent the brave on a mission in which he was killed. The chief then claimed the princess. To escape, she climbed Beacon Rock and hurled herself and her baby from the top. If you listen carefully, you can still hear her sad wail near the rock when the wind blows.

Poems and Poets

A waterfall's a poet
Performing daily for the crowd
Who writes its verse in watery rhyme.

A waterfall's a poem
That must be shared and read out loud
Of love and beauty lost in time.

47   Rodney Falls

A Falls Splits a Rock and Forms a Pool — Wow!

Height: 115'   **Difficulty:** 6   **Romance:** 9

Type: Narrow Contact Plunge, Cascade.

Description: A truly amazing and unique falls which is almost impossible to fully explain or depict. Hardy Creek drops over a cliff and plunges straight down. Beneath its plunge, an enormous rock, larger than a house, once sat. Over time, the force of the water drilled a hole through the rock and made a vertical crack through which the water squeezes. Within the circle of rock and under the falling water is a tiny, ice cold pool, The Pool of the Winds, in which the brave and overheated cool off on hottest days. Even if you don't try that, you can walk along a rock ledge protected by a steel guard rail to peer within the mysterious region.

Distance/Time From Portland: 43 miles, 55 minutes.

Directions to Parking/Trailhead: Follow directions to Hardy Falls (#46).

Distance/Time From Parking: 45 minutes.

Distance/Time From Other Landmark: 5 minutes from Hardy Falls (#46); trail continues to top of Hamilton Mountain, a fantastic hike, a great view, and a terrific feeling of accomplishment for the non-mountain climber!

Directions From Parking: Follow directions to Hardy Falls; continue .2 miles, 5 minutes on the trail upstream to the bridge across the creek and on the trail to the base of the falls.

Elevation Change: 650 feet.

Restroom: At Parking; at Beacon Rock (not always open).

Picnic Area: At Beacon Rock Camp Ground.

View & Kissing Spots: At bridge below falls, at base of falls, in pool.

Accessibility to the Physically Challenged: None.

Hazards: Very wet, slippery rocks require care.

Information: On Hardy Creek, Skamania County, Washington, USGS Beacon Rock Quadrangle, Green Trails Maps: Bonneville Dam; listed in USGS Geographic Names Information System.

We're sure that you, like many others, assume that this waterfall is named for Rodney Dangerfield. Although relatively few people take the trouble to visit this fabulous falls and, therefore, it really does "get no respect" (at least in proportion to its splendor). We are pretending to be experts, right? And, thus, we should know everything, right? Well, we don't know for whom this falls was named. We'll learn all about it as soon as the book goes to press and it's too late. But...we know it's not Rodney Dangerfield, ok!

See detailed map at falls #46, Hardy Falls.

You and I

Your cheeks are rosy from exertion
Of climbing up the trail
And now the spray upon your face
Makes sparkles match your smile.

How full you make my heart today.
We've left the world behind.
And now we stand in nature's realm
To kiss beneath the falls.

Washington Lily

48   Sweeney Falls

A Small Falls in an Intimate Glen Hidden Right off the Road

Height: 40'   Difficulty: 5   Romance: 4

Type: Narrow Steep Slide.

Description: Within a small leafy glen, a small creek slides down a lava rock wall to create a pool.

Distance/Time From Portland: 55 miles, 60 minutes.

Directions to Parking/Trailhead: Either take SR14 east from Vancouver or take Interstate 84 to Cascade Locks(exit 44) and cross the river on the Bridge of the Gods toll bridge (75¢) to SR14. In either case, drive 3 miles east of the Bridge of the Gods to and through Stevenson, then continue east to near milepost 47 until you see one of the few roads heading to the right (toward the river), marked by a sign "Sweeney Road"; a few parking places can be found on the left side of the road on either side of a small, tree-filled canyon. The falls can be seen through the trees from the road at the east side of the opening.

Distance/Time From Parking: Less than 100 yards, 5 minutes.

Distance/Time From Other Landmark: Only about 2 miles from Stevenson; 2 miles east to the Wind River Road to Carson.

Directions From Parking: From a remnant of a dirt road intersecting SR14 on the west (left) side of the Sweeney Creek canyon, walk into the woods a short distance then either scramble 20 to 30 feet down a leafy slope to a rock outcropping with a view of the falls or continue until you reach a rock wall blocking your path and slide down a steep slope beside the cliff to reach the creek from which you can traverse a few yards to the base of the falls.

Elevation Change: 20 feet

Restroom: In Carson, at area campgrounds, at the park in Stevenson, or in Cascade Locks.

Picnic Area: No formal picnic area.

View & Kissing Spots: At a rock outcropping which projects beyond the near slope a short distance downhill from the trail near the bridge; from creekside at the bottom of the rock wall; from the base of the falls.

Accessibility to the Physically Challenged: None.

Hazards: Be careful on the steep and often slippery slopes.

Information: On an unnamed creek, Skamania County, Washington, USGS Carson Quadrangle, Green Trails Maps: Bonneville Dam.

Local kids often party here. Several young people we met said "everyone" calls it "The Place". Linda at the Skamania County Chamber of Commerce in Stevenson says "everyone" calls it "The Falls at Sweeney's Corners". We have named it "Sweeney Falls" for the road directly across the highway from it. Hopefully, "everyone" will like the name.

Although very close to Highway 14, Sweeney Falls is a secluded, even hidden, place to cool off, frolic, hide, meditate, or neck. Enjoy!

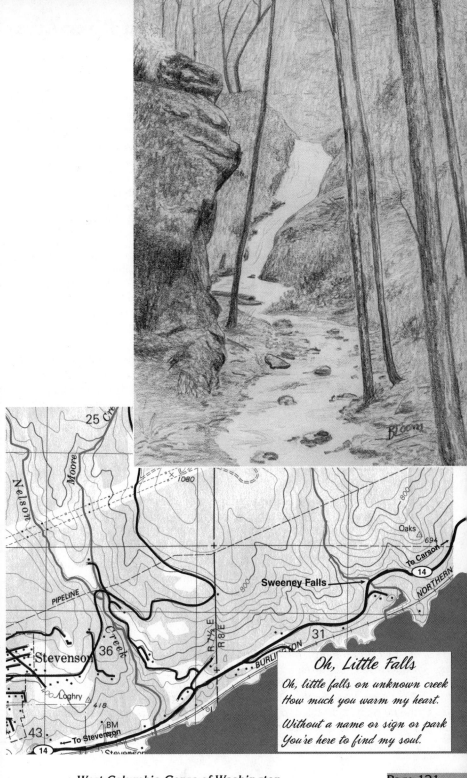

Bloom

Sweeney Falls

Oh, Little Falls

Oh, little falls on unknown creek
How much you warm my heart.

Without a name or sign or park
You're here to find my soul.

West Columbia Gorge of Washington

V. Wind River & White Salmon River Area

From Washington State Route 14 along the Columbia River from Carson to Bingen, one can access a number of waterfalls from roads lead far inland, ultimately climbing to the slopes of Mount St. Helens and Mount Adams. The increase in elevation heading northward is proportional to the likelihood of snow or reaching roads closed in Winter. Please consider the season and the weather when planning excursions to the upper reaches of this region.

Unlike the Oregon side of the Columbia, most falls on this side are beyond a barrier range of hills on tributary streams which originate in the gradually increasing heights of the Cascades as you travel north. Three significant watersheds are represented: Wind River, White Salmon River, and Lewis River (named, of course, by the Lewis and Clark expedition in 1805 for Meriwether Lewis, its co-leader). Nearly all the falls in this section are related to one of them.

Although we believe we have included the most attractive, significant, and accessible to visits, there are many more. One is Shipherd Falls off Shipherd Springs Road in Carson, on the Wind River a mile upstream from the Carson Hot Mineral Springs. Incidentally, a visit to the Carson Hot Mineral Springs is a real trip! The restaurant is pretty good and a soak in the waters must be much the same as in the last century. In fact, the whole place seems to be left over from the nineteenth century.

Another well known falls is Rock Creek Falls in Stevenson, which theoretically can be reached from Iman Cemetery Road. Unfortunately, the falls is at a curve in the stream, hidden from public view and the stream has recently eroded a very deep chasm preventing any practical access. We've tried to reach it several times and met only discomfort and frustration.

There are several falls along the lower Lewis River. The only one we found interesting was one which we saw falling a great distance before reaching the surface of one of the reservoirs over a mile away. What a wonder it must have been before its course was ended artificially.

Closer to Mount St. Helens and Mount Adams, there are several other falls. Frankly, we had to stop somewhere and probably went too far north as it was. If we hadn't exercised restraint, we would have never stopped, including Spokane Falls and beyond and never getting the book finished!

Near the mouth of the White Salmon River, across the Columbia from the city of Hood River, are the twin cities of White Salmon and Bingen. Obviously, White Salmon is named for the river (or vice versa). Bingen is named after a city on the Rhine River in Germany. Thanks to an irreconcilable dispute, the railway whistle stop at this location is the only one in the nation named for two towns.

Just west of the mouth of the White Salmon River is the tiny town of Underwood, the terminus of the 9 mile long Broughton Flume, a wooden trough down which logs were floated from the rim of the gorge to the Broughton Lumber Mill. The last log was sent down it in 1989, after which the flume was disabled to prevent fools from attempting to ride down it. Although its remains will continue to be visible for years to come, its passing is the end of an era in the wild Pacific Northwest.

Where Did We Come From?

Did we begin in desert plains
Where water was a luxury
Or did we come from mountain slopes
Where water fell so bountifully?

Is our great love of waterfalls
From times of water's scarcity
Or did we see it every day
To love familiarity?

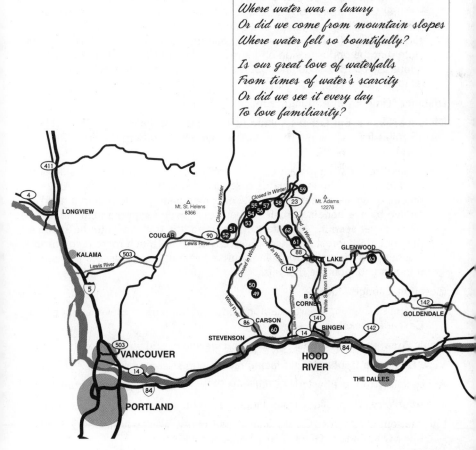

Wind River & White Salmon River Area

49   **Panther Creek Falls**

Two Streams, Two Beautiful Falls Side-By-Side, Unbelievable!

Height: 125'   Difficulty: 5   Romance: 8

Type: Twin: Wide Contact Plunge, Arched Plunge.

Description: One creek slides 125 feet down the side of a narrow, deep canyon. The falls spreads to cover the cliff to a width of 40 feet or more. Another creek comes down the canyon itself lower than the top of the first falls. As the second creek nears the first, part of it drops over the lip of a cliff, while the rest turns sharply and runs along a trough-like ledge to the side of the first falls, from which it blasts 65 feet beside its sister. During higher water, water pours down in a 90° curve. Amazingly, the viewpoint for all this is no more than 100 feet straight across the canyon from the main portion of the falls and right beside the right hand portion. Wow!

Distance/Time From Portland: 70 miles, 80 minutes.

Directions to Parking/Trailhead: Either take SR14 east from Vancouver or take Interstate 84 to Cascade Locks (exit 44), cross the river on the Bridge of the Gods toll bridge (75¢) to SR14. In either case, drive 5.9 miles east of the Bridge of the Gods to the Wind River Road #30 to Carson; drive about 7 miles north; turn right on "Old State Road" and then left within 100 feet onto Panther Creek Road #65; drive about 7.5 miles until you see the overgrown, gated road #6511 on your right; within a couple of hundred yards, a rock slide hillside with a small, rough parking area adjoins the road on the right. Note that the opposite side of the road is clear of trees and characterized by a long, steep rock slide and that the road makes a switchback which crosses the creek a couple of hundred yards past the parking area.

Distance/Time From Parking: .1 miles, 5 minutes.

Distance/Time From Other Landmark: 19 miles from Falls Creek Falls (#50); 13 miles from Carson. The roads to both falls lead from the Wind River Road.

Directions From Parking: Walk back downhill along the left (stream) side of the road for about a hundred yards carefully observing the roadside. After reaching roadside trees, you will see a steep, sandy slide of a trail nearly hidden by overhanging brush. If there were ever a sign marking the trail, we've never seen it. A few feet off the road, the trail dips into the shade of the cool, dark forest and, though steep, becomes much more recognizable. Continue on the trail downhill for only a few hundred yards and perhaps 5 minutes until you see the falls.

Elevation Change: 200

Restroom: In Carson, at area campgrounds, at the park in Stevenson, or in Cascade Locks.

Picnic Area: Potential ad hoc spots round viewpoint and streamside.

View & Kissing Spots: At cliff facing falls; along stream above falls.

Accessibility to the Physically Challenged: None, no view possible from road.

Hazards: Very steep, slidey trail; dangerous at unguarded cliff-top viewpoint!

Information: On Panther Creek, Skamania County, Washington, USGS Wind River Quadrangle, Green Trails Maps: Wind River.

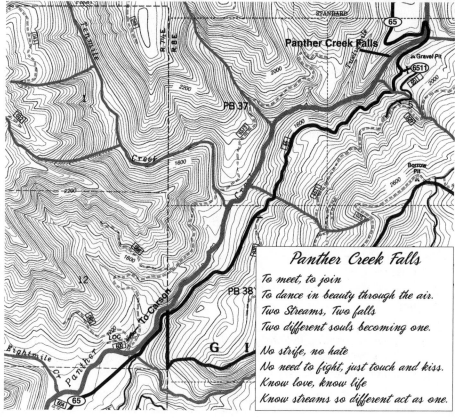

Panther Creek Falls

To meet, to join
To dance in beauty through the air.
Two Streams, Two falls
Two different souls becoming one.

No strife, no hate
No need to fight, just touch and kiss.
Know love, know life
Know streams so different act as one.

Wind River & White Salmon River Area

50   Falls Creek Falls

The Falls with Everything in Three Towering Tiers

Height: 250'   **Difficulty:** 6 by lower trail, 8 by upper trail   **Romance:** 10

Type: Wide Slide, Triplet Contact Plunge, Free Plunge.

Description: This amazing falls cannot all be seen at one time but each of its three tiers is so remarkable, big, and beautiful that it would be a destination by itself! Falls Creek begins its display by dipping over the crest of the canyon and sliding 100 feet or so down a steeply angled cliff. At the end of this first tier, the stream flows out onto the top of a huge hexagonal column of rock from which it drops over three sides forming three parallel contact plunges 100 feet tall. At the base of the third tier, the water gathers in a pool from which it plunges 50 to 75 feet into a punch bowl no more than 50 feet from a raised viewpoint

Distance/Time From Portland: 75 miles, 90 minutes.

Directions to Parking/Trailhead: Either take SR14 east from Vancouver or take Interstate 84 to Cascade Locks(exit 44) and cross the river on the Bridge of the Gods toll bridge (75¢) to SR14. In either case, drive 5.9 miles east of the Bridge of the Gods to the well marked Wind River Road #30 to Carson; drive 16 miles north through Carson; turn right on road #3032-057 and drive a little over 2 miles to a supermarket-size parking lot next to the road. You may see signs for lower trail. If so, follow them. Depending upon road and trail conditions, the parking may be the end of the road.

Distance/Time From Parking: 2.2 miles, 75 minutes via the lower falls trail; 2.5 miles, 110 minutes via the upper trail.

Distance/Time From Other Landmark: 19 miles from Panther Creek Falls (#49); 18 miles from Carson. The roads to both falls lead from the Wind River Road north of Carson.

Directions From Parking: Follow the trail from the parking lot through the woods; soon you will be hiking along the right bank of a creek; within a few minutes, you will reach and cross a narrow chasm with deep blue water; the area near the bridge is exceedingly beautiful and romantic; from the bridge, hike upstream along the left bank of the stream, gradually climbing away from it on the hillsides of the canyon; within 45 minutes to an hour, you will glimpse the falls through the trees far ahead; in 5 more minutes, you will reach the viewpoint at the bottom of the falls.

Elevation Change: 500 feet by the lower trail; 1,100 feet by the upper trail.

Restroom: In Carson, at area campgrounds, at the park in Stevenson, or in Cascade Locks.

Picnic Area: Informally at base of falls and at various scenic spots along the trail.

View & Kissing Spots: View of top tier of the falls from the trail a couple of minutes before reaching the base; middle and bottom tiers are viewed from a rock-top perch right in front of the bottom falls tier. Lots of kissing spots!

Accessibility to the Physically Challenged: None.

Hazards: Be careful on viewpoint rocks. Brush along edges conceal a sudden and severe drop into the stream and rocks downstream of the falls!

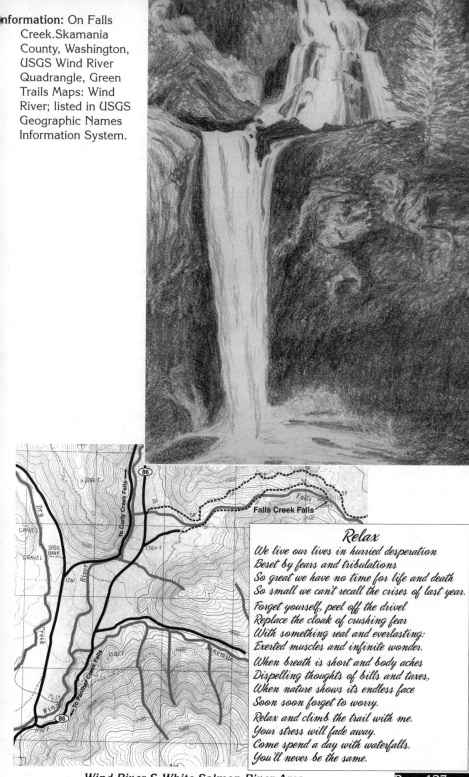

Information: On Falls Creek.Skamania County, Washington, USGS Wind River Quadrangle, Green Trails Maps: Wind River; listed in USGS Geographic Names Information System.

Falls Creek Falls

Relax

We live our lives in hurried desperation
Beset by fears and tribulations
So great we have no time for life and death
So small we can't recall the crises of last year.

Forget yourself, peel off the drivel
Replace the cloak of crushing fear
With something real and everlasting:
Exerted muscles and infinite wonder.

When breath is short and body aches
Dispelling thoughts of bills and taxes,
When nature shows its endless face
Soon soon forget to worry.

Relax and climb the trail with me.
Your stress will fade away.
Come spend a day with waterfalls.
You'll never be the same.

51   Curly Creek Falls

A One of a Kind — Ducking Under Two Rock Arches

Height: 80'   **Difficulty:** 1 from bridge, 0 from viewpoint parking   **Romance:** 8

Type: Angle Slide, Spread Contact Plunge.

Description: From the cliff-top viewing platform, you look little more than 100 feet directly across the Lewis River to Curly Creek Falls dropping down the opposite bank. This amazing falls has a powerful flow which issues from a narrow gap in a cliff, roars down a slope behind a large rock arch to a bounce point from which it blasts out from under another, smaller, tighter arch to stream down to its pools below, connected to the river.

Distance/Time From Portland: 93 miles, 1 hour and 45 minutes.

Directions to Parking/Trailhead: Either take SR14 east from Vancouver or take Interstate 84 to Cascade Locks (exit 44) and cross the river on the Bridge of the Gods toll bridge (75¢) to SR14. In either case, drive 5.9 miles east of the Bridge of the Gods to the well marked Wind River Road #30 to Carson; drive through Carson and continue on Wind River Road #30 to mile post 28 where you reach Curly Creek Road #51; turn left on Curly Creek Road and drive approximately 7 miles to Lewis River Road #90; turn left on Lewis River Road and continue for about a quarter mile until you reach the continuation of Curly Creek Road on your right; take Curly Creek Road for 1 mile downhill to the bridge over the Lewis River. Either park next to the bridge for a nice relatively short hike to the falls along the river or drive across the bridge for .25 mile to the well marked Falls Viewpoint parking lot on your left for a short, quick, level walk. **Alternative Route:** Curly Creek Falls and all those along the Lewis River may be reached from Interstate 5 instead of the Columbia River Gorge. Take I-5 to the Woodland, Washington exit from which you drive east along the Lewis River and its three dam-made lakes on State Route 503 for about 24 miles to its junction with State Route 90 at the "Eagle Cliff Bridge", cross the bridge and drive east on route 90 for about 5 miles to Curly Creek Road.

Distance/Time From Parking: .25 miles, 10 minutes from bridge; .1 miles, 2 minutes from viewpoint parking area.

Distance/Time From Other Landmark: .1 miles, 5 minutes to Miller Creek Falls (#52).

Directions From Parking: From Bridge Parking: After parking at the Lewis River bridge, cross the bridge and take the trail on the left side of the road a few feet beyond the bridge and head downstream for .25 miles, 10 minutes to the well designed log-rail viewing platform directly across the river from the falls. **From Viewpoint Parking:** Follow the trail near the restrooms for 2 minutes to the platform.

Elevation Change: 100 feet (via bridge trail); 0 feet (via viewpoint parking area).

Restroom: At viewpoint parking lot (primitive), at campgrounds along the road or in Carson.

Picnic Area: No formal spots but plenty of possible sites from which to choose.

View & Kissing Spots: Along the trail and at the viewpoint—very romantic!

Accessibility to the Physically Challenged: Should be accessible from parking area on the wide, level trail and on the excellent, well built viewing platform.

Hazards: Slippery slopes and a very deep, swift river could be lethal if you are very fool-hardy.

Information: On Curly Creek, Skamania County, Washington, USGS Burnt Peak Quadrangle, Green Trails Maps: Lone Butte; listed in USGS Geographic Names Information System.

Who knows how long the arches of Curly Creek Falls will survive the power of the water. Someday, they will be gone. Don't miss this amazing natural wonder.

Beside the bridge over the Lewis River may be seen giant logs which formed the base of a former bridge long ago.

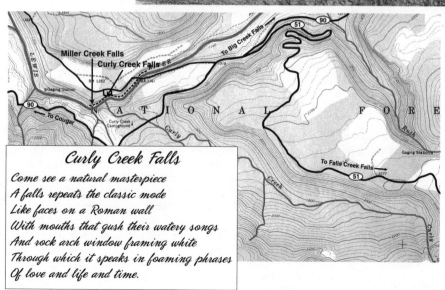

Curly Creek Falls

Come see a natural masterpiece
A falls repeats the classic mode
Like faces on a Roman wall
With mouths that gush their watery songs
And rock arch window framing white
Through which it speaks in foaming phrases
Of love and life and time.

52   Miller Creek Falls
A Strong and Scenic Plunge in the Woods

Height: 65'   **Difficulty:** 1 from bridge, 0 from viewpoint parking   **Romance:** 6

Type: Arch Plunge.

Description: Miller Creek blasts like a giant fire hose from cliff-top of its natural bowl into its pool next to the Lewis River. Viewed from the picturesque log-rail viewing platform, the falls resembles Metlako Falls. Below the base of the falls, the stream divides to form a striking "V" on its short path to its entry into the river.

Distance/Time From Portland: 93 miles, 1 hour and 45 minutes.

Directions to Parking/Trailhead: Follow directions to Curly Creek Falls (#51).

Distance/Time From Parking: .3 miles, 15 minutes from bridge; .2 miles, 7 minutes from viewpoint parking area.

Distance/Time From Other Landmark: .1 miles, 5 minutes to Curly Creek Falls (#51) viewing platform; 5 miles, 10 minutes drive to Big Creek Falls (#53).

Directions From Parking: Hike to Curly Creek Falls then continue downstream for .1 miles, 5 minutes to the end of the trail at Miller Creek Falls viewing platform.

Elevation Change: 100 feet (via bridge trail); 0 feet (via viewpoint parking area).

Restroom: At viewpoint parking lot (primitive), at campgrounds along the road or in Carson.

Picnic Area: No formal spots but plenty of possible sites from which to choose.

View & Kissing Spots: Along the trail and at the viewpoint—very romantic!

Accessibility to the Physically Challenged: Should be accessible from parking area on the wide, level trail and on the excellent, well built viewing platform.

Hazards: Slippery slopes and a very deep, swift river could be lethal if you are very foolhardy. Note: Do not continue on the rude path past the viewing platform. It's dangerous, doesn't go anywhere useful, ends soon, and presents no useful views of the falls.

Information: On Miller Creek, Skamania County, Washington, USGS Burnt Peak Quadrangle, Green Trails Maps: Lone Butte.

In the Fall, the woods near these falls explodes with mushrooms of many kinds, shapes and colors. Don't eat them!

If you are interested in visiting Mount Saint Helens and witnessing the devastation wrought by its famous 1980 eruption. you can drive about 5 miles west on route 90 to the Eagle Cliffs junction with route 25. This route will take you straight north along the east side of the mountain all the way to route 99 which takes you to the Windy Ridge Viewpoint which looks into the volcano's crater. There is a visitor center and other facilities there. Ultimately, route 25 would take to the town of Randle on U.S. Route 12 which would, in turn, take you east to Mount Rainier or west back to Interstate 5 about 75 miles north of Portland. The drive to Randle from Eagle Cliffs is about 35 miles—subject to closure due to snow during Winter. Call the headquarters in Amboy or the visitors center in Castle Rock for road conditions and suggestions (see page 247).

In case you have forgotten or never knew, Mount Saint Helens erupted explosively on Sunday morning, May 18, 1980 with a force equal to a great many atom bombs. The sound from the explosion was reflected in strange ways so that some people nearby did not hear it but others hundreds of miles away, (as far as Vancouver, British Columbia) heard it. The blast blew more that a cubic mile of material off the top of the mountain, cost it about 2,000 feet of its former height, flattened an old growth forest, and killed about 50 people. You should see it!

See detailed map at falls #51, Curly Creek Falls.

The Critic

How can you rate a masterpiece?
Is Shakespeare best, Rembrandt, or Bach?
Do literary reference explain perfection?
Lean back, relax, absorb the beauty, love,
and waterfalls.

Queens Cup

53   Big Creek Falls
A Big, Powerful Plunge in a Magnificent Setting

Height: 125'   **Difficulty:** 1   **Romance:** 7

Type: Narrow Free Plunge.

Description: A wonderful falls which reminded us of South Falls at Silver Falls State Park as it thunders down from the clifftop to its deep, wide pool. Its power often raises spray to the viewpoint.

Distance/Time From Portland: 96 miles, 1 hour and 50 minutes.

Directions to Parking/Trailhead: Follow directions for Curly Creek Falls (#51) to State Route 90 but at the intersection of Routes 51 and 90, turn east (right) on 90; drive east to past milepost 24 where you will see the well marked Big Creek Falls parking area on your left.

Distance/Time From Parking: .1 mile, 5 minutes to view next to top of falls; less than 1 mile and 5 minutes to viewing platform; loop nature trail total .25 miles, 15 minutes.

Distance/Time From Other Landmark: 5 miles, 10 minutes drive from Curly Creek Falls (#51) and Miller Creek Falls (#52); 15 minute walk to the Cave Falls viewpoint on the narrower clifftop trail downstream from the Big Creek Falls viewing platform; 5 miles, 8 minutes drive to Lower Lewis River Falls (#54).

Directions From Parking: The wide, level dirt trail begins next to the kiosk.

Elevation Change: 0 feet.

Restroom: No restroom at this location. Nearest would be Lower Lewis River Falls Campground.

Picnic Area: No picnic area at this location.

View & Kissing Spots: Romantic views of Big Creek Falls from near its top and on viewing platform; lovely spots in the woods; along the cliff edge trail downstream, especially at the view of Cave Falls.

Accessibility to the Physically Challenged: Excellent unpaved but accessible loop trail from parking area to the falls, a platform viewpoint, and through a lovely visit to an old growth forest. Trail to Cave Falls is not accessible.

Hazards: Be careful at edge of the cliffs near the falls. Do not test the stability of the cliff edges, Newton's laws of gravity, or your ability to fly!

Information: On Big Creek, Skamania County, Washington, USGS Burnt Peak Quadrangle, Green Trails Maps: Lone Butte.

There is an excellent informational kiosk at the parking lot and markers denoting specific points of interest along the loop trail.

A 15 minute walk downstream from Big Creek Falls, there is a view across the canyon of the amazing falls we called "Lower Big Creek Falls", turns out to be called "Cave Falls" according to the rangers of Gifford Pinchot National Forest. We just have to describe it to you! Big Creek continues downstream to a very narrow spot in the canyon where the falls drops perhaps 80 feet over a cliff. So far, no big deal. However, where the stream forms the falls, the force of the water has undercut the cliff at the level of the top of the falls to form a horizontal slot of a cave in the far cliff into which most of the water of the creek disappears for 100 feet or so, reemerging straight out of the cliff as a falls, perpendicular to its sibling. Wow!

About 5 minutes further downstream from Cave Falls is a spectacular view looking downstream at the Lewis River Valley from the clifftop at the end of the trail.

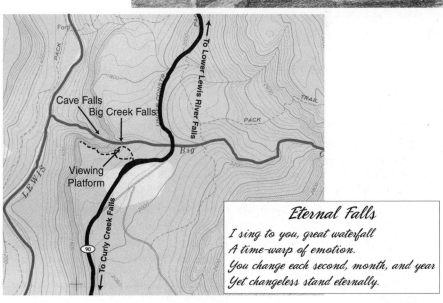

Eternal Falls
I sing to you, great waterfall
A time-warp of emotion.
You change each second, month, and year
Yet changeless stand eternally.

Wind River & White Salmon River Area

54   Lower Lewis River Falls
A Powerful, River-Wide Falls

Height: 35 feet   **Difficulty:** 3   **Romance:** 4

Type: Wide low tumble.

Description: The wide and very full Lewis River flows on a series of flat layers of bedrock. Where the bedrock breaks, the power of the river carves out a striking waterfall. Lower Lewis River Falls is the furthest downstream of three examples of this phenomenon. While quite a bit smaller than Niagara Falls, this delightful attraction is best described as a miniature of it.

Distance/Time From Portland: 101 miles, 1 hour and 58 minutes.

Directions to Parking/Trailhead: Follow directions to Big Creek Falls (#53); continue east on Lewis River Road #90 about 5 miles, 8 minutes to the marked "Lower Falls Campground" near milepost 29. Bear right on road marked with appropriate icon to parking for the falls.

Distance/Time From Parking: .1 mile and 5 minutes to top of falls viewpoint.

Distance/Time From Other Landmark: 8 minutes, 5 miles drive from Big Creek Falls (#53); 1 mile, 3 minute drive to parking for Copper Creek Falls (#55) and Middle Lewis River Falls (#56); 30 minutes and 1.2 miles walk upstream to Middle Lewis River Falls (#56).

Directions From Parking: A loop trail begins near the parking and restroom. Other, better views are available somewhat downstream.

Elevation Change: 300 feet.

Restroom: At parking (primitive).

Picnic Area: In the campground.

View & Kissing Spots: At riverside viewpoints on the trail near the falls.

Accessibility to the Physically Challenged: Although it is not an ideal trail, the trail and viewpoint for this falls is considered accessible.

Hazards: Slippery conditions on the trail near the falls; the river is more powerful and dangerous than it looks. Always be very careful in the water or near it.

Information: On Lewis River. Skamania County, Washington, USGS Quartz Creek Butte Quadrangle, Green Trails Maps: Lone Butte. An "official" USGS-Geographic Names Information System feature (with the name "Lower Falls"). We have somewhat renamed this falls to express which of the dozens of "Lower Falls" we are talking about!

This falls was once a favorite salmon fishing spot of the local Native Americans before the arrival of the Europeans. Unfortunately, the ill conceived dams which create the three downstream reservoirs block the passage of the fish so they can no longer reach this spot.

The falls are within the Lower Lewis Recreation Area Campground with complete but rustic amenities near the parking area.

Sadly, until the late 1960s, this entire area was a lush old growth forest with huge, centuries old trees, including cedars over eight feet in diameter. They say that if we simply wait a half a millennium or so, it will grow back to its former splendor. New trees have gown already but they are but tiny memories of their giant ancestors.

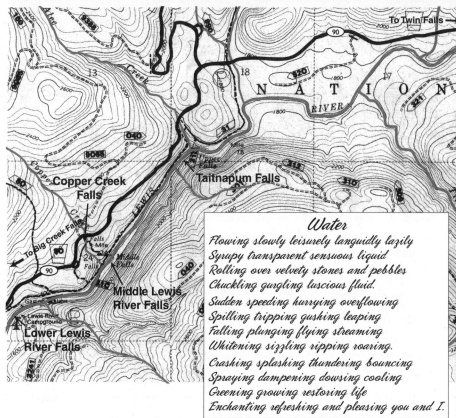

Water

Flowing slowly leisurely languidly lazily
Syrupy transparent sensuous liquid
Rolling over velvety stones and pebbles
Chuckling gurgling luscious fluid.

Sudden speeding hurrying overflowing
Spilling tripping gushing leaping
Falling plunging flying streaming
Whitening sizzling ripping roaring.

Crashing splashing thundering bouncing
Spraying dampening dowsing cooling
Greening growing restoring life
Enchanting refreshing and pleasing you and I.

55   Copper Creek Falls
A Romantic Plunge in a Bower of Green

Height: 60 feet   **Difficulty:** 2   **Romance:** 7

Type: Narrow Free Plunge.

Description: Copper Creek flows through deep green brush and forest, cuts a smooth but twisted channel in its bedrock below a rustic footbridge, then dips over an undercut cliff to land in a cool pool, all of which can be viewed head-on from the trail.

Distance/Time From Portland: 102 miles, 2 hours and 1 minute.

Directions to Parking/Trailhead: Follow directions to Lower Lewis River Falls (#54) and either park there and hike upstream to Copper Creek Falls and Middle Lewis River Falls or drive 1 mile further upstream (east by northeast) to the marked parking area for "Middle Falls" (#56).

Distance/Time From Parking: About 5 minutes from the nearby, roadside parking area for "Middle Falls".

Distance/Time From Other Landmark: 1 mile, 3 minute drive from parking for Lower Lewis River Falls (#54); 1 mile, 3 minutes drive to parking for Taitnapum Falls (Upper Lewis River Falls) (#57); .25 miles, 10 minutes walk down hill to Middle Lewis River Falls (#56).

Directions From Parking: Alternative #1: Hike upstream for about 1 mile from Lower Lewis River Falls (#55) to Middle Lewis River Falls (#56), crossing a bridge near it in between halves of Lower Copper Creek Falls; turn left on the trail to the parking just beyond this bridge. Copper Creek Falls is up slope from this area and upstream from the Lower Copper Creek Falls. **Alternative #2:** If you've driven to the Middle Lewis River Falls parking area, walk toward the river on the very obvious trail; the trail winds downhill until it crosses Copper Creek just above the falls; continuing downhill, the trail swings around to offer a splendid frontal view of this fabulous, intimate waterfall.

Elevation Change: 100 feet.

Restroom: At Lower Lewis River Falls Campground.

Picnic Area: At Lower Lewis River Falls Campground.

View & Kissing Spots: On the bridge above the falls, at the trailside viewpoint.

Accessibility to the Physically Challenged: This trail is likely to be too steep and narrow to be considered accessible.

Hazards: Minor, at worst.

Information: On Copper Creek (tributary of Lewis River), Skamania County, Washington, USGS Quartz Creek Butte Quadrangle, Green Trails Maps: Lone Butte.

Note that Lower Copper Creek Falls is downstream at the point where Copper Creek enters the Lewis River. Its 2 tiers, reminiscent of Dutchman Falls on Multnomah Creek, is wonderful but impossible to adequately sketch or photograph unless you are in the middle of the river. Make sure to visit it from the scenic footbridge between its tiers—another great kissing spot!

In case you wonder why we did not include Lower Copper Creek Falls (which is, in fact really fascinating, different, and attractive) there is a simple answer: We could not find a way to get a view of it which didn't involve drowning or hanging from a balloon! It's really neat when you are standing there looking around at all of it. It would be great to find a spot across the river (or suspended over the middle of it) where we could see it perfectly to draw it. Even if we had done that, you'd look at Barbara's picture and say, "How in the devil do we see it like that?" So...it ain't here!

See detailed map at falls #54, Lower Lewis River Falls.

From There to Here and Beyond

Who stood here looking at you, falls
Before my time or language?
I know he felt as me,
As those in eons to come
Will likewise feel in awe,
Connected to the earth and time,
In wordless praise of thee.

Black Capped Chickadee

Middle Lewis River Falls

Big, Beautiful Niagara-like Falls.

Height: 35 feet   Difficulty: 4   Romance: 4

Type: Wide tumble.

Description: Like Lower Lewis River Falls, Middle is a giant stair step in the river. It is different, however, in that it has several smaller steps below the main one. If you are careful, you can stand on the bedrock layer downstream of the falls.

Distance/Time From Portland: 102 miles, 2 hours and 1 minute.

Directions to Parking/Trailhead: Follow directions to Copper Creek Falls.

Distance/Time From Parking: .3 miles, 15 minutes.

Distance/Time From Other Landmark: .25 miles, 10 minutes walk from Copper Creek Falls (#55); 1 mile, 3 minute drive from parking for Lower Lewis River Falls (#54); 1 mile, 3 minute drive to parking for Taitnapum Falls (Upper Lewis River Falls) (#57); 1.2 miles, 30 minute walk upstream from Lower Lewis River Falls; 1 mile, 25 minutes walk upstream to Taitnapum Falls (Upper Lewis River Falls).

Directions From Parking: Follow directions to Copper Creek Falls (#55) then continue downhill for another quarter mile until you reach the riverside trail; walk downstream (right) until you reach the top of the falls. Additional views of the falls and of the delightful Lower Copper Creek Falls can be had a little bit further downstream.

Elevation Change: 200 feet.

Restroom: At Lower Lewis River Falls or Twin Falls Campgrounds.

Picnic Area: At Lower Lewis River Falls or Twin Falls Campgrounds.

View & Kissing Spots: At several viewing spots next to the top of the falls and downstream to the bridge and beyond.

Accessibility to the Physically Challenged: Pretty difficult (read as probably impossible) to negotiate with a wheelchair.

Hazards: This is a very powerful river and always quite cold. Wading or swimming in it is, therefore, extremely dangerous, especially near the falls. Be very careful!

Information: On Lewis River. Skamania County, Washington, USGS Quartz Creek Butte Quadrangle, Green Trails Maps: Lone Butte. An "official" USGS-Geographic Names Information System feature (with the name "Middle Falls"). As you can see, once again we have slightly renamed it to better differentiate it.

This area, as well as much of the rugged, forested part of the Pacific Northwest, is thought by some to be the habitat of the legendary Sasquatch or "Big Foot". As you visit some of the more remote areas, such as the upper Lewis River, you will appreciate how easily seemingly quite obvious things (such as downed airplanes) could disappear even without trying to hide. A recent example put this in perspective. Just as we finished the book and had it ready to take to the printer, something happened that we just had to include. A Bulgarian criminal, wanted in his home country for

murder and an illegal alien in the United States, was caught in Skamania County after hiding alone in the forest for something like twenty years. If he can manage that, who knows what could be hiding out there!

See detailed map at falls #54, Lower Lewis River Falls.

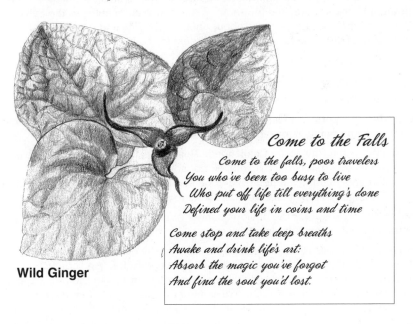

Wild Ginger

Come to the Falls

Come to the falls, poor travelers
You who've been too busy to live
Who put off life till everything's done
Defined your life in coins and time

Come stop and take deep breaths
Awake and drink life's art:
Absorb the magic you've forgot
And find the soul you'd lost.

57   **Taitnapum Falls**

Powerful White Water Spanning the River

Height: 35 feet   **Difficulty:** 4   **Romance:** 4

Type: Wide tumble.

Description: An exciting and powerful though not very tall falls containing a whole river full of water. Standing beside it, especially if the river is running high, is to be almost a part of the falls, feeling its power in every pore.

Distance/Time From Portland: 103 miles, 2 hours and 3 minute.

Directions to Parking/Trailhead: Alternative #1: Park at either Lower Lewis River Falls (#54) or at Middle Lewis River Falls (#56) and hike the Lewis River Trail to this falls. **Alternative #2:** Drive east about a mile beyond the parking area for Middle Lewis River Falls (2 miles past the Lower Lewis River Falls parking area) to a very roughly developed parking area along the south side of the road just before the bridge for Straight Creek.

Distance/Time From Parking: .5 miles, 15 minutes from the roadside parking lot for this falls.

Distance/Time From Other Landmark: 1 mile, 3 minutes drive from Middle Lewis River Falls (#56) parking area; 9.5 miles, 15 minutes drive to Twin Falls (#58); 1 mile, 30 minute walk upstream from Middle Lewis River Falls (#56) on the Lewis River Trail.

Directions From Parking: Alternative #1: Continue upstream from Middle Lewis River Falls (#56) on the Lewis River Trail for about a mile and 30 minutes to the viewpoint. **Alternative #2:** From the "Upper Falls" parking area, hike downstream (south) on the trail leading from parking along the west rim of Straight Creek's watershed for about .3 miles and 10 minutes to the Lewis River and then downstream for about another .2 miles and 5 minutes to the view of the falls. The falls thunder right next to the trail.

Elevation Change: 100 feet.

Restroom: At Lower Lewis River Falls or Twin Falls Campgrounds.

Picnic Area: At Lower Lewis River Falls or Twin Falls Campgrounds.

View & Kissing Spots: Wonderful views from right beside the top of the falls and from vantage points somewhat downstream.

Accessibility to the Physically Challenged: This trail is not rated as accessible. Despite its rating, it is relatively level, not so narrow, and with no major impediments. Perhaps a determined person accompanied by someone to help if things get too sticky would be able to navigate the trail to the falls.

Hazards: Minor, except for the obvious danger of venturing into the seductively attractive but potentially deadly river.

Information: On Lewis River. Skamania County, Washington, USGS Quartz Creek Butte Quadrangle, Green Trails Maps: Lone Butte. An "official" USGS-Geographic Names Information System feature (with the prosaic and repetitive name "Upper Falls"). We would have unofficially renamed it "Upper Lewis River Falls" but we prefer the Native American name carved into an old wooden sign nailed to a tree above the falls. Hopefully, the word doesn't translate to "restroom" or "caution"!

The Lewis River area may be open during weather which closes most of the

ways into it with snow. When you are here, you are very close to both Mount Saint Helens and Mount Adams. Their weather spills over to the Lewis River area and the elevation of Taitnapum Falls is about 2,300 feet above sea level, more than high enough to encourage snow!

The Lewis River Horse Camp is located on Forest Service Road #93 near Quartz Creek east of the Taitnapum Falls parking area—a delight for those with an equestrian turn of mind.

Another waterfalls, Straight Creek Falls, is located about 2 miles upstream on Straight Creek (which is just east and across the road from the Taitnapum Falls parking area).

See detailed map at falls #54, Lower Lewis River Falls.

Write to the Falls

Write as you walk to waterfalls
Or sing, or draw, or dance, or kiss
Express the beauty, sounds, and joy
Discover veins from stream to heart.

American Robin

58   **Twin Falls**

One Beautiful White Curtain after Another in a Deep Wooded Setting

Height: 80 feet   **Difficulty:** 1   **Romance:** 5

Type: Double (not twin) Wide Contact Plunges.

Description: This is a smaller version of Bridal Veil Falls set in a green bower with a wide, flat curtain of water dropping to a deep ledge from which it descends again in a similar wide, white curtain of water to a small stream leading directly to the river. The park and its views of Twin Falls is directly across the narrow river from this lovely scene.

Distance/Time From Portland: 109 miles, 2 hours and 18 minute.

Directions to Parking/Trailhead: Follow directions to Upper Lewis River Falls. Continue east on State Route 90 past the road to the Saw Tooth Berry Fields and Trout Lake Road to between mileposts 41 and 42. The marked entrance is on the right, a driveway which goes steeply downhill to the campground at the river level.

Distance/Time From Parking: A short walk across the campground to the river-side viewpoints.

Distance/Time From Other Landmark: 9.5 miles, 15 minutes drive from Taitnapum Falls (#57); 6 miles, 7 minutes to Big Spring Creek Falls (#59).

Directions From Parking: Walk through the campground to the bank of the Lewis River, then walk upstream a short distance (still in the park) until you see Twin Falls across the river.

Elevation Change: 0 feet.

Restroom: Rustic facilities in the park.

Picnic Area: Several scenically located picnic tables are scattered strategically about the small park.

View & Kissing Spots: Streamside and within view of the falls.

Accessibility to the Physically Challenged: Relatively accessible open spaces.

Hazards: No significant hazards unless you act silly in the river.

Information: On Twin Falls Creek (tributary of the Lewis River), Skamania County, Washington, USGS Steamboat Mountain Quadrangle, Green Trails Maps: Mt. Adams West; listed in USGS Geographic Names Information System.

This is a lovely, secluded park. It is a great place to spend a quiet, romantic time alone. Camping spaces are also available at this park.

Note that a "twin" falls is usually considered to be one with two side-by-side flows. A "double" falls is one with one tier followed by another. Obviously, the name is wrong but it's a well established one. Oh, well!

Watery Inspiration

Somehow the water which falls before us
Inspires a need in us to find
A means to express in art or word or music
The swell of feelings in our hearts
That fills to overflowing.

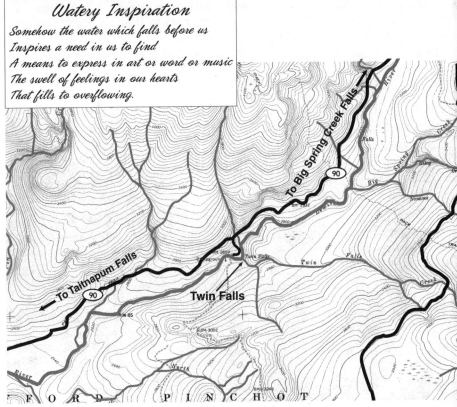

Wind River & White Salmon River Area

59   Big Spring Creek Falls
A Small but Charming and Cool Wayside Waterfall

Height: 30 feet   Difficulty: 0   Romance: 5

Description: Big Spring Creek comes out of the forest into the deepest, darkest forest glen where it drops once, splits and changes directions, drops again and then slides sideways to rejoin and redirect itself at you. One can walk beside the falls almost to its top and at any point, virtually reach out and touch it.

Type: Narrow Steep Slide with Multiple Steps.

Description: This small, complex falls emerges from the deep green of the forest and bounces over rock ledges and logs to the clearing and undeveloped parking area next to the highway.

Distance/Time From Portland: 115 miles, 2 hours and 25 minutes.

Directions to Parking/Trailhead: Follow Directions to Twin Falls. Continue driving east for a little over 5 miles on State Route 90 to its intersection with State Route 23 to Trout Lake; bear right on SR 23 and drive less than a quarter mile until you see a large, unpaved parking area on the left side of the road. Big Spring Creek is the first creek which crosses the road after the intersection. The falls is visible in its deeply wooded cleft.

Distance/Time From Parking: 0. It's right at the parking area.

Distance/Time From Other Landmark: 6 miles, 7 minutes from Twin Falls (#58); approximately 19 miles and 35 minutes to Trout Lake; 29 miles and 50 minutes to Little Goose Creek Falls (#61).

Directions From Parking: A short walk upstream to stopping places next to the falls.

Elevation Change: 0 feet.

Restroom: None here. Twin Falls Campground.

Picnic Area: No formal picnicking but plenty of room.

View & Kissing Spots: Next to the falls.

Accessibility to the Physically Challenged: The falls is visible from the road and from the level area near the falls which should be relatively easy to negotiate in a wheelchair.

Hazards: Really none here.

Information: On Big Spring Creek (tributary of the Lewis River), Skamania County, Washington, USGS Steamboat Mountain Quadrangle, Green Trails Maps: Mt. Adams West.

This is a wonderful place for a family to stop and play on a Summer excursion. There is deep, cool shade next to the falls, a sunny clearing, and the children (or youthful feeling grownups) could splash and wade in the creek below the falls.

Dipper

The Water Sprite

The waterfall's a water sprite
Who dances in the spray
On stage of trees and moss and rocks
Unseen, yet felt and long remembered.

60   Dog Creek Falls

An Exciting Falls at a Secluded Wayside

Height: 25'   **Difficulty:** 1   **Romance:** 3

Type: Arch Spreading Plunge.

Description: In a secluded but barren small canyon just off the highway, a powerful though small falls is produced as the creek squeezes through a narrow crack.

Distance/Time From Portland: 64 miles, 75 minutes.

Directions to Parking/Trailhead: Either take SR14 east from Vancouver or take Interstate 84 to Cascade Locks (exit 44) and cross the river on the Bridge of the Gods toll bridge (75¢) to SR14. In either case, drive east of the Bridge of the Gods to the east side of Dog Mountain near milepost #56 where you will see an informal parking area on the north side of the road where Dog Creek crosses under the road.

Distance/Time From Parking: Less than a hundred yards and 5 minutes.

Distance/Time From Other Landmark: 39 miles, 50 minutes drive to Little Goose Creek Falls (#61).

Directions From Parking: An informal and often changing foot path leads from parking along Dog Creek the very short distance to the falls. Note that floods on Dog Creek cause severe changes in the course of the creek and the path to the falls.

Elevation Change: 15 feet

Restroom: In Carson or Bingen.

Picnic Area: None but many likely spots can be used near the falls.

View & Kissing Spots: From the road, parking, and several good spots on the way to the falls. Kiss in the surprisingly secluded area near the falls.

Accessibility to the Physically Challenged: Visible from the road and parking.

Hazards: Some potential danger during high stream flow if you are really foolish.

Information: On Dog Creek. Skamania County, Washington, USGS Mt. Defiance Quadrangle, Green Trails Maps: Hood River.

Salmonberry

Bloom

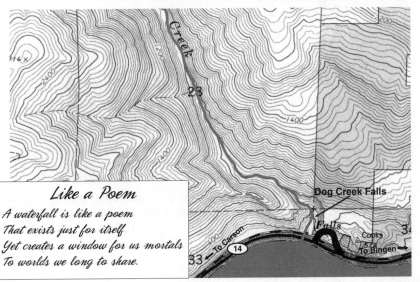

Dog Creek Falls

Falls

To Carson

14

To Bingen

Cooks

Like a Poem

A waterfall is like a poem
That exists just for itself
Yet creates a window for us mortals
To worlds we long to share.

Wind River & White Salmon River Area

61   Little Goose Creek Falls

Fabulous but Undeveloped, Nearly Hidden, and Dangerous

Height: 90'   Difficulty: 3   Romance: 4

Type: Contact Plunge.

Description: Little Goose Creek traverses a wide, flat layer of rock then plunges over a sheer cliff through several clefts in its lip to fall in rivulets into the deep canyon faced with cliffs eroded into rows of rounded shapes.

Distance/Time From Portland: 103 miles, 2 hours and 5 minutes.

Directions to Parking/Trailhead: From The Bridge of the Gods across the Columbia from Cascade Locks, drive east on Washington State Route 14 about 25 miles until you cross the White Salmon River from which you take State Route 141 north about 21 miles to Trout Lake. Drive west from Trout Lake on State Route 141 past the ranger station on your left about 1.5 miles to Route 88 (Trout Lake Creek Drive); turn right and drive north a little over 8 miles to just before the bridge for Little Goose Creek where you will find a dirt road on the left which opens into an ad hoc campground. Park out of the way. **Alternative #1:** You could take Interstate 84 to Hood River, cross the Columbia and pick up Route 141 in the town of White Salmon or drive west on SR 14 to SR 141 at the White Salmon River. **Alternative #2:** You could reach Trout Lake on your way from Big Spring Creek Falls and the other falls on the Lewis River and then drive to Little Goose as stated above.

Distance/Time From Parking: .25 miles, 10 minutes.

Distance/Time From Other Landmark: 39 miles, 50 minutes drive from Dog Creek Falls (#60); 4.5 miles, 7 minutes drive to Langfield Falls (#62); 29 miles and 50 minutes to Big Spring Creek Falls (#59).

Directions From Parking: Walk across the road to the large burned over clear cut. Find your own route (there is no trail) to the left toward the creek and along the clifftop, peeking at the creek whenever possible for about 5 minutes until you see Upper Little Goose Creek Falls (about 40 feet tall) and 3 minutes further to views of the much larger and more impressive Little Goose Creek Falls (Lower?).

Elevation Change: Less than 100 feet.

Restroom: None here. Try in Trout Lake.

Picnic Area: There is a very, very rustic campground and picnic area in the woods across the road from the field near the falls. It appears to be no longer maintained by anyone or else it was never actually an official campground. However, we have often encountered people camping here.

View & Kissing Spots: At the clifftop viewpoints. Unfortunately, there is no developed trail or viewpoints and it is somewhat difficult to get as good a view of the larger falls as one would like.

Accessibility to the Physically Challenged: Really not accessible due to terrain too uneven and blocked by brush and downed timber.

Hazards: Be very careful around the unmarked, unguarded viewpoints. This is the primal world where, if you get too close to the edge, you fall into the abyss! Do not do that!

Information: On Little Goose Creek, Skamania County, Washington, USGS

Sleeping Beauty Quadrangle, Green Trails Maps: Mt. Adams West.

A short distance upstream from the main falls, a picturesque smaller narrow plunge falls drops about 40 feet to the strata which is ultimately the top of Little Goose Creek Falls. Because both falls are very attractive, they each deserve a name. Perhaps they should be "Upper Little Goose Creek Falls" and "Lower Little Goose Creek Falls". Names too long? Oh Well.

A Little Girl

A little girl stood near the falls
Her hand inside her dad's.
She seemed amazed with eyes so wide
Just staring at the falls.

She stood so still except a smile
That grew across her face
Then laughed and pulled her dad
Who stooped to give a hug.

62   Langfield Falls
Beautiful Big Falls in a Well Maintained Setting

Height: 110'   **Difficulty:** 4   **Romance:** 7

Type: Spreading Contact Plunge.

Description: Langfield slides down a rock cliff in a deep, wooden glen. Its shape and appearance varies quite widely depending upon which way the water chooses to slide and how much water is available at the time of your visit. This is a very romantic, almost mystical setting, well cared for and carefully developed to provide wonderful views from many locations and elevations.

Distance/Time From Portland: 108 miles, 2 hours and 12 minutes.

Directions to Parking/Trailhead: Follow directions to Little Goose Creek Falls. Continue north on State Route 88 for about 4.5 miles until you see the sign on your right for Langfield Falls just before the intersection with Route 8851.

Distance/Time From Parking: Walk less than .25 miles and 10 minutes down the well maintained, wide dirt trail and staircase to the viewpoint.

Distance/Time From Other Landmark: 4.5 miles, 7 minutes drive from Little Goose Creek Falls (#61).

Directions From Parking: The trail is quite obvious from the parking area next to the road. Follow the trail to the falls.

Elevation Change: 200 feet.

Restroom: None at this location.

Picnic Area: A wonderful place to spend time and to picnic even without formal sites.

View & Kissing Spots: From many locations from the end of the trail, along the gently sloping switchbacked trail to the creek level.

Accessibility to the Physically Challenged: Not really designed to be accessible but might be possible with assistance or if quite athletic.

Hazards: Few if any hazards about which to be concerned.

Information: On Mosquito Creek, Skamania County, Washington, USGS Sleeping Beauty Quadrangle, Green Trails Maps: Mt. Adams West; listed in USGS Geographic Names Information System.

In Summer, the shallow pool at the base of the falls can be a delightful place to cool off. Although quite secluded and often very lonely, don't forget that a bus full of elementary school kids or a bible study group is bound to show up if you aren't discrete in your swimming attire!

Note that this falls can be reached by driving from Twin Falls and Big Spring Creek Falls as part of a loop tour from the Wind River area through Trout Lake and back to the Columbia at White Salmon.

This romantic falls is named for a retired Forest Service Ranger, K.C. Langfield, who discovered the falls.

While you are in the vicinity of the town of Trout Lake, you will have a chance to admire the fascinating and different terrain of this alpine valley. It is beautiful and unique. One feature we spent a lot of time trying unsuccessfully to find was the lake! The best information we could get was that there was once a lake here but it's gone because of natural changes in the water table or the streams or the depth of the lake or overuse of irrigation or introduced plants or draining swamps or erosion or any number of other theories. In other words, don't come here to fish because Trout Lake has neither trout nor a lake!

See detailed map at falls #61, Little Goose Creek Falls.

For Whom?

A waterfall's for children
To laugh and play beneath the spray.

A waterfall's for lovers
To share their love in solitude.
A waterfall's for poets
To hear new rhymes and verses.

A waterfall's for parents
To find again forgotten dreams.

A waterfall's for oldsters
To find the promise of eternity.

Steller's Jay

63   Outlet Falls

Gorgeous Big Falls in a Remarkable Rock Canyon

Height: 150'   **Difficulty:** 2   **Romance:** 4

Type: Narrow Free Plunge.

Description: Water from the snows of the high mountains pours down the glacier created canyon, further cut by the power of the stream. As the canyon becomes a huge, deep crack with vertical walls of columnar basalt, the bedrock on which the stream travels suddenly reaches a cliff over which it falls in a spectacular plunge to the deeper canyon below. From an unmarked wide spot on the roadside, one can see the canyon. A short walk on a very improvised trail takes you to an outcrop from which you can see the majesty of this obscure natural wonder.

Distance/Time From Portland: 115 miles; 2 hours and 15 minutes (via SR #14).

Directions to Parking/Trailhead: From Portland, follow directions for Little Goose Creek Falls as far as the intersection of routes 14 & 141 by the Columbia. **Alternative #1:** Drive north from the gorge on route 141 until you reach the town of B Z Corners where you will intersect the B Z Corners-Glenwood Road (that's right, there's no number). Take it about 20 miles to Glenwood. **Alternative #2:** Follow directions (from the north or the south) to Trout Lake (see directions for Little Goose Creek Falls #61). Drive east from Trout Lake on the Trout Lake-Glenwood Road (also no number) for about 17 miles. **Then:** From Glenwood (however you got there) drive east for between 4 and 5 miles on what is now called the Glenwood-Goldendale Road to an unmarked pull-off on the left (north) side of the road. From this dirt parking area, you will be able to see the yawning gorge of Outlet Creek.

Distance/Time From Parking: 0. The viewpoint is immediately beyond the parking area.

Distance/Time From Other Landmark: 31 miles, 50 minutes from Little Goose Creek Falls (#61).

Directions From Parking: Walk carefully away from the road to the edge of the cliff from which you can see the falls.

Elevation Change: 0 feet.

Restroom: None here. Try Glenwood, Trout Lake, B Z Corners, or Goldendale.

Picnic Area: No picnic tables here either.

View & Kissing Spots: Views are along and among large rock outcrops which project up from the cliff. Be very careful! Although you can work your way down to improve your vantage point, eventually gravity and the bottomless canyon will get you if you make any mistake! We stayed very near the top.

Accessibility to the Physically Challenged: Partially visible from parking and trail areas but the rude viewpoint is currently totally inaccessible.

Hazards: Very, very dangerous undeveloped cliff-top viewpoint! Be careful!

Information: On Outlet Creek, Klickitat County, Washington, USGS Outlet Falls Quadrangle; listed in USGS Geographic Names Information System.

This little known falls is not only beautiful in itself, it is surrounded by some of the most remarkable rock formations we have ever seen. They're almost other worldly!

Outlet Falls is on the Glenwood-Goldendale Road. If you're looking for something else to do, drive to Goldendale where you'll find an astronomical observatory. South to the gorge, look for signs for "Stonehenge". This replica of the famous ancient English circle of rocks is a war memorial. There's a nice park by the river. Better yet, the Maryhill Museum is a short distance west on SR 14. The museum is an amazing place with the artifacts of the royal family of Rumania, the only miniature Parisian fashion manikins, a collection of Rodin's sculpture models and drawings, American paintings, chess sets. and lots of other stuff.

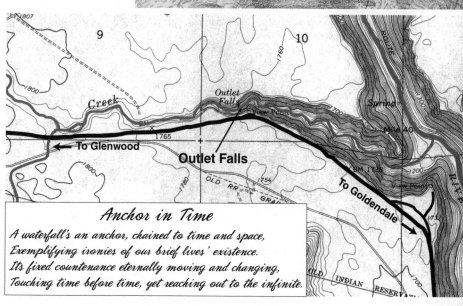

Anchor in Time

A waterfall's an anchor, chained to time and space,
Exemplifying ironies of our brief lives' existence.
Its fixed countenance eternally moving and changing,
Touching time before time, yet reaching out to the infinite.

Wind River & White Salmon River Area

VI. North Oregon Coast & Coast Range

The Northern Coast and Coast Range of Oregon offers a great diversity of outdoor delights: quaint country towns, seashore resorts, beaches, forests, and waterfalls. You can visit these waterfalls as part of a day trip from Portland or other areas in the Willamette Valley or as part of a visit to the beach.

Fortunately, there are only a few routes leading from the Willamette Valley to the coast. All of the falls in this section are on or relatively near one of these primary routes.

Much of the mountains in Oregon between the sea coast and the Willamette Valley, the Coast Range, was ravaged by a series of huge forest fires beginning in the 1930s. These fires and the enormous area effected is collectively called "The Tillamook Burn". The first of these cataclysms occurred in 1933, burning 290,000 acres of huge old growth trees. You will see evidence of it on the way to virtually every waterfall in this section, particularly those on highway 6 between the cities of Forest Grove and Tillamook (University Falls, Fern Rock Creek Falls, and Bridge Creek Falls).

This section covers the largest geographical area in the book but it does not contain a very large

A Waterfall's a Poem

A waterfall's a poem
From nature's pen to you
But written in her flowing hand
Its touch to teach your heart and soul.
Each drop a word of perfect rhyme
Its stanzas sweep and splash
The verses sing and soar,
Recited loudly by the muse.

Elk (wapiti)

number of waterfalls. There are several falls which we did not include for a variety of reasons, including:

Beaver Falls on Beaver Creek just off Old Route 30 near Delena, a curtain plunge below a ford across Beaver Creek by which one reaches partying and viewing areas. The frightening slopes by the falls and fording a stream just above a 75 foot drop are too dangerous for us—and you!

Kilchis Falls on the Kilchis River is too long a drive on too lousy a gravel road for the romance of the falls. Maybe conditions will improve.

Nehalem Falls on the Nehalem River off the Nehalem River Road isn't too bad. It isn't near anything else and we just didn't have room for it.

There's Silver Falls, Echo Falls, Euchre Falls, Alsea Falls, and more.

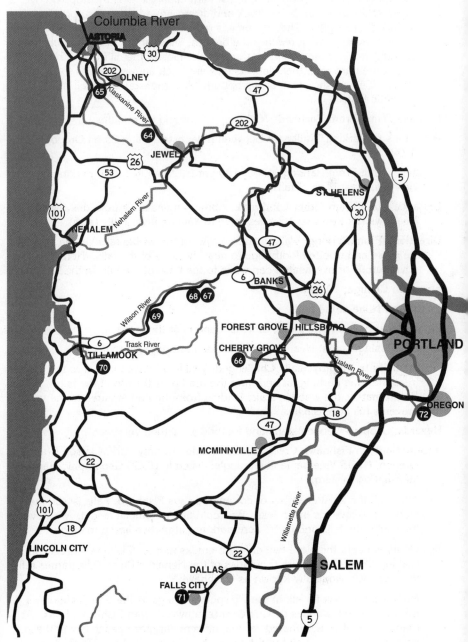

North Oregon Coast & Coast Range

64   Fishhawk Falls

A Surprising, Complex Fan of White Water in a Quiet Little Park

Height: 55'   Difficulty: 1   Romance: 7

Type: Spreading Slide

Description: Fishhawk Creek meanders alongside the road for miles with little change of elevation. Suddenly, the stream changes level by dropping over a steep, rocky break in the bedrock and drops into a lush and surprisingly secluded forest glen. The falls begins rather narrow, widening to three times its width by the time it reaches the bottom. Most of the water is deflected to the right (facing), and continues across the face of the cliff until it hits the wall at the right side, then deflects leftward back across the falls to recombine as it enters the creek at the bottom. A complex, interesting and romantic falls.

Distance/Time From Portland: 76 miles, 1 hour and 27 minutes.

Directions to Parking/Trailhead: Between mileposts 24 and 25 on Oregon Route #202.

Distance/Time From Parking: About 100 yards, 2 minutes from parking to viewpoint near base of falls.

Distance/Time From Other Landmark: About 4 miles drive from the Jewell Meadows Elk Reserve; 16 miles drive to Youngs River Falls (#65).

Directions From Parking: Walk upstream toward the visible falls via the wooden staircase and wooden footbridge to near the base of the falls. Note that the adventurous or overheated can wade to the base of the falls in the Summer.

Elevation Change: 10 feet.

Restroom: None at the park.

Picnic Area: At least one picnic table is found near the creek.

View & Kissing Spots: Near base of falls, on footbridge, in the woods.

Accessibility to the Physically Challenged: Visible at close range through the trees from the parking lot and from the road near the top of the falls. Unfortunately, the wooden stairs leading from the parking area to the falls prevents full accessibility.

Hazards: Slippery wooden steps and footbridge, getting very wet.

Information: On Fishhawk Creek, in Lee Wooden County Park, Clatsop County, Oregon, USGS Vinemaple Quadrangle; listed in USGS Geographic Names Information System.

Although the local chamber of commerce says Fishhawk Falls is 100 feet high, we believe it's much less. We could find no official height. Whatever its height, the falls and its 55 acre park are attractive and romantic.

Oddly enough, there are two different creeks named 'Fishhawk Creek" in Clatsop County which are tributaries of the Nehalem River. The names refer the Osprey, colloquially known as "Fishhawk".

Make sure to look for elk at the viewpoints alongside the Jewell Meadows Elk Reserve a few miles downstream (southwest) from Fishhawk Falls. At many times of year, hundreds of magnificent elk graze peacefully in these pastures, oblivious to all but the most obnoxious onlookers. These horse-size members of the deer family can simply melt into the woods almost before your eyes. It is amazing how quiet and virtually invisible they can be while moving through the forest. I once saw a group of hunters moving up a hillside on the other side of a valley. A herd of forty or more elk were in ahead of them and simply circled around the hunters and followed them up the hill. It was quite obvious that the hunters were unaware of their quarry just a few yards away all around them.

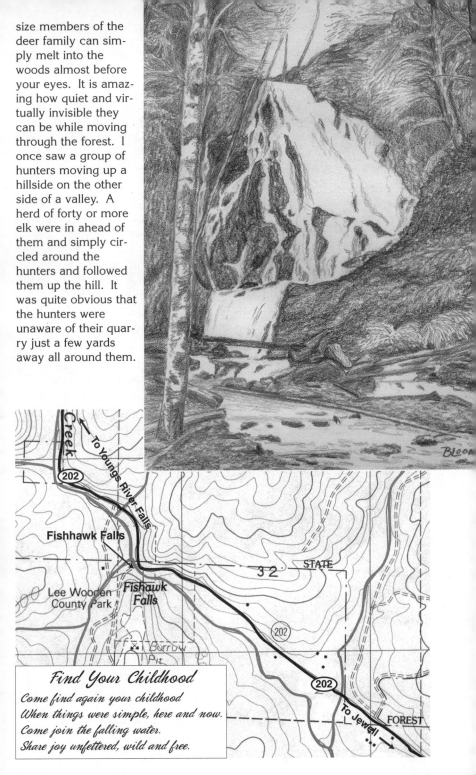

Fishhawk Falls

Lee Wooden County Park

Fishhawk Falls

To Youngs River Falls

To Jewell

STATE

FOREST

Find Your Childhood

Come find again your childhood
When things were simple, here and now.
Come join the falling water.
Share joy unfettered, wild and free.

65   Youngs River Falls
A Thundering Tumbling Torrent in a Romantic Glen

Height: 65'   Difficulty: 4   Romance: 6

Type: Square Contact Plunge.

Description: Youngs River tumbles out of the clear-cut woods and roars down a rock face with great power and excitement. Amazingly, this huge falls and great power becomes an almost stagnantly motionless stream within a few hundred yards.

Distance/Time From Portland: 87 miles, 1 hour and 40 minutes.

Directions to Parking/Trailhead: Follow Oregon Route 202 southwest from Astoria or northwest from Jewell then turn south at the northwest end of the town of Olney at the "Youngs River Falls" sign. Just across a small concrete bridge about 1 mile from Olney, bare sharp right. Follow this road for about 3 miles until you reach the first paved road on your left. It may be marked by a "Scenic Tour #7" sign. This road (part of the original highway, now eliminated by a "short-cut") ends in view of the falls in a few hundred yards.

Distance/Time From Parking: .1 miles, 10 minutes.

Distance/Time From Other Landmark: 16 miles and 25 minutes drive from Fishhawk Falls (#64); 10 miles and 20 minutes drive from Astoria.

Directions From Parking: A trail begins on the left side of the parking and upper viewing area. Follow it switching back and forth down to the streamside then upstream to as near to the falls as the ever changing course of the stream and your determination allows.

Elevation Change: 30 feet.

Restroom: In Olney or Astoria, none at the park.

Picnic Area: No formal picnic area but plenty of delightful spots in the woods and along the creek below the falls can be used.

View & Kissing Spots: Visible from parking, along the trail to streamside, and along the stream up to near the base of the falls.

Accessibility to the Physically Challenged: Beautifully visible from parking.

Hazards: Steep, muddy trail, slippery rocks near the falls, getting wet in the stream or from spray.

Information: On Youngs River, Clatsop County, Oregon, USGS Olney Quadrangle; listed in USGS Geographic Names Information System.

Youngs River Falls, which was discovered by members of the Lewis and Clark expedition while hunting game during their Winter near the mouth of the Columbia in 1805-6. The falls appeared in the motion picture "Free Willy II". Unfortunately, Youngs River Falls seems to have fallen out of favor, lost financial support, or at least lost its physical and political visibility. Hopefully, some private or public organization will find the time and money to restore its surroundings to its former status as a first class attraction. Trail maintenance, picnic tables, a restroom, or at least a sign would improve things. Thankfully, mother nature continues to create beauty even if ignored, unassisted, and unheralded!

You can loop back to Astoria through the rich and interesting countryside by continuing northeast on the winding county road which brought you to the falls.

After the Lewis and Clark expedition spent the Winter of 1805-6 at Fort Clatsop near present day Astoria, they spent a year getting back to President Jefferson in Washington, D.C. Their report was so exciting to everyone that in 1811. John Jacob Astor founded Astoria, the first U.S. settlement west of Saint Louis, Missouri.

A 1949 map (and the GNIS) shows "Barth Falls" 2 to 4 miles southeast of Olney and a few hundred yards south of the road. Maybe you can find it! Let us know.

Youngs River Falls

A Big Falls

We hear the noise from far ahead
Hiking on the trail
Then see the whiteness through the trees
Walking to the falls.

We see the water tumbling down
Looking from the view
Then feel the spray upon our skin
Standing at the edge.

We sense the power of the flow
Pulsing though our feet
And stand awestruck at the sight
Loving all we feel.

66   Lee Falls

A Surprisingly Huge, Powerful Falls Beside a Forest Lane

Height: 25'   **Difficulty:** 3   **Romance:** 4

Type: Wide low tumble.

Description: Near the headwaters of the Tualatin River, the stream gently flows until it reaches a break in the bedrock and roars to a lower level.

Distance/Time From Portland: 38 miles, 45 minutes.

Directions to Parking/Trailhead: From Portland, drive west on U.S. 26 to Oregon #47; drive south on 47 to 7 miles south of Forest Grove; turn west on Patton Valley Road (Old Highway 47) and follow directions to Cherry Grove, about 6.5 miles; follow the main road through town (it eventually becomes Summit Avenue); at about the end of the pavement on Summit Avenue (which may have a sign "Nixon Road" at that point), a dirt road (which may bear a sign "Lee Falls Road") drops off to the left and ends at a gate in about 25 yards. Park alongside the road near the gate. Do not block the gate and do not drive beyond it even if it happens to be open unless there are signs saying its open for public use. It is subject to being locked without warning!

Distance/Time From Parking: 2.3 miles, 65 minutes from gate.

Distance/Time From Other Landmark: 1.5 miles, 40 minutes from Little Lee Falls; 2 miles to Haines Falls (inaccessible!).

Directions From Parking: Follow crushed rock road from gate upstream to falls.

Elevation Change: 90 feet.

Restroom: None available, try in Cherry Grove or Forest Grove.

Picnic Area: No picnic areas but there are beautiful areas along the stream.

View & Kissing Spots: View the falls from many scenic spots along the road.

Accessibility to the Physically Challenged: The nearly level, well maintained, crushed rock road should be a delightful wheelchair hike.

Hazards: The only apparent hazards are the swift cold water and foolishness near the falls or discussions with those who mark the area "No Trespassing".

Information: On the Tualatin River, Washington County, Oregon, USGS Turner Creek Quadrangle; listed in USGS Geographic Names Information System.

Little Lee Falls, a charming, 5 to 10 foot falls in a lovely setting, can be found on the river near the metal maintenance building.

Note that the road has a locked gate marked "No Trespassing". Despite the signs, no one chased us out. In fact, we met hikers and horseback riders. If you enter, however, be certain to respect the property and be a good steward of the resource. We hope this area will ultimately be fully opened. Haines Falls and two other falls are upstream of Lee Falls but are "off limits" or "inaccessible". <u>Update</u>: Jerry Rogers, Water Master of Washington County, told us that the road and the adjoining land is a mix of private and public property ownerships. The gate was erected and locked because of vandalism, littering, and general hooliganism, culminating in an altercation resulting in a death. Since the gate was locked, the area has been quiet, clean, and safe and you should be welcome to visit. Have fun!

Nearby Henry Haag Lake, also in the Tualatin River watershed, on Scoggins Valley Road off Route 47, is a popular and delightful picnic spot and swimmin' hole to enjoy on warm and lazy Summer days. A great Summer day is an early morning hike to Lee Falls followed by a short drive to Haag Lake for a picnic lunch and a cool dip. "It's a good thing!"

Your Soul in the Falls

You sit alone and watch TV
Or join a club for make-work sport.
Somehow your loneliness persists
In meaningless and hollow acts.

Go see a falls and find yourself
Among the trees and spray.
Their art and life and time and place
Will help you find the way.

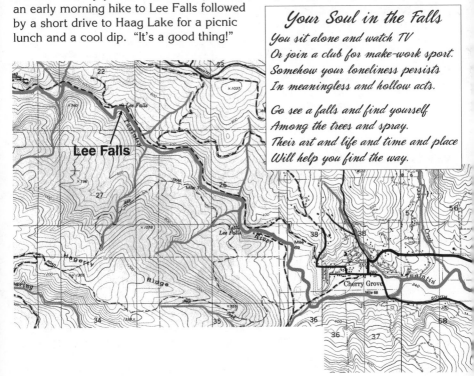

67   University Falls

A Big, Powerful Falls Hidden in the Woods

Height: 65'   **Difficulty:** 3   **Romance:** 5

Type: Spreading tumble

Description: Elliott Creek quietly meanders over a broad, level rock shelf until it reaches a deep crack in the strata into which it thunders as a broad, spreading falls, bouncing over square blocks on its way down.

Distance/Time From Portland: 44 miles, 60 minutes.

Directions to Parking/Trailhead: Drive west from Portland on U.S. 26 to its junction with State Route #6. Follow Route #6 to just past the summit of the coast range. Look for a sign saying "University Falls" on your right pointing across the road. There is also a sign saying "Browns Camp". Turn just east of the large highway department lot and shed filled with gravel. Follow "University Falls" signs when present but always bearing right at every fork or intersection. When you reach University Falls Road, follow it to near mile marker 2.5 where you should see a "University Falls" sign just before crossing Elliott Creek. Park in a small turnout alongside the road near a trailhead for the "Historic Trail" before the bridge.

Distance/Time From Parking: .3 miles, 15 minutes.

Distance/Time From Other Landmark: 7 miles (3 miles west on Route 6 from the entrance to the side road), 19 minutes to Fern Rock Creek Falls (#68).

Directions From Parking: Follow trail uphill toward falls crossing two dirt roads en route; after which you walk steeply downhill for some distance; at the bottom of the slope, the trail turns left toward the creek; a sign marks the trail back-tracking upstream toward the falls which are, by then, visible through the trees; a short walk will bring you to a viewpoint near the base.

Elevation Change: 90 feet.

Restroom: No restrooms in this area. Try one of the quaint roadside restaurants along the highway such as at Jordan Creek.

Picnic Area: Although there are no picnic tables, the grassy area near the stream should be ideal for a picnic on a blanket.

View & Kissing Spots: From roadside (barely visible through the trees); from near the base of the falls.

Accessibility to the Physically Challenged: Barely visible through the trees from the road a short distance past the bridge but otherwise inaccessible due to the steep, narrow, and rough trail.

Hazards: Few if any hazards except for slipping on the steep, slippery trail.

Information: On Elliott Creek (tributary of Devils Fork of the Wilson River), Tillamook County, Oregon, USGS Woods Point Quadrangle; listed in USGS Geographic Names Information System.

There is the mangled evidence that a bridge once crossed the stream just downstream from the base of the falls. It also demonstrates the enormous power of the water to dispatch human works. Hopefully, this hidden little park will be rehabilitated.

The "Historic Trail' which you cross repeatedly in this area, is a terrific 12 or more mile hike which begins at Gales Creek Forest Park, a campground about a mile north of route 6 east of the road to University Falls.

This entire area is a maize of roads, many of them less suitable for normal passenger vehicles than for off-road vehicles, motorcycles, and bulldozers. Although most of the roads are marked by names or numbers, they are all one lane dirt roads. You could easily get lost and/or stuck if you aren't careful. Please note that in our little Toyota hatchback, we were able to wander around this area for many miles in rainy weather due to very poor directions and had no problems but were very, very careful!

The condition of the roads encourages a great many people to use the area to practice driving their off-road motorcycles and 4-wheel drive trucks. Don't get run over!

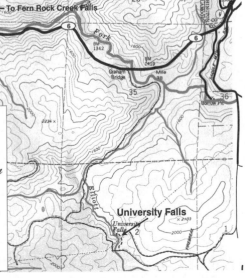

University Falls

Ten thousand years you've waited here
Providing beauty for itself
While fires have raged and trees regrown
Along your mighty flow.

So now we're here to share your charms,
To witness art in nature's realm,
To join our love and life with yours
And dream you know we're here.

68   Fern Rock Creek Falls
A Lovely, Complex Falls in a Glen Beside the Highway

Height: 40'   Difficulty: 1   Romance: 3

Type: Narrow Spreading Steep Slide

Description: Fern Rock Creek courses through the thick second growth timber of the Tillamook Burn until it reaches a steep rock cliff down which it plunges within 100 yards of the highway.

Distance/Time From Portland: 44 miles, 50 minutes.

Directions to Parking/Trailhead: Follow directions as for University Falls (#67) but continue west on State Route #6 another 3 miles to past mileposts 30. Before you reach milepost 29 you will see a large parking area on the south (left) side of the road opposite a small sign on the right which simply says "Falls" with an arrow.

Distance/Time From Parking: 0 minutes, it's just beyond the parking area and visible from it.

Distance/Time From Other Landmark: 7 miles (3 miles east on Route 6 from the entrance to its side road), 19 minutes from University Falls (#67); 10 miles, 12 minutes to Bridge Creek Falls (#69).

Directions From Parking: The falls is visible from your parking spot.

Elevation Change: 0 feet.

Restroom: None at this location. Try restaurants or gas stations along the highway.

Picnic Area: No formal picnic area, however, this area is a terrific place to stop and cool off or picnic when traveling along this highway.

View & Kissing Spots: Visible from the highway and from the large, convenient gravel parking area.

Accessibility to the Physically Challenged: Completely visible from your car. Paths on either side of the creek are level and should be relatively easy for wheelchairs although they do not seem to be actively maintained and might, therefore, vary in condition over time.

Hazards: No meaningful hazards except cars.

Information: On Fern Rock Creek (tributary of Devils Fork of the Wilson River), Tillamook County, Oregon, USGS Woods Point Quadrangle.

Although we can find no "official" listing of this falls under any name, our original guess as to its name is correct according to Clyde Zeller of the Oregon Department of Forestry.

When you are parked at this falls, you will notice a rough forest road heading upward into the forest from the west edge of the open parking area by the highway. On our first falls hunting trip to this area, the awful directions we were given to University Falls (#67) led us to discover Fern Rock Creek Falls and Bridge Creek Falls, which is all to the good. However, our desperation trying to find the right road, led us to take the road from this parking lot. At that time (and probably today) it was suitable only for 4-wheelers. We backtracked and found University Falls Road entering route 6 further west. Although that ultimately reached the falls, we spent over an hour wandering around on really terrible dirt roads before we got there. On the way out, we found the right way—a much shorter, much better road. If you have a really husky off-road vehicle, this would be a great place to go nuts!

On your way from Portland on route 6, you will pass the junction for the town of Timber at milepost 49 and the Trolley Museum at milepost 37. If you have time, visit the very rustic Trolley Museum where they save and refurbish abandoned streetcars from all over. Some of their work is in use in Portland and elsewhere. They always seem encouraged by the interest of any visitor.

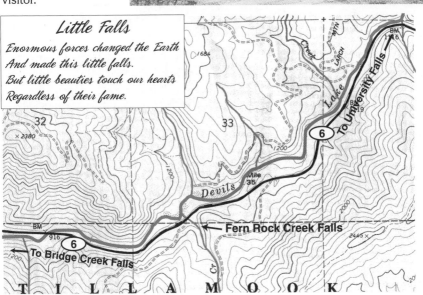

Little Falls

Enormous forces changed the Earth
And made this little falls.
But little beauties touch our hearts
Regardless of their fame.

North Oregon Coast & Coast Range

69 Bridge Creek Falls

Between Streets, a River Blasts Through a Crack

Height: 45'   **Difficulty:** 2   **Romance:** 6

Type: Narrow contact plunge, narrow arched plunge.

Description: A narrow contact plunge descends a vertical cliff at the head of a very narrow crack of a canyon, lands on a flat stone shelf where a gutter has been carved to lead some of the water to a handmade stone catch basin for a long-abandoned fresh water system. From the shelf, the water arches a few feet more to reach its final streambed along which it courses rapidly over exposed bed rock.

Distance/Time From Portland: 54 miles, 1 hour.

Directions to Parking/Trailhead: Follow directions to Fern Rock Creek Falls (#68) but continue west on route 6 for about another 10 miles (but before the town of Jordan Creek) to near milepost 20 until you see a slightly wider shoulder of the road on the left (south) side next to a vertical cliff. Just beyond this spot, the cliff is split by a narrow cleft through which you can see the falls upstream. Unfortunately, there's no sign. You may want to slow down to look for it or have your companion do so. We don't want you to miss it but neither do we want you to end up driving into the Wilson River!

Distance/Time From Parking: 5 minutes.

Distance/Time From Other Landmark: 10 miles, 12 minutes from Fern Rock Creek Falls (#68); 29 miles, 40 minutes to Munson Creek Falls (#70).

Directions From Parking: Walk upstream from the road about 200 yards following the obvious stone steps and short trail to the base of the falls.

Elevation Change: 30 feet.

Restroom: None at this location.

Picnic Area: No picnic area but a rustic bench at the base of the falls.

View & Kissing Spots: Lovely spots along the short trail to the falls and at the base of the falls.

Accessibility to the Physically Challenged: Visible through the trees from parking next to the road (especially in the Winter) but not accessible beyond the road due to stone steps.

Hazards: No real hazards except slippery,wet stone steps and rocks, especially near the base of the falls.

Information: On Bridge Creek, Tillamook County, Oregon, USGS Jordan Creek Quadrangle.

Although the degree of careful development and maintenance of this attraction lead us to believe it must have an official name, we found no name for it and named it for its creek. According to Clyde Zeller of the Oregon Department of Forestry, this is the right name.

Despite the obscurity of this nearly unknown falls, its roadside location and artfully built stone walls and stairs should make it a favorite spot to visit. We're sure you will be happy you visited it too.

We have no information as to the history of this falls and its obvious, well built but very old development. In the picture, you can see the rock railing which meets and crosses the base of the upper, larger portion of the falls. "On the ground", it is obvious that there were once trails on both sides of this very, very narrow crack in the rock and that a great deal of work went into its walls, steps, and trails. Someone continues to maintain it quite beautifully. Whoever it is deserves praise for his unheralded efforts on our behalf. As a tribute to that unnamed hero, leave it better than you found it!

Wilson Falls is purported to be in the vicinity of Jones Camp, on the River or, we suspect, coming into the river from the north.

The Jones Camp bridge spans a deep, clear, and powerful "pinch point".

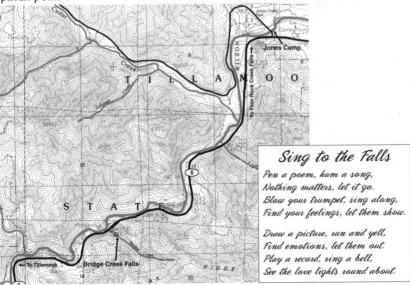

Sing to the Falls

Pen a poem, hum a song,
Nothing matters, let it go.
Blow your trumpet, sing along,
Find your feelings, let them show.

Draw a picture, run and yell,
Find emotions, let them out.
Play a record, ring a bell,
See the love lights round about.

70   **Munson Creek Falls**

A Beautiful, Complicated, and Dizzyingly Tall Falls in a Wilderness

Height: 256'   Difficulty: 4 to base, 7 to top   Romance: 6

Type: Steep Slide, Contact Plunge, Contact Plunge.

Description: This stately falls drops virtually from out of sight to ground level in a series of awe inspiring plumes of white. Those willing to brave the thick undergrowth and wet conditions can go right to the base of the falls. For another, more comprehensive view of this very tall spectacle, one can traverse a hillside trail for a view with the middle of the falls at eye level. From one year to another, trail conditions are quite variable but the relatively short and reasonably level walk is well worth the trip. You will love it.

Distance/Time From Portland: 83 miles; 1 hour and 40 minutes.

Directions to Parking/Trailhead: Take U.S. Route 26 west from Portland to its junction with State Route #6; follow route 6 to Tillamook; turn south on U.S. Route 101 at its intersection in Tillamook; drive approximately 7 miles south passing the very noticeable "Blimp Hangar" to the sign for Munson Creek Falls County Park; turn left onto this small road and drive for about one and a half miles to the gravel road which almost immediately leads to the small parking area.

Distance/Time From Parking: Lower Trail: .2 miles, 10 minutes; Upper Trail: .5 miles. 25 minutes.

Distance/Time From Other Landmark: 15 minutes from Tillamook.

Directions From Parking: From the parking area, either turn left and walk uphill on the marked upper trail to cliffside views of the falls or walk upstream on the much easier lower trail to views near the bottom of the falls. Note that downed timber and other storm debris usually chokes the path before you can conveniently reach the base of the falls. Views from the end of the trail are wonderful and adequate for most of us. The extremely athletic and determined can overcome these obstacles and reach the bottom of the falls if they really want to!

Elevation Change: 0 to near base of falls; 150 feet or less to upper view point.

Restroom: None at the day use area.

Picnic Area: At parking area.

View & Kissing Spots: At the views nearest the falls.

Accessibility to the Physically Challenged: Unfortunately, the narrow, uneven, and often muddy trail is not suitable for wheelchairs.

Hazards: Frequent washouts and nasty trail conditions on the upper trail; mud and thick undergrowth (including berry vines) on the lower trail.

Information: On Munson Creek, in Munson Creek Falls County Park, Tillamook County, Oregon, USGS Beaver Quadrangle; listed in USGS Geographic Names Information System.

At 256 feet, Munson Creek Falls is the highest west of the Willamette River.

Munson Creek and its falls were named for Goran Munson who settled near the creek in 1889. One of the highest and certainly one of the most beautiful waterfalls in Oregon.

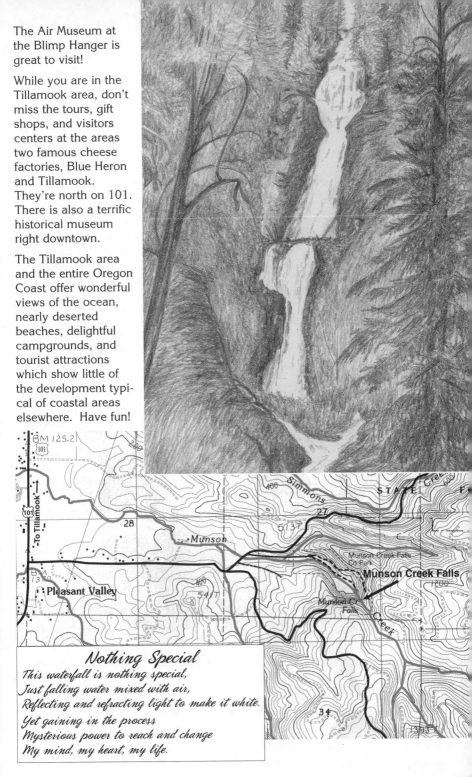

The Air Museum at the Blimp Hanger is great to visit!

While you are in the Tillamook area, don't miss the tours, gift shops, and visitors centers at the areas two famous cheese factories, Blue Heron and Tillamook. They're north on 101. There is also a terrific historical museum right downtown.

The Tillamook area and the entire Oregon Coast offer wonderful views of the ocean, nearly deserted beaches, delightful campgrounds, and tourist attractions which show little of the development typical of coastal areas elsewhere. Have fun!

Nothing Special
This waterfall is nothing special,
Just falling water mixed with air,
Reflecting and refracting light to make it white.
Yet gaining in the process
Mysterious power to reach and change
My mind, my heart, my life.

North Oregon Coast & Coast Range

71 Falls City Falls

Between Streets, a River Blasts Through a Crack

Height: 35' Difficulty: 2 Romance: 3

Type: Narrow Complex Contact Plunge

Description: Right in the center of town there's a bridge over a very narrow crack of a rock-walled gorge. A short distance upstream, a rather large river is squeezed through a very, very narrow crack in the bedrock, at which point the river drops over the end of the rock shelf on which it has traversed and roars down and into the slot. Though not an enormous falls, your proximity to it, its raw power, and the uniqueness of its "design" makes it a real wonder that will draw you back despite the bleak surroundings.

Distance/Time From Portland: 70 miles, 73 minutes.

Directions to Parking/Trailhead: Take Interstate 5 south to exit 260B (Salem Business Bypass 99E); drive south toward downtown Salem until the road intersects State Route 22; turn right (west), drive across the bridge and drive approximately 13 miles to the intersection of State Route 223 (signs for Dallas); drive south through Dallas; drive south another 6 miles until you reach the road to Falls City; turn right (west) and drive about 4 miles to Falls City; continue through the small town until you see and cross the river; immediately after crossing the bridge, turn right and drive a short way close to the river until you see the remains of a tiny park. Park near it.

Distance/Time From Parking: 1 minute (it's right there!).

Distance/Time From Other Landmark: Well, it's not really near enough to say.

Directions From Parking: Walk toward the river until you reach the fence which guards against people walking off the cliff. Once you've seen the falls from this side, look carefully at the street and houses on the other side then drive over there, park at a suitable wide spot and walk down to the falls view from the rocky cliffs on that side. It's a better view (Barbara drew the falls from that viewpoint) but it's a little bit more slippery walking down from the road and definitely more dangerous on the rocks next to the torrent.

Elevation Change: 0 feet (south side); 50 feet (north side).

Restroom: Perhaps at the restaurant in town.

Picnic Area: There is obvious archeological evidence of a picnic area which once existed on the south side of the river.

View & Kissing Spots: Next to the falls on both sides.

Accessibility to the Physically Challenged: Some views should be accessible.

Hazards: Please be careful on the wet, slippery rocks and near the cliffs from which one could fall into the maelstrom.

Information: On Little Lukiamute River, Polk County, Oregon, USGS Falls City Quadrangle.

Falls City was named for the falls sometime before 1889, possibly at the suggestion of a family which emigrated from Falls City, Nebraska.

Maybe it's only a trick of the light at the exact moment we were there or just our imagination, but we could clearly see the profile of a face—Chief Lukiamute, perhaps.

Although this remarkable falls gives the town its name and is a scenic attraction which would be the envy of virtually any other small town in the country, the "park" on both sides of the falls has had very little development. Sadly, the few improvement have been totally destroyed by vandalism. One can only wonder what inspires someone to do this. Perhaps the appreciation of this natural feature by you and other visitors will inspire the appreciation and pride which is so sorely lacking in Falls City. A little publicity might make the town a destination for enough visitors to improve the local economy and the attitude of its people. We dream that it will happen.

Science
Attraction of gravity pulling the stream
And hormones released by our brains.
Pure science explains the pertinent facts
Mysterious emotions and beauty remains.

VII. North Willamette Valley & Cascades

Between the Willamette Valley and the valleys east of Mount Hood and between Mount Hood and the North Santiam River, a number of remarkable and romantic falls can be found, some right beside the road, others a good hike from your car. Their settings vary from areas of obvious human influence to extremely remote ones, from lush lowland forest to near alpine situations. All of them are splendid and enjoyable in their own special way.

The watersheds in which the falls in this section lie can be divided into those whose water flows to the Columbia (east or west of Mount Hood) and those

Varied Thrush

in the Willamette River's watershed. They include the largest (in width and volume) extant waterfall in the Pacific Northwest (and one of the largest by those criteria in the country) and others which vary greatly from each other in size and appearance. They are spread out over a wide area. Some, such as those east of Mount Hood, could be included in a day excursion with falls from the East Columbia Gorge of Oregon section. Tamanawas Falls (#76) is on the road to Punchbowl Falls (#41). Others could be included in a day outing with some of the falls in the North Oregon Coast & Coast Range section or with the Mid Willamette Valley & Cascades section. From Whispering Falls (#80), you can drive south to Sahalie Falls (#97) with relative ease.

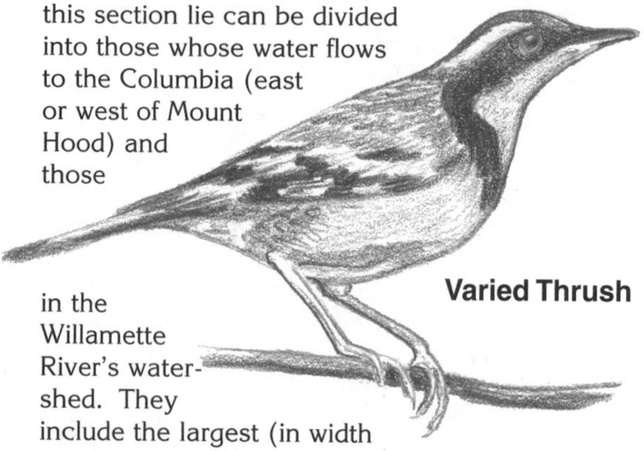

Western White Pine

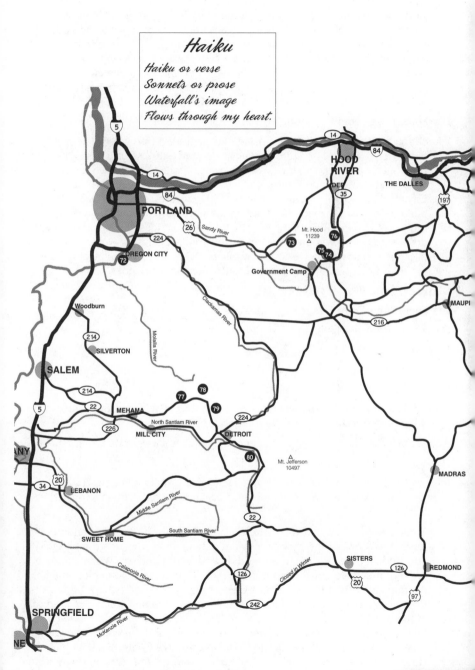

Haiku

Haiku or verse
Sonnets or prose
Waterfall's image
Flows through my heart.

North Willamette Valley & Cascades

Willamette Falls

The Biggest Falls in the Northwest: "Oregon's Niagara"

Height: 42' **Difficulty:** 0 **Romance:** 3

Type: Extremely wide, low tumble.

Description: Willamette Falls is the largest existing waterfall in the Pacific Northwest measured by width, volume of water, volume multiplied by height, width multiplied by height, or any measure except height alone. It is an enormous, river wide horseshoe (470 feet across, .25 mile in length) along which water pours in a "Niagara-like" cascade. During low water (such as in Summer), the falls is limited to part of the horseshoe, revealing its ancient rocks and man-made additions. Its flow varies from 10,000 to 50,000 cubic feet per second. That's a lot of water!

Distance/Time From Portland: 21 miles, 23 minutes.

Directions to Parking/Trailhead: For an excellent view from the west, visit the Falls Viewpoint on Interstate 205 eastbound at exit 7. For a head-on view (as drawn here), take exit 8, West Linn; turn right and drive 2 blocks to the West Linn Police Station; park and take the pedestrian walk on the Oregon City Bridge. To see the historic locks, drive further into the Police Station parking lot, then through the gate on left and immediately down the wooden ramp to the paper company parking lot. Follow signs. To see the east side, drive across the Oregon City Bridge; turn right and follow Route 99E up the hill to the rock walled viewpoint at milepost 13. The best view of all is from the third floor of the Clackamas County Museum of History.

Distance/Time From Parking: 0

Distance/Time From Other Landmark: At historic Oregon City.

Directions From Parking: See directions above..

Elevation Change: 0 feet.

Restroom: In Oregon City and West Linn.

Picnic Area: At locks.

View & Kissing Spots: At viewpoints on I-205 and 99W; from the historic Willamette Falls Locks; on the Oregon City Bridge.

Accessibility to the Physically Challenged: All listed viewpoints are accessible.

Hazards: No unusual ones unless you jump or fall off any of the cliffs or bridges!

Information: On the Willamette River, Clackamas County, Oregon, USGS Oregon City Quadrangle; listed in USGS Geographic Names Information System.

The barrier formed by Willamette Falls has always made this area important. It was one of the most important fishing spots and was the meeting and trading place for upstream and downstream peoples. When Europeans arrived, they also considered it important. Founded by John McLoughlin, it's the site of the first U.S. Court west of the Mississippi (where San Francisco's plat had to be filed and still hangs), the first water powered mill in the west, the first locks in the west (for boats to get around the falls), the first "long distance electric power transmission", and the end of the Oregon Trail. Visit the End of the Oregon Trail Interpretive Center, McLoughlin House, and the Clackamas County Museum of History. As you drive around

town, watch for the "Historic House" plaques on houses from as far back as the 1850s. This is a very historic place that barely seems to realize it.

The small dark spots in front of the falls in the picture are power boats full of fishermen. It gives you an idea how big Willamette Falls really is!

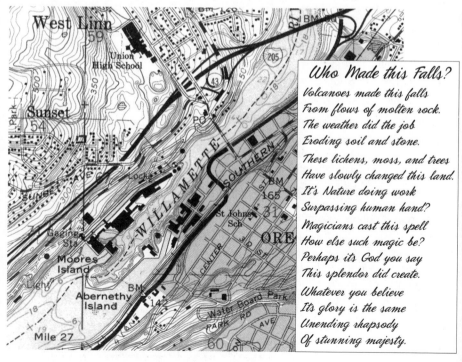

Who Made this Falls?

Volcanoes made this falls
From flows of molten rock.
The weather did the job
Eroding soil and stone.

These lichens, moss, and trees
Have slowly changed this land.
It's Nature doing work
Surpassing human hand?

Magicians cast this spell
How else such magic be?
Perhaps it's God you say
This splendor did create.

Whatever you believe
Its glory is the same
Unending rhapsody
Of stunning majesty.

73   **Ramona Falls**

One of the Most Fun, Personal, and Romantic Falls Anywhere

Height: 50'   **Difficulty:** 5   **Romance:** 7

Type: Spreading Steep tumble.

Description: In a lush grove of trees, stands a high, wide rock wall appearing as if it were made of giant blocks. Water pours over the top of the wall splashing over each block on its way down. Stand as close as you want, from camera distance to ground zero, becoming part of the falls and very wet.

Distance/Time From Portland: 49 miles, 65 minutes.

Directions to Parking/Trailhead: Route 26 east from Portland 42 miles to town of Zigzag, left (east) on Lolo Pass Road, 4.9 miles to Road 1825, turn right on Road 100 for .7 mile, cross Sandy River Bridge, .1 mile bear right on dirt road (marked by Ramona Falls sign), 1.4 miles on this miserable dirt road to trailhead. Note: if you'd rather walk an extra 2.4 miles than drive the washboard road, you can bear left and park at a large, gravel parking lot.

Distance/Time From Parking: 2.25 miles, 45 minutes.

Distance/Time From Other Landmark: 8 miles, 15 minutes to Zigzag by road.

Directions From Parking: 4.5 mile loop hike to falls and back (6.9 miles if you choose the "paved road only parking spot"). In either case, you ultimately start from the same place. Follow trail from parking to footbridge; cross bridge and choose left fork (cooler, easier, more scenic but longer path) or right fork (harder, hotter, drier but shorter path) depending upon time of day and weather; follow path to falls. Return on other path.

Elevation Change: 700 feet.

Restroom: In Zigzag, about 8 mile drive from trailhead.

Picnic Area: Lovely picnicking in a lush grove of giant trees around the base of the falls. On hot Summer days, you'll want to spent the day here!

View & Kissing Spots: Every place within the grove near the falls.

Accessibility to the Physically Challenged: Inaccessible due to stairs on bridge.

Hazards: Poison oak and getting wet!

Information: On the Sandy River, Clackamas County, Oregon, USGS Bull Run Lake Quadrangle, Green Trails Maps: Government Camp; listed in USGS Geographic Names Information System.

Ramona Falls was named by a USFS employee supervising CCC trail building in the 1930s who was in love and humming a popular song, Ramona from a popular movie of the same name starring Loretta Young.

Ramona is one of the most delightful waterfalls anywhere and one of the most visited spots in the Mount Hood area. It is personal, available, and unpretentious. Although there is a significant elevation change over the course of the hike, you will think it's relatively level. The trail passes through a number of different habitats, including Ramona Creek which presents a cool, safe wading spot for kids and adults and through dry oak woods, cool evergreen woods, etc. Look for examples of nearly every major tree species in the region (Douglas Fir, Subalpine Fir, Western Larch, Western White Pine, Grand, Western Hemlock, etc.), and many different

plants, birds, and mammals.

The Lolo Pass Road is often closed by snow during Winter. Check weather

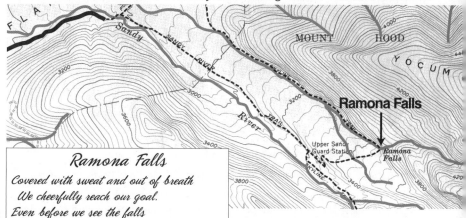

Ramona Falls

Covered with sweat and out of breath
* We cheerfully reach our goal.*
Even before we see the falls
* We're chilled by the change in the weather.*

Air conditioned by falls and trees
* We bask in the cool of the glen.*
Drawn like a moth to a flame,
* We walk to the glorious falls.*

Rushing to reach the base of the falls
* We gambol like kids with new toys.*
Feeling the spray we're lured underneath
* And kiss as we laugh at ourselves.*

reports to avoid snow or other severe weather—but prepare for the worst!

Driving northeast on the Lolo Pass road, you will get lots of gravel road driving experience but you will see wonderful scenery, get close to Mount Hood, cross the Pacific Crest Trail, and end up at Lost Lake and/or the Hood River Valley— very dicey in Winter though!

74   Sahale Falls

A Wonderful Falls which Crosses Under a Scenic Bridge

Height: 100'   **Difficulty:** 0   **Romance:** 4

Type: Spreading Contact Plunge, Arched Plunge.

Description: In a cut in the deep, dark forest, a mighty falls bursts through a cleft in the briefly visible bedrock and plunges powerfully, spreading white as it drops to a flatter strata along which it runs to the graceful arched bridge, under which it drops again to a far lower level on its long course from its birthplace at the nearby glacier to its conjunction with the Columbia at Hood River and ultimately to the sea.

Distance/Time From Portland: 66 miles, 1 hour and 25 minutes.

Directions to Parking/Trailhead: Drive east from Portland on Route #26 as if you were going to Mount Hood (which, of course, you are); continue through Government Camp and past the well marked road to Timberline Lodge until you see signs for Route 35 north to Hood River; go north on 35 about 2.5 miles past Bennett Pass to the huge sign on the left for Mount Hood Meadows Ski Resort; turn left into their access road and almost immediately turn right on another road which more or less parallels the highway; drive for less than a half mile to a scenic old bridge; park on the roadside at either end of the bridge.

Distance/Time From Parking: 0 minutes (visible from the road).

Distance/Time From Other Landmark: Less than a 5 minute drive to the Umbrella Falls (#75) trailhead; 7 miles to Tamanawas Falls (#76)

Directions From Parking: The falls is just upstream of the bridge and under it. Views are from the bridge.

Elevation Change: 0 feet.

Restroom: In the town of Government Camp, at the ski lodge, at Timberline Lodge, and at nearby campgrounds—but none here.

Picnic Area: None here.

View & Kissing Spots: From the bridge and from the highway looking upstream the short distance to the bridge and falls.

Accessibility to the Physically Challenged: Yes, visible from bridge and road.

Hazards: Getting stuck in the snow (you or your car) if you try to visit the falls from October through May depending upon the weather; leaning too far out from the bridge (it's a very long way down).

Information: On the East Fork of Hood River, Hood River County, Oregon, USGS Mount Hood South Quadrangle, Green Trails Maps: Mt. Hood; listed in USGS Geographic Names Information System.

Note that this is also the "official" spelling of the name! Its name was the result of a nineteenth century contest by the Portland Telegram newspaper. Sahale, a Chinook word meaning "high", was the winning entry. Almost everyone seems to mix up this falls and that of "Sahalie Falls" on the McKenzie River. Even the quadrangle map has the wrong spelling!

Note Pencil Falls north of Umbrella on the Timberline Trail and Switchback Falls next to the highway but very disappointing as an attraction. One is a good, long hike to a small falls, the other is a hunt with a "could that be it?" result.

The map shows a network of trails around Mount Hood Meadows which link Sahale with Umbrella and traverse the entire area. The Timberline Trail circumnavigates Mount Hood and is linked to the local trails. In Winter, many trails and lesser roads become cross country ski routes. Winter sports enthusiasts may witness the falls in an entirely different environment and with a changed visage.

Sunday in the Woods

It's Sunday in the woods
Cathedral place untouched by hand of man
Where feathered chorus and splashing organ
Sings hymns before the watery altar
And God is smiling as she works.

North Willamette Valley & Cascades

75   Umbrella Falls
A Really Different and Fun Falls — Should Be In Yellowstone!

Height: 60'   Difficulty: 3   Romance: 6

Type: Spreading Angled Slide.

Description: A creek flows gently through cool woods until it drops over a fine-textured stone outcrop composed, perhaps, of compressed glacial sand. The surface of the rock makes the water sizzle as it dances down its face to a pool at the base.

Distance/Time From Portland: 67 miles, 1 hour and 30 minutes.

Directions to Parking/Trailhead: Follow directions for Sahale Falls (#74) as far as the beginning of the Mount Hood Meadows road. Instead of turning off, follow the road uphill to the ski area parking lot (when the gate is open); turn right and drive along the down slope edge of the parking lot until you find the trail near the visible stream which leads to the falls. Park here. **Or:** Look for a badly marked but well worn trail on the right hand roadside within sight of the gate. Park on the shoulder.

Distance/Time From Parking: .3 miles, 15 minutes from roadside trailhead; .2 miles, 10 minutes from ski area parking lot at streamside trailhead.

Distance/Time From Other Landmark: Less than a mile up the ski area's road from Sahale Falls (#74).

Directions From Parking: From the Mount Hood Meadows parking lot: Try to find and follow something that looks like a trail (from among several possibilities) until you reach the stream; by the stream you will find a definite path; head downstream and downhill at an increasing rate until you reach the top of the falls, which is to your left; continue down the path beside the falls to the bridge below. From the roadside parking spot, walk toward the mountain, paralleling the stream downhill until the trail swings round to cross the small stream; after a short distance across the open area, climbing slightly until you see the falls ahead of you.

Elevation Change: 150 feet

Restroom: At the ski lodge or in Government Camp when the ski area isn't open.

Picnic Area: Informal spots near base of falls.

View & Kissing Spots: On bridge at bottom of falls, at top of falls.

Accessibility to the Physically Challenged: None.

Hazards: Being stupid at the top of the falls or getting off the trail and discovering that the fields of wildflowers are concealing a very deep layer of very sticky mud underneath.

Information: On the East Fork of Hood River, Hood River County, Oregon, USGS Mount Hood South Quadrangle, Green Trails Maps: Mt. Hood; listed in USGS Geographic Names Information System.

The name, Umbrella Falls, was inspired by its shape and became official in 1925.

While in this area, you have to make your pilgrimage to Timberline Lodge. If you've never been there, you're in for a real treat! The lodge was hand

made by amazing artisans working for "the W.P.A." during the depression of the 1930s. Its architecture and monumental log construction is truly remarkable. In addition, it has a wonderful pub, a world class restaurant, fabulous views, huge fireplaces, Saint Bernard dogs, and, if that weren't enough, it's a terrific hotel with pool, sauna, and unique rooms which are still as they were designed in the 1930's.

In addition to the waterfalls, Mount Hood, and Timberline Lodge, there are worthwhile hostelries, restaurants, and watering holes in Government Camp and in sister mountain villages along the road to Mount Hood (Rhododendron, Welches, Zig Zag, Wemme, Brightwood, etc.). These hamlets are as eccentric and charming as their names. We'll leave it to you to uncover the stories of their names. Other attractions are the "Alpine Slide" at the ski area in Government Camp, remnant stretches of the original 1846 Barlow Toll Road over which the emigrants from the east traveled the last and often most dangerous portion of their journey from Saint Louis to the Willamette Valley, the uncharacteristicly modern "Inn at the Mountain" resort with its golf course, other recreational facilities, accommodations, restaurant, and condominiums. Oh, don't forget the skiing and other Winter sports. Thanks to its "Palmer Lift", which takes you to a glacier high on the Mount Hood, Timberline Lodge has skiing year-round. It's where world-class and Olympic skiers from around the world train during the off-season.

See detailed map at falls #74, Sahale Falls.

Someday
Once I saw a waterfall
And once I read a book.
I know they both were wonderful.
Someday again I'll look.

76   Tamanawas Falls

A Big, Powerful Plunge Falls Like the Gorge but in a Different Setting

Height: 150'   Difficulty: 5   Romance: 6

Type: Curtain Plunge.

Description: In a natural bowl of cliffs, a wide wall of water falls straight down from the lip of the cliff past a crescent shaped grotto which allows a torturous one way walk behind—truly a beautiful destination.

Distance/Time From Portland: Alternative #1: 73 miles, 1 hour and 33 minutes; **Alternative #2:** 88 miles, 1 hour and 30 minutes.

Directions to Parking/Trailhead: Alternative #1: Drive east from Portland on Route #26 through Government Camp to Route 35; go north on 35 about 6 miles past Mount Hood Meadows to a good, unpaved parking area on west side of road near milepost 72 .25 miles north of the Sherwood Campground. **Alternative #2:** Take Interstate 84 63 miles east from Portland through Hood River to the exit for Highway 35; then drive about 25 miles south on Highway 35 to the same parking area.

Distance/Time From Parking: 1.4 miles, 91 minutes.

Distance/Time From Other Landmark: 7 miles (by car) from Sahale (#74); 27 miles to Punchbowl Falls (#41).

Directions From Parking: From the campground, hike to the single log bridge across the East Fork of Hood River; cross the bridge and immediately turn right on trail # 650A; Hike 22 minutes and about .5 mile to a single-log bridge over Cold Spring Creek; continue upstream along the creek for .5 miles, 47 minutes to another single-log bridge and a fork in the trail (take the left fork); continue .3 miles, 17 minutes to your first view of falls; .1 miles, 5 minutes to behind the falls.

Elevation Change: 500 feet

Restroom: At the Sherwood Campground near the trailhead.

Picnic Area: At trailhead and at the campground.

View & Kissing Spots: Wonderful views of forest and stream along trail and approaching the falls itself are excellent vantage points for photos. Many kissing spots on trailside and near falls.

Accessibility to the Physically Challenged: Not accessible due to single-log bridges and narrow trail.

Hazards: Steep off-trail slopes and very narrow, potentially dangerous areas due to slides on portion of trail along the north fork; the trail along Cold Spring Creek is continuously surfaced with large, sharp edged rocks which make good, sturdy shoes a must; poison oak in sunny spots; totally thorn-covered gooseberry bushes line the trail along Cold Spring Creek; very hot, dry conditions in mid-Summer; mud and slippery, loose rocks in area behind and near the falls.

Information: On Cold Spring Creek, Hood River County, Oregon, USGS Dog River Quadrangle, Green Trails Maps: Mt. Hood; listed in USGS Geographic Names Information System.

Excellent camping and picnicking at the scenic Sherwood Campground.

The U.S. Forest Service gave this falls its Chinook name meaning friendly guiding or guardian spirit.

Look for golden mantled ground squirrels near the falls. Though friendly, they are not guiding spirits!

This is a mixed regrowth forest with grand fir; douglas fir, western red cedar, western white pine, white bark pine, ponderosa pine, western hemlock, englemann spruce and even a few rare Pacific Yew.

This area is drier than the gorge and shows signs of cold Winters. Elevation and climate make seasons about 6 weeks later: trillium in May not March. Forest floor plants are gooseberry, huckleberry, bunchberry, and Oregon Grape.

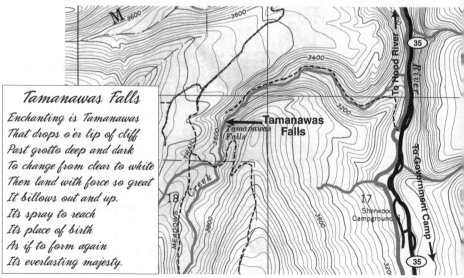

Tamanawas Falls

Enchanting is Tamanawas
That drops o'er lip of cliff
Past grotto deep and dark
To change from clear to white
Then land with force so great
It billows out and up.
Its spray to reach
Its place of birth
As if to form again
Its everlasting majesty.

77   **Salmon Falls**

A Fun, Wide, and Powerful Falls with Fish and a Fish Ladder!

Height: 35'   **Difficulty:** 1   **Romance:** 4

Type: Twin Arched Contact Plunges.

Description: The Little North Santiam River reaches a very wide rock shelf into which it has carved channels along which it courses during lower water while spreading over the whole ledge during Spring floods. The rock shelf ends abruptly in a cliff, down which the stream descends to a large, placid, blue pool. A fish ladder ends at the near bank assists migrating fish in their upstream trip. The huge rock shelf provides picnic spots, pools and small channels in which to cool off, and lots of fun nooks and crannies to explore.

Distance/Time From Portland: 87 miles, 90minutes.

Directions to Parking/Trailhead: Take Interstate 5 46 miles south to Exit 253, Route 22, in Salem; drive 27 miles east on Route 22 to North Fork Road #2209 1 mile past Mehama (on the left bank of the Little North Santiam River); drive 14 miles on North Fork Road to the well marked Salmon Falls County Park on your right. Park at Salmon Falls County Park next to falls.

Distance/Time From Parking: 5 minutes.

Distance/Time From Other Landmark: 5 minutes (by car) to Henline Falls (#78); 7 miles to Sullivan Creek Falls (#79); 43 miles to Whispering Falls (#80).

Directions From Parking: You can't miss the falls from the park.

Elevation Change: 20 feet.

Restroom: At the park (primitive).

Picnic Area: At picnic area in the park and informally on rocks at top and bottom of falls.

View & Kissing Spots: From shore, downstream along trail, at base and top of falls.

Accessibility to the Physically Challenged: None except views from road.

Hazards: Be very, very careful around the falls and the rocks near them and especially in the strong currents just above the falls. A trip down the falls would almost certainly be fatal! Do not attempt to get into the fish ladder. It actually goes across the river to reenter the stream below the falls through a concrete tunnel—a deadly trip if you're not a fish!.

Information: On Little North Santiam River, in Salmon Falls County Park, Marion County, Oregon, USGS Elkhorn Quadrangle; listed in USGS Geographic Names Information System.

An interesting nearby place to visit is Niagara Park. From the intersection of Routes 22 and 2209, drive east on 22 about 13 miles to the relatively well marked park on your right. In addition to being a pleasant, rustic, and verdant park, you can visit the remains of a stone dam which was built in 1889 to generate power for a proposed mill (which was never built). Abandoned in 1912, the place is a fascinating place to explore and experience the past. The falls which inspired the dam is still visible in its narrow rock channel, though somewhat altered by the dam. Be careful on the rocks!

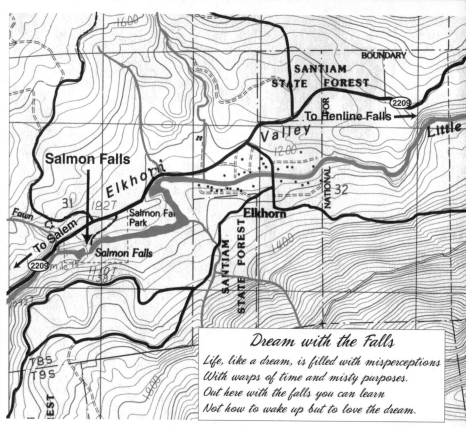

Dream with the Falls

*Life, like a dream, is filled with misperceptions
With warps of time and misty purposes.
Out here with the falls you can learn
Not how to wake up but to love the dream.*

78 **Henline Falls**

A Remarkable Miniature Version of Victoria Falls

Height: 100'   **Difficulty:** 4   **Romance:** 6

Type: Wide Contact Plunge.

Description: At the head of a very narrow canyon, the 100 foot high cliffs on each side suddenly form no more than a crack perhaps 30 feet wide, 200 feet long, and 100 feet high. Instead of descending from the point of the crack, Henline Creek spreads to cover the entire length of the crack on one side and drops in a fantastic curtain the full length of the crack then spews forth to form a pool just outside the crack, then tumble through a maze of huge rocks and logs. Just to the right of the falls next to its pool is a black hole of a horizontal mine shaft, the long abandoned Silver King Mine.

Distance/Time From Portland: 90 miles, 95minutes.

Directions to Parking/Trailhead: Follow directions to Salmon Falls; continue past Salmon Falls County Park on North Fork Road #2209 for 3 miles to junction of Road #2207; drive straight ahead on #2209 (don't turn right onto #2207) for less than .1 miles until you find a skid road on your left blocked by huge boulders. Although there may or may not be any indication that this is a trail, this is it! There may be a sign saying: "2209 3 0 1". Park at the trailhead or along the road nearby.

Distance/Time From Parking: 30 minutes.

Distance/Time From Other Landmark: 5 minutes (by car) from Salmon Falls (#77); 4 miles to Sullivan Creek Falls (#79).

Directions From Parking: Leave parking spot at roadside on remnant road; hike for 15 minutes to fork in road (perhaps with sign marked "Henline Falls Trail #3348"); turn left and hike for 15 minutes downhill on narrowing trail to falls.

Elevation Change: 300 feet.

Restroom: At Salmon Falls County Park.

Picnic Area: Atop giant boulders or logs at base of falls.

View & Kissing Spots: Everywhere near base of falls. Kiss in the mine shaft.

Accessibility to the Physically Challenged: None.

Hazards: Few except being stupid in pitch black mine shaft or fooling around on huge rocks. Please be careful in the mine. Who knows whether it's about to cave in or if it has a bottomless vertical shaft waiting patiently for an unwary hiker to discover in the dark!

Information: On Henline Creek, Marion County, Oregon, USGS Elkhorn Quadrangle; listed in USGS Geographic Names Information System.

Henline Creek, Falls, and Mountain were named for a Mr. Henline who was a pioneer miner in the area.

Notice the abandoned shaft of the Silver King Mine and the remnants of its waterwheel stamp mill near the falls. The shaft goes about .3 miles into the cliff and has been without maintenance for a very long time. A strong flashlight or lantern is needed to go even a few feet into the mine. Do not enter (unless you've made out your will with us as beneficiary)! Seriously though, wondering around an abandoned mine shaft is probably the craziest and most dangerous thing you can do! Stay out!

For an interesting and delightful side trip, try driving the right hand fork just before the Henline Falls trailhead to "Three Pools" (there should be a sign), a short drive to a small county park containing startlingly unique water scenes—a great place for a cooling dip after a long hike on a hot day.

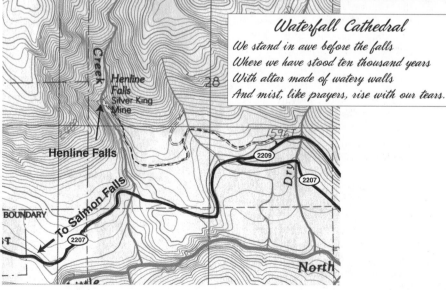

Waterfall Cathedral
We stand in awe before the falls
Where we have stood ten thousand years
With altar made of watery walls
And mist, like prayers, rise with our tears.

79   Sullivan Creek Falls

An Exciting Tumble and Bounce of Water Right by the Road

Height: 60'   Difficulty: 0   Romance: 2

Type: Narrow Steep Slide, Narrow Steep Slide, Narrow Steep Slide.

Description: Right next to a gravel road, a beautiful falls descends a cliff in several steps to a small but clear and beautiful pool at its base.

Distance/Time From Portland: 93 miles, 100 minutes.

Directions to Parking/Trailhead: Follow directions to Henline Falls except turn right on Road #2207 (rather continuing straight on #2209 to Henline); drive for 3 miles on this gravel road until you see Sullivan Creek Falls on your right. Park on the roadside near the falls.

Distance/Time From Parking: 0 minutes.

Distance/Time From Other Landmark: 7 miles from Salmon Creek Falls (#77); 4 miles, 5 minutes (by car) from Henline Falls trailhead (#78).

Directions From Parking: It's right there.

Elevation Change: 0.feet.

Restroom: At Salmon Falls County Park.

Picnic Area: Only informal spots roadside or near base of falls.

View & Kissing Spots: From road and near base of falls.

Accessibility to the Physically Challenged: Visible from road.

Hazards: None.

Information: On Sullivan Creek, Marion County, Oregon, USGS Elkhorn Quadrangle.

Sullivan Creek is a tributary of Cedar Creek, which runs along the left side of the road on your way to the waterfall. About two miles on the road before you reach the falls, you will pass the Shady Grove Campground, a very rustic but pleasant spot to stop and picnic.

The area around Sullivan Creek Falls was clear cut in recent decades. When we first visited it, the area around the falls was very bleak—scarred and raw looking. Although it is hardly the lush rainforest that once adorned the area, trees and shrubs are rapidly growing back, greatly improving the appearance and enjoyment of the area. Hopefully, someday in the distance future, a generation of our ancestors will witness its former splendor.

Western Hemlock

Sullivan Creek Falls

To Salmon Falls →

Cedar

Creek

Creek

A Falls

Can I hold you, hug you, kiss you?
Can we stand beneath the falls?

How I want you, need you, love you.
Do you feel the same for me?

North Willamette Valley & Cascades

80   Whispering Falls

A Waterfall Across the Creek from a Campground, Wow!

Height: 60'   **Difficulty:** 0   **Romance:** 6

Type: Steep Slide.

Description: The Whispering Falls Campground is a secluded and deeply forested park situated along the north bank of the North Santiam River. Whispering Falls is visible from streamside within the campground as it slides down the cliff to terminate in the river about 50 feet away. During the Summer, campers wade across the narrow river to stand under the shower of Whispering Falls.

Distance/Time From Portland: 106 miles, 100 minutes.

Directions to Parking/Trailhead: Take Interstate 5 46 miles south to Exit 253, Route 22, in Salem; drive 60 miles east on Route 22 (4 miles east of Idanha) to Whispering Falls Campground where a small amount of parking is available.

Distance/Time From Parking: 0

Distance/Time From Other Landmark: 43 miles from Salmon Falls (#77); 32 miles, 35 minutes to Sahalie Falls (#97).

Directions From Parking: The falls are visible from the campground.

Elevation Change: 0 feet.

Restroom: At the campground.

Picnic Area: At park.

View & Kissing Spots: Along the river and in the woods near the falls.

Accessibility to the Physically Challenged: Fully accessible.

Hazards: Extremely cold and swift river requires caution.

Information: On Misery Creek (tributary of the North Santiam River), in Whispering Falls Campground, Marion County, Oregon, USGS Idanha Quadrangle.

What a terrific place to camp or picnic! The rustic and secluded campground is set in a lush, wooded spot along the stream directly across from the falls.

Two other waterfalls in the vicinity of Whispering Falls but which are not the subject of a full discussion in this book are Gatch Falls and Gooch Falls. Both are located on Marion Creek downstream from Marion Lake. Gooch Falls was originally called Gatch Falls to honor Professor Thomas M. Gatch, the President of Willamette University. Unfortunately, Nathan Gooch homesteaded near the falls in the 1880s. As you can imagine, a great deal of confusion and controversy arose. Finally, in 1970 they decided the name should be Gooch Falls and found another nearby falls (previously called Orla Falls or Lower Marion Falls) was renamed Gatch Falls. I guess we're lucky they didn't name it Falls Creek Falls or Salmon Falls! To reach them, take Route 22 about 8 miles southeast to Marion Forks and turn on road #2255. Drive about 3 miles to a lesser road which intersects on the right. A short walk will take you to a very underdeveloped trail and a very, very dangerous cliffside overlook from which you will see the powerful curtain

So Many Falls

How can there be so many falls
In infinite shapes ad kinds
With gauze like mist or firehose blast
In roaring plunge or sensuous curve.

Each twist of the current or jut of a rock
Forms shapes in the speeding flow
To ever excite the fortunate few
Who peak at their glorious art.

plunge of Gooch Falls. Be Careful! This is really dangerous! Reach Gatch Falls after a 2 mile hike from the trailhead 1 mile ahead at the end of road #2255. Follow signs for Lake Ann and Marion Lake. It's a far safer wilderness experience.

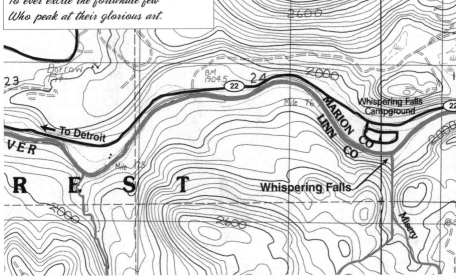

VIII. Silver Falls State Park

Silver Falls State Park is Oregon's largest state park with 8,700 acres, a 100 space overnight campground, lodge, conference center, hiking, mountain biking, and horse trails. It offers a remarkable collection of truly romantic waterfalls in a secluded space, including four "walk behind falls". The state deserves applause for its outstanding development and management.

Silver Falls State Park is a must destination for peaceful contemplation in one of nature's most beautiful settings, for expressing new love, to rekindle a fading relationship, to share the warmth of togetherness with family and friends, or just to have an invigorating hike in a beautiful setting.

Several falls are so convenient that you can drive to the park, kiss behind a fabulous falls, and return to Portland—all in about four hours! In addition, several can be seen from viewpoints close to the road.

A Day Use Pass must be purchased (currently $3.00 per vehicle) at a gate-house near South Falls. A comfortable lodge with crackling fireplace, gift shop, snack bar, and restrooms is also located in this area.

The lodge was built by the Civilian Conservation Corps in the 1930s. Employees of the lodge are volunteers who have connection to the park. Many were residents of "Silver Falls City" or descendants of nearby home-steaders. They answer your questions with joy, patience, and authority. Incidentally, there are some remaining remnants of the town within the park. Laid out in 1888, it was liquidated in 1933 with the creation of the park.

Hiking note: All trails lead downhill to the falls, a "reverse hike". The fur-thest point from all three trailheads—is the lowest point! Keep in mind that you will have to climb back up. Make certain you make your return to "the surface" before sundown. It could be quite unpleasant in the dark on narrow trails and trying to pick your way through the grottos behind falls.

In addition to the eleven falls depicted in the book, which are above the junction of the North Silver Creek and South Silver Creek, there are at least five more smaller ones downstream on Silver Creek within the park. They are: Crag Falls (12 feet), Elbow Falls (20 feet), Canyon Falls (10 feet), Lisp Falls (5 feet), and Sunlight Falls (5 feet).

#81	North Falls	pg 194	A short steep hike
#82	Upper North Falls	pg 196	A short walk
#83	Twin Falls	pg 198	Beyond North Falls
#84	Middle North Falls	pg 200	Beyond Twin Falls
#85	Drake Falls	pg 202	Beyond Middle North Falls
#86	Double Falls	pg 204	Beyond Drake Falls
#87	Lower North Falls	pg 206	Beyond Double Falls
#88	Winter Falls	pg 208	A short hike
#89	South Falls	pg 210	A short walk and/or hike
#90	Frenchie Falls	pg 212	On the way to South Falls
#91	Lower South Falls	pg 214	Beyond South Falls

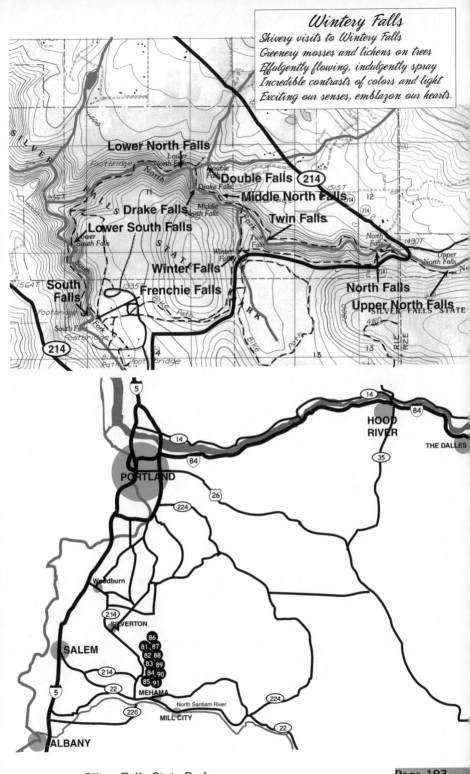

81 North Falls

A Huge Water Blast from a Slit with Deep 180° Walk Behind Grotto

Height: 136'   Difficulty: 3   Romance: 10

Type: Narrow Arched Plunge.

Description: A 180° "Walk-Behind" Falls with a very deep grotto high up. A large body of water forces itself through a narrow slit and blasts over the lip of a high cliff and falls powerfully into its canyon. The force of the water makes it one of the loudest falls you'll visit and the effects of the grotto seems to magnify and modulate the sound. This is one of the most awesome, accessible, and romantic large falls anywhere. The grotto formed by the falls is uncharacteristically deep but with a very low ceiling and is located almost at the top of the falls, rather than near its base as is the case in most other walk-behind falls. This is a real winner!

Distance/Time From Portland: 57 miles, 75 to 90 minutes via Alternative #1; although the distance is greater via Salem and Route 22, the time is not significantly longer because of the better, faster roads.

Directions to Parking/Trailhead: Alternative #1: Interstate 5 to the Woodburn exit, east through Woodburn to Route 99E, south (right) on 99E until you reach a sign for State Route 214 to Silverton, route 214 through Silverton (about 6 miles) to Silver Falls State Park (15 miles). **Alternative #2:** Interstate 5 to Route 22 (Bend) exit on the south side of Salem, east (left) on route 22 about 5 miles to Silver Falls State Park exit (route 214), north (left) on Route 214 20 miles to park. There is a huge parking area at South Falls, a tiny wayside at Winter Falls, a small pull-off viewpoint for North Falls, and a medium sized parking area at North Falls (used in this hike).

Distance/Time From Parking: .2 miles, 9 minutes to behind falls from North Falls trailhead; 4.3 miles, 153 minutes from South Falls trailhead.

Distance/Time From Other Landmark: .4 miles, 14 minutes from Upper North Falls (#82); .9 miles, 31 minutes to Twin Falls (#83).

Directions From Parking: Paved trail leads from North Falls parking downstream (away from the road). Paving on trail ends as you approach the grotto.

Elevation Change: 70 feet to behind falls.

Restroom: Several modern year round restrooms at South Falls activities areas.

Picnic Area: At main park grounds near South Falls.

View & Kissing Spots: At a viewpoint on the road between North and South Falls; on the trail to the falls from the parking lot; from behind the falls; on the trail beyond it. There are many romantic places to pause and kiss. Have fun!

Accessibility to the Physically Challenged: Falls are visible from the road between North Falls and South Falls parking areas; accessible to good close up views via the paved trail to the falls, but unfortunately, 88 stone steps prevents access to the falls itself.

Hazards: A "reverse hike", which has a substantial downhill portion (to behind falls) with an uphill return. Do not attempt to fall off trails! Do not swim or wade immediately above the falls. Sometimes slippery. Very, very dark in the deep grotto after sundown. Be carefully about returning to trailhead late.

Unofficial paths lead to the pool below the falls require special care if used. They're slippery and the rocks can slide out from under you!

formation: On North Fork Silver Creek, in Silver Falls State Park, Marion County, Oregon, USGS Elk Prairie Quadrangle; listed in USGS Geographic Names Information System.

Notice house size squared rocks in the stream below the falls.

In the ceiling of the cavern behind the falls are lava casts of trees.

North Falls is particularly powerful and beautiful in Winter when it's as loud as a 747 taking off!

The area near and behind this falls was a Native American ceremonial site.

See detailed map at section head, VIII. Silver Falls State Park.

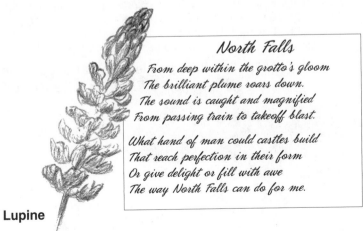

Lupine

North Falls

From deep within the grotto's gloom
The brilliant plume roars down.
The sound is caught and magnified
From passing train to takeoff blast.

What hand of man could castles build
That reach perfection in their form
Or give delight or fill with awe
The way North Falls can do for me.

Upper North Falls

A Pleasant Falls Overshadowed by Other Fabulous Ones Nearby

Height: 65' **Difficulty: 1** **Romance: 3**

Type: Wide Square Contact Plunge.

Description: A beautiful, wide falls with a lovely pool.

Distance/Time From Portland: 57 miles, 75 to 90 minutes via Alternative #1; although the distance is greater via Salem and Route 22, the time is not significantly longer because of the better, faster roads.

Directions to Parking/Trailhead: Follow Directions to North Falls.

Distance/Time From Parking: .2 miles, 5 minutes from North Falls trailhead.

Distance/Time From Other Landmark: .4 miles, 14 minutes to North Falls (#81).

Directions From Parking: Trail goes upstream under the road from the North Falls Parking lot.

Elevation Change: 50 feet.

Restroom: Several modern year round restrooms at South Falls activities areas.

Picnic Area: At main park area near South Falls.

View & Kissing Spots: Along trail approaching the falls and near the falls.

Accessibility to the Physically Challenged: Via a wide, relatively level, paved path, including underpass. There are numerous other accessible facilities in the park.

Hazards: Getting wet.

Information: On North Fork Silver Creek, in Silver Falls State Park, Marion County, Oregon, USGS Elk Prairie Quadrangle; listed in USGS Geographic Names Information System.

Although this is nowhere near as exciting a falls as its downstream neighbor, if it were in most other states in the U.S., it would be a park of its own!

Every Spring, the Lady Slipper Orchids are particularly showy at various places within Silver Falls State Park. Lady Slippers are hardly suitable for a corsage, but they are really quite a respectable size, really quite impressive and very beautiful. Because their bloom time varies depending upon the weather, check with the park staff for the best times and places to look.

See detailed map at section head, VIII. Silver Falls State Park.

Canada Goose

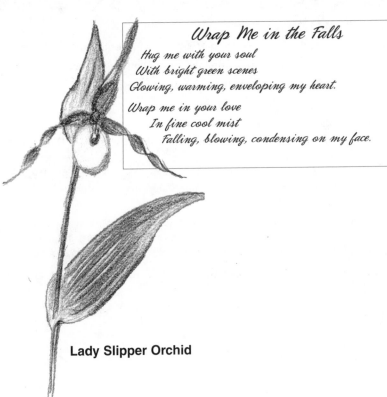

Wrap Me in the Falls

Hug me with your soul
With bright green scenes
Glowing, warming, enveloping my heart.

Wrap me in your love
In fine cool mist
Falling, blowing, condensing on my face.

Lady Slipper Orchid

Silver Falls State Park

83   Twin Falls

A Powerful and Attractive Falls Right Beside You — Great Fun

Height: 31'   Difficulty: 5   Romance: 7

Type: Twin: Arched Slides.

Description: As the creek approaches a sharp right turn, it flows over a wide, flat shelf of rock, splits as it goes around a large rock then immediately roars down a sharp incline. A gentle slope inside the curve allows a romantic grove (and visitors) to reach right up to the waterside above and at the falls.

Distance/Time From Portland: 57 miles, 75 to 90 minutes via Alternative #1; although the distance is greater via Salem and Route 22, the time is not significantly longer because of the better, faster roads.

Directions to Parking/Trailhead: Follow Directions to North Falls, South Falls, or Winter Falls (depending upon which way you want to start your hike).

Distance/Time From Parking: 1.1 miles, 40 minutes from North Falls trailhead; 3.4 miles, 122 minutes from South Falls trailhead.

Distance/Time From Other Landmark: .9 miles, 31 minutes from North Falls (#81); .3 miles, 9 minutes to Winter Falls (#88) trail bridge; .6 miles, 18 minutes to Middle North Falls (#84).

Directions From Parking: Follow Directions to North Falls; continue downstream for .9 miles, 31 minutes to a shady viewing and resting area at the top of Twin Falls.

Elevation Change: 350 feet.

Restroom: Several modern year round restrooms at South Falls activities areas.

Picnic Area: Informal spot beside the falls. Excellent places near South Falls.

View & Kissing Spots: Beside falls and at downstream trail.

Accessibility to the Physically Challenged: None.

Hazards: A "reverse hike", with subtle but continuous downhill trail (from North Falls) and an uphill return. Often muddy trail conditions. Possible danger of falling if being foolish around or above falls.

Information: On North Fork Silver Creek, in Silver Falls State Park, Marion County, Oregon, USGS Drake Crossing Quadrangle; listed in USGS Geographic Names Information System.

When you reach the rock ledge at the top of Twin Falls, make sure to stay here a while, have a snack, dip your feet in the cold water, hug and kiss your partner, enjoy the spot. It's a great place to just hang around!

See detailed map at section head, VIII. Silver Falls State Park.

Twin Falls

We stand atop your splitting drop
   Amid the trees and spray.
   Your mist is cold yet warms our hearts
Inspiring us to kiss.

   We walk downstream along the trail
   To see your frontal view.
   You make us smile then laugh out loud
   In sudden childish glee.

Fawn Lily

Silver Falls State Park

84   Middle North Falls
A Secluded and Romantic One-Way Walk-Behind Falls
Height: 106'   Difficulty: 6   Romance: 10

Type: Wide Curtain Plunge.

Description: A wide curtain of white water pours from a ledge into a cool, dark, green 180° bowl of cliffs. A comfortable side trail leads behind the falls to a dead end with a great view looking back at the falls from the other side.

Distance/Time From Portland: 57 miles, 75 to 90 minutes via Alternative #1; although the distance is greater via Salem and Route 22, the time is not significantly longer because of the better, faster roads.

Directions to Parking/Trailhead: Follow Directions to North Falls, South Falls, or Winter Falls (depending upon which way you want to start your hike).

Distance/Time From Parking: 1.7 miles, 58 minutes from North Falls trailhead; 2.8 miles and 104 minutes from South Falls trailhead.

Distance/Time From Other Landmark: .3 miles, 9 minutes from Winter Falls (#88) trail bridge; .6 miles, 18 minutes from Twin Falls (#83); .2 miles, 7 minutes to Drake Falls (#85).

Directions From Parking: Follow directions to Twin Falls; continue downstream for 9 minutes to Winter Falls bridge; continue on the trail (don't cross bridge) for 5 minutes until you reach the view from the top of Middle North Falls; walk downhill for 2 minutes to the Middle North Falls cut-off; take the cut-off for 5 minutes to walk behind and beyond the falls.

Elevation Change: 390 feet.

Restroom: Several modern year round restrooms at South Falls activities areas.

Picnic Area: At many spots along the trail and at main park grounds near South Falls.

View & Kissing Spots: At the top of the falls; downstream; at the end of the side trail, and, especially, a kiss behind the falls.

Accessibility to the Physically Challenged: None.

Hazards: Do not go beyond railings and other barriers. Be careful near steep edges. An adult couple of experienced hikers fell to their deaths here in January, 1998.

Information: On North Fork Silver Creek, in Silver Falls State Park, Marion County, Oregon, USGS Drake Crossing Quadrangle; listed in USGS Geographic Names Information System.

See detailed map at section head, VIII. Silver Falls State Park.

Pacific Yew

Descartes

"I think, therefore, I am"
Perhaps Descartes was not quite right
For standing in this holy place
I find myself in nature's web
No need of thoughts to validate
Or prove I'm in existence.

Silver Falls State Park

85   Drake Falls

A Complex and Exciting Falls Close-Up

Height: 27'   Difficulty: 6   Romance: 4

Type: Wide Square Slide.

Description: From the amazingly engineered viewing platform, the falls is seen sizzling down a sloped slide which seems to be made of small black cobble stones with their corners pointing out to catch the water. The sound and sight makes you smile or even giggle.

Distance/Time From Portland: 57 miles, 75 to 90 minutes via Alternative #1; although the distance is greater via Salem and Route 22, the time is not significantly longer because of the better, faster roads.

Directions to Parking/Trailhead: Follow Directions to North Falls, South Falls, or Winter Falls (depending upon which way you want to start your hike).

Distance/Time From Parking: 1.9 miles, 65 minutes from North Falls trailhead; 2.6 miles, 97 minutes from South Falls trailhead.

Distance/Time From Other Landmark: .2 miles, 7 minutes from Middle North Falls (#84) trail bridge; .2 miles, 5 minutes to Double Falls (#86).

Directions From Parking: Follow Directions to Middle North Falls; continue hiking for 7 minutes to Drake Falls viewing platform.

Elevation Change: 470 feet.

Restroom: Several modern year round restrooms at South Falls activities areas.

Picnic Area: At many spots along the trail and near South Falls.

View & Kissing Spots: At viewing platform and trailside locations.

Accessibility to the Physically Challenged: None.

Hazards: Be careful on and around the viewing platform.

Information: On North Fork Silver Creek, in Silver Falls State Park, Marion County, Oregon, USGS Drake Crossing Quadrangle; listed in USGS Geographic Names Information System.

Named after J.D. Drake, a Silverton Photographer who helped create the park in 1935.

See detailed map at section head, VIII. Silver Falls State Park.

Oregon Grape

The Children

The children skipped and laughed
and sang
Along the trail in front of us.
They rushed to find each new surprise
And be the first to see the falls.

We walked behind more slow than fast
No need to race to reach the fall
Our time of skipping long has passed
But slower children see it all.

Silver Falls State Park

Double Falls
A Very Tall Skinny Fall in Two Tiers

Height: 178'

Difficulty: 6

Romance: 5

Type: Narrow Contact Plunge, Contact Plunge.

Description: Up a side canyon from the main Silver Falls Canyon, Double Falls sips over the lip of the high, shear canyon wall, drops in a narrow plunge, reaches a ledge about halfway down (which may very well shelter a pool but which is all but impossible to view by anything but birds), then drops again in a similar tall, narrow plunge to its base ahead of you on the footpath.

Distance/Time From Portland: 57 miles, 75 to 90 minutes via Alternative #1; although the distance is greater via Salem and Route 22, the time is not significantly longer because of the better, faster roads.

Directions to Parking/Trailhead: Follow Directions to North Falls, South Falls, or Winter Falls (depending upon which way you want to start your hike).

Distance/Time From Parking: 2.1 miles, 70 minutes from North Falls trailhead; 2.4 miles and 94 minutes from South Falls trailhead.

Distance/Time From Other Landmark: .2 miles, 5 minutes from Drake Falls (#85); .1 miles, 3 minutes to Lower North Falls (#87).

Directions From Parking: Follow Directions to Drake Falls; continue for .2 miles, 5 minutes to bridge below Double Falls. A side trail leads upstream for .1 miles, 10 minutes to base of falls.

Elevation Change: 510 feet.

Restroom: Several modern year round restrooms at South Falls activities areas.

Picnic Area: At many spots along the trail and near South Falls.

View & Kissing Spots: At the footbridge on the main trail below the falls and near the base of the falls on its side trail.

Accessibility to the Physically Challenged: None.

Hazards: Similar hazards to other falls in the area, thorns, slippery rocks, mud, and sore feet.

Information: On an unnamed tributary of the North Fork Silver Creek, in Silver Falls State Park, Marion County, Oregon, USGS Drake Crossing Quadrangle; listed in USGS Geographic Names Information System.

See detailed map at section head, VIII. Silver Falls State Park.

Rufous Hummingbird

I Guess I Lost My Mind

Have I ever felt this way
Did I simply lose my brain
Is there magic in this day
Am I crazy from the rain

I forgot what worried me
What's the project, where's the boss
All selections here are green
Rhododendron, fern, or moss

Peaceful beauty in the wood
Water falling from above
All the bad things turned to good
There is nothing here but love.

Paintbrush

Silver Falls State Park

87   Lower North Falls

A Symmetrical Block of Water Slides from One Level to Another

Height: 30'   **Difficulty:** 6   **Romance:** 3

Type: Wide Square Slide.

Description: The North Fork Silver Creek runs for a time over a broad, flat, more or less level shelf of bedrock until it reaches a break in level of this shelf. At this point, the water slides and tumbles down in a wide, square, angled block of white water.

Distance/Time From Portland: 57 miles, 75 to 90 minutes via Alternative #1; although the distance is greater via Salem and Route 22, the time is not significantly longer because of the better, faster roads.

Directions to Parking/Trailhead: Follow Directions to North Falls, South Falls, or Winter Falls (depending upon which way you want to start your hike).

Distance/Time From Parking: 2.2 miles, 73 minutes from North Falls trailhead; 2.3 miles, 89 minutes from South Falls trailhead.

Distance/Time From Other Landmark: .1 miles, 3 minutes from Double Falls (#86); .3 miles, 10 minutes to bridge to Lower South Falls; 1.3 miles, 50 minutes to Lower South Falls (#91).

Directions From Parking: Directions From Parking: Follow directions to Double Falls; continue for .1 miles, 5 minutes to Lower North Falls.

Elevation Change: 550 feet.

Restroom: Several modern year round restrooms at South Falls activities areas.

Picnic Area: At many spots along the trail and near South Falls.

View & Kissing Spots: At trailside views more or less beside the falls through a wide arc to squarely in front of the falls. A very simple marked trailside viewpoint is probably the best view (from which our drawing was made).

Accessibility to the Physically Challenged: None.

Hazards: No special hazards for this falls or its environs.

Information: On North Fork Silver Creek, in Silver Falls State Park, Marion County, Oregon, USGS Drake Crossing Quadrangle; listed in USGS Geographic Names Information System.

Although both bears and cougars have been quite numerous in Silver Falls State Park in recent years, they are so shy (or stealthy) that they are rarely seen. Before you start looking over your shoulder and listening for the hot breath of predators, don't worry! They not only avoid people at all costs, they never go into the deep gorge where the falls are located. There's no prey there and far too many people!

See detailed map at section head, VIII. Silver Falls State Park.

Feelings

Shimmering, falling, spreading,
Sizzling, chuckling, tumbling.
Splashing, blowing, misting,
Raising, warming, loving.

Douglas Squirrel
(Chickaree)

88   Winter Falls
A Tall but Delicate Falls of the Winter and Spring

Height: 136'   **Difficulty:** 3 from viewpoint, 6 from North Falls   **Romance:** 6

Type: Narrow Contact Plunge.

Description: 4

Distance/Time From Portland: 57 miles, 75 to 90 minutes via Alternative #1; although the distance is greater via Salem and Route 22, the time is not significantly longer because of the better, faster roads.

Directions to Parking/Trailhead: Take Interstate 5 to the Woodburn exit, go east through Woodburn to route 99E, go south (turn right) on 99E until you reach a sign for State Route 214 to Silverton. Continue through Silverton 15 miles to Silver Falls State Park. Continue past the North Falls parking area toward the South Falls facilities; watch for the Winter Falls viewpoint, parking area, and trailhead alongside the road.

Distance/Time From Parking: .1 miles, 5 minutes to base of falls from Winter Falls trailhead; 1.8 miles, 65 minutes from North Falls trailhead via the Winter Falls Bridge; 3.6 miles, 129 minutes from South Falls trailhead via Winter Falls Bridge.

Distance/Time From Other Landmark: .7 miles, 25 minutes from Twin Falls (#83); .7 miles, 25 minutes to Middle North Falls (#84).

Directions From Parking: From Winter Falls Viewpoint parking area, take trail downhill for .1 miles, 5 minutes to base of falls. From North Falls parking area, hike 1.4 miles, 49 minutes to Winter Falls Trail Bridge; cross bridge and hike upstream .5 miles, 18 minutes to base of Winter Falls.

Elevation Change: 0 feet to top of falls viewpoint; 140 feet to base of falls.

Restroom: Several modern year round restrooms at South Falls activities areas.

Picnic Area: At main area near South Falls.

View & Kissing Spots: Visible from parking area at trailhead above the falls; approaching the falls on Winter Falls spur of the canyon trail; at base of falls.

Accessibility to the Physically Challenged: Roadside viewpoint (above falls) is accessible; not otherwise.

Hazards: The Winter Falls Trail is a steep, narrow, and slippery downhill path upon which care must be taken, especially in Winter and rainy conditions. The trail from the Winter Falls Trail bridge to the falls often becomes very poor after storms and floods. Likewise, the bridge itself has been destroyed by storms in the past and will be again.

Information: On Winter Creek (tributary of North Fork Silver Creek), in Silver Falls State Park, Marion County, Oregon, USGS Drake Crossing Quadrangle; listed in USGS Geographic Names Information System.

Note that, as the name implies, Winter Falls is spectacular in the Winter and Spring but nearly dries up in the Summer.

See detailed map at section head, VIII. Silver Falls State Park.

Winter Falls

So sad your yearly cycle
By which you show your lacy plunge
When no one's here to see your glory
But birds and trees and moss and fern.

Your Winter splendor is revealed
When rain and cold provide your flow
And paint in crystal ice and snow
The majesty the tourists never see.

Indian Pipe

Silver Falls State Park

89   South Falls

A Wide Wall of Water with Scenic Walk-Behind — Views Everywhere

Height: 177'   **Difficulty:** 4   **Romance:** 10

Type: Curtain Plunge.

Description: A "Walk-Behind" Falls! A wide, flat wall of water drops from the lip of the cliff and streams downward to the floor of the canyon. A nearly 180° shallow grotto behind the base of the falls provides space for the trail. The water falls almost near enough to touch it.

Distance/Time From Portland: 57 miles, 75 to 90 minutes via Alternative #1; although the distance is greater via Salem and Route 22, the time is not significantly longer because of the better, faster roads.

Directions to Parking/Trailhead: Take Interstate 5 to the Woodburn exit, go east through Woodburn to route 99E, go south (turn right) on 99E until you reach a sign for State Route 214 to Silverton. Continue through Silverton 15 miles to Silver Falls State Park. Continue past the North Falls parking area to the South Falls parking area, the main facilities portion of the park.

Distance/Time From Parking: 2 minutes from the Lodge to the viewpoint above falls (at trailhead); .3 miles, 9 minutes to behind falls; 4.5 miles, 162 minutes from North Falls trailhead.

Distance/Time From Other Landmark: 5 minutes from Frenchie Falls (#90) (on short side trail); .8 miles, 30 minutes to Lower South Falls (#91).

Directions From Parking: Trail begins near lodge. Follow signs.

Elevation Change: 0 to the upper viewpoint, 170 feet to behind the falls.

Restroom: Several modern year round restrooms at South Falls activities areas.

Picnic Area: Many locations all over main park grounds above falls.

View & Kissing Spots: Above falls and on trail before and after the falls. Kiss behind the falls and at all view spots and hiding spots along the way.

Accessibility to the Physically Challenged: Accessible above falls; steep, narrow, paved trail is possible.

Hazards: Paving of trail is sometimes slippery. Do not swim or wade in stream immediately above the falls. The rocks are very slippery and the current is more than strong enough to carry away a foolish wader. There are better times and places to learn to fly! Do not go beyond railings above the steep drops. Cliffs may be undercut and give way. Don't be a dead daredevil!

Information: On South Fork Silver Creek, in Silver Falls State Park, Marion County, Oregon, USGS Drake Crossing Quadrangle; listed in USGS Geographic Names Information System.

Look for casts of trees trapped and destroyed in the lava which formed the cliffs of the falls and giant bubbles creating strange holes and hiding places around the falls. These are believed to have been formed when the hot lava flowed into cold water, perhaps a lake or the original South Silver Creek.

The moisture of the falls creates and sustains the lush growth of wildflowers, moss, ferns, and other plants. This spray literally creates its own weather. Notice the strong, cool breeze in the canyon produced by the cold water of the falls and its motion. This is a great place to visit and cool off when it's too hot elsewhere else!

Silver Creek Falls City was once near South Falls. We owe our visit to this natural wonder to the hardy residents of this place who publicized and popularized it before it had trails or bridges. Unfortunately, the town was destroyed and the residents sent packing when the park was created. The lodge has a display of photos and memorabilia of this era. All the volunteers who work in the gift shop and lodge are former residents of the town or their relatives. Please treat them with the respect and appreciation that they richly deserve for their generous labors on our behalf.

See detailed map at section head, VIII. Silver Falls State Park.

South Falls

Who first saw this falls
　　Nature's fluid art?
　　Neolithic man
　　Searching this new land.

Long ago they came
　　Ancient visitors
　　Gazing from behind
　　South Falls' liquid wall.

Did they stand in awe
　　Feeling near to God?
　　Could they sense the peace
　　Hidden in this place?

Were they just excited
　　Filled with love and joy
　　Bursting with delight
　　Laughing like a child.

We can know them now
　　Ancestors and friends.
　　Feeling like they did
　　Seeing the same sight.

90   Frenchie Falls

A Lush Setting for a lovely, Intimate Falls among Giants

Height: 48'   Difficulty: 2   Romance: 10

Type: Narrow Contact Plunge.

Description: A creek flows out of the woods near the rim of the canyon and flows over the edge into a narrow side canyon overgrown with berries, shrubs, wildflowers, and trees, creating a small but scenic falls which would be totally hidden around a corner of the South Falls trail were it not for a short spur provided. Nestled a few feet from the busy South Falls trail, Frenchie Falls may be the most romantic spot in the park. Steal a kiss and see for yourself!

Distance/Time From Portland: 57 miles, 75 to 90 minutes via Alternative #1; although the distance is greater via Salem and Route 22, the time is not significantly longer because of the better, faster roads.

Directions to Parking/Trailhead: Follow Directions to South Falls.

Distance/Time From Parking: .1 miles, 4 minutes from lodge at South Falls; 4.4 miles, 160 minutes from North Falls trailhead.

Distance/Time From Other Landmark: 5 minutes from South Falls (#89) walk-behind.

Directions From Parking: Take trail to South Falls then make a right turn on marked trail about 2 minutes from the start.

Elevation Change: 50 feet.

Restroom: Several modern year round restrooms at South Falls activities areas.

Picnic Area: Many locations all over main park grounds above falls.

View & Kissing Spots: At the falls at the end of the Frenchie Falls spur trail.

Accessibility to the Physically Challenged: Accessible from trail to bottom (and behind) South Falls.

Hazards: Berry vines.

Information: On Frenchie Creek (tributary of South Fork Silver Creek), in Silver Falls State Park, Marion County, Oregon, USGS Drake Crossing Quadrangle.

Named for Roland "Frenchie" Lecompte, Assistant Park Manager in the 1960s.

Interestingly, despite the many famous and exciting falls in the park, we are told Frenchie Falls is the most popular place in the park for marriage proposals. We are proud that so many people feel as strongly about it as we do. When we first decided Frenchie would be in the book, everyone thought we were nuts!

See detailed map at section head, VIII. Silver Falls State Park.

Calypso Orchid

Frenchie Falls

A lovely falls unknown to most
You fall just off the path
Where crowds go by without a look
And miss your smaller charm.

Silver Falls State Park

91   Lower South Falls

A Powerful Wall of Water so Close You Can Reach Out and Touch It

Height: 93'　　　　　　　Difficulty: 6　　　　　　　Romance: 10

Type: Curtain Plunge.

Description: A "Walk-Behind" Falls! Even more powerful than South Falls with an even longer grotto trail and its water even closer to the trail. You can reach out and touch it. In the Winter, it may reach out and touch you!

Distance/Time From Portland: 57 miles, 75 to 90 minutes via Alternative #1; although the distance is greater via Salem and Route 22, the time is not significantly longer because of the better, faster roads.

Directions to Parking/Trailhead: Follow Directions to North Falls, South Falls, or Winter Falls (depending upon which way you want to start your hike).

Distance/Time From Parking: .7 miles, 26 minutes to viewpoint on trail above falls; .8 miles, 30 minutes to behind falls from South Falls trailhead; 3.5 miles, 123 minutes from North Falls trailhead.

Distance/Time From Other Landmark: .8 miles, 30 minutes from South Falls (#89); 1.3 miles, 50 minutes to Lower North Falls (#87). To loop back to the trailhead at South Falls via the Ridge Trail: .3 miles, 13 minutes to junction of Canyon Trail and Ridge Trail (downstream); .5 miles, 22 minutes to the rim of the canyon, .4 miles, 13 minutes to the top of Frenchie Falls (#90), and .1 miles, 2 minutes to the South Falls viewpoint.

Directions From Parking: Trail begins near lodge. Follow signs to South Falls and continue downstream on the Canyon Trail.

Elevation Change: 300 feet to above the falls; 385 feet to behind the falls.

Restroom: Several modern year round restrooms at South Falls activities areas.

Picnic Area: Many locations in main park grounds at South Falls activities areas.

View & Kissing Spots: On trail approaching and leaving falls and behind falls.

Accessibility to the Physically Challenged: Not accessible due to stairs and other barriers.

Hazards: Some slippery places when wet.

Information: On South Fork Silver Creek, in Silver Falls State Park, Marion County, Oregon, USGS Drake Crossing Quadrangle; listed in USGS Geographic Names Information System.

Look for berries of all kinds along the trail.

Throughout Silver Falls State Park, but particularly in the area between South Falls and Lower South Falls, the Mountain Beaver, *aplodontia rufa*, is found in grassy areas near water. The "boomers", as they are called, are not beavers despite their name. Because they are nocturnal and very shy, you will have to be very lucky (and very quiet) to ever see one.

See detailed map at section head, VIII. Silver Falls State Park.

Bear Grass

Lower South Falls

Behind a crystal curtain at your base
We stand and peer at forest glen
    And canyon formed by your
    Unending flow o'er untold millennia.

We feel your spray upon our face
And stretch our hands to touch you
As if the magic of existence
Could flow to us from your sweet water.

IX. Mid Willamette Valley & Cascades

This section of the book contains waterfalls within three primary watersheds, the Santiam, the McKenzie, and Salt Creek. Although there are many more streams in this region and, in fact, many more waterfalls, we are limiting our examination to these nine. They are all particular favorites of ours. In future volumes, we promise to include others, some of which might be your favorites. Please let us know what you would like.

A number of beautiful waterfalls can be found near US Route 20 more or less in the Lebanon and Sweet Home area. They include those in McDowell Creek County Park and near Cascadia State Park.

The McKenzie River is a very big, powerful stream which is born high in the Cascades and travels almost straight south for much of its length before finally turning west toward the Willamette. The two falls on the McKenzie which we've shown are both very dramatic ones with great power and volume.

The waterfalls on Salt Creek and one of its tributaries are simply amazing and delightful, especially Salt Creek Falls, which is certainly higher than any other waterfall in

**Belted Kingfisher
(with fish)**

Oregon south of the Columbia River Gorge. It is a favorite of a great many people in addition to the two of us.

We're certain that you will find all of these falls to be among your favorites too. Have fun!

The Blackboard of Life

On the blackboard of life the chalk often squeaks
And report cards are rarely so great,
But whatever your age, your life is a stage
Where solace is always at hand.

You can visit the woods and look at the falls
Where silence is broken by life,
And stay for a while till finally you'll smile
Your outlook restored and refreshed.

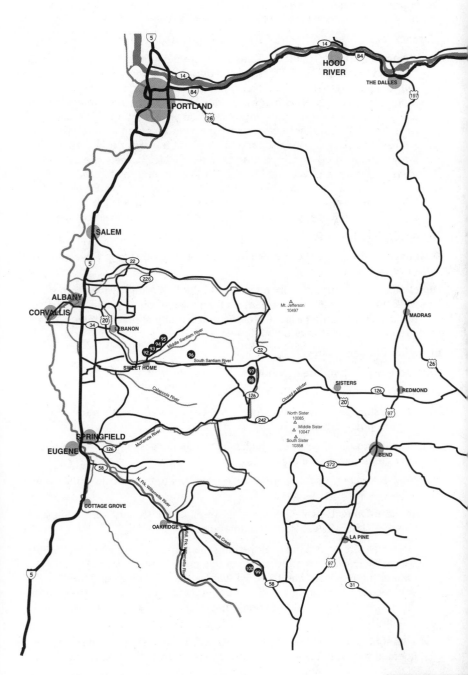

Mid Willamette Valley & Cascades

92   Lower McDowell Creek Falls
A Wonderful, Delightful Watery Playground

Height: 15'   **Difficulty:** 0 to bridge, 2 to streamside   **Romance:** 4

Type: Stepped Slides.

Description: A delightful Summer playground—a series of slides connecting broad, flat, smooth rock shelves—perfect for wading, sitting, and splashing.

Distance/Time From Portland: 95 miles, 1 hour and 31 minutes.

Directions to Parking/Trailhead: Take Interstate 5 south to the Albany exit 233, "Santiam Highway US 20"; drive east through Lebanon toward Sweet Home to the relatively well marked McDowell Creek Road, onto which turn left; jog around through Waterloo following signs for the park; the primary parking lot for McDowell Creek Falls Park will be on your right approximately 7 miles from US 20. There is an excellent paved parking lot just off the road; a large, unpaved secondary parking lot about a quarter mile further; the larger, unpaved upstream parking area near Majestic Falls is a quarter mile even further on a paved road on the left just beyond the highway bridge over McDowell Creek up ahead. The first lot is best if you are to see all the falls. Otherwise, you either have a reverse hike or you will be parking in the middle. In any case, parking is good, convenient and close to everything.

Distance/Time From Parking: 2 minutes.

Distance/Time From Other Landmark: 9 minutes upstream to Royal Terrace Falls (#93).

Directions From Parking: Walk a few feet to the footbridge visible from parking; walk 50 to 100 feet downstream on the maize of paths parallel to the stream (on parking lot side of creek) to one of the many short scrambles to the streamside (pick the one you find easiest).

Elevation Change: 10 feet.

Restroom: At parking area, primitive.

Picnic Area: At all three parking areas.

View & Kissing Spots: From bridge, along trail through woods paralleling stream, at streamside.

Accessibility to the Physically Challenged: Fully accessible short path to bridge over creek just above the falls.

Hazards: Take care reaching streamside from trail to avoid a short but painful fall.

Information: On McDowell Creek, in McDowell Creek County Park, Linn County, Oregon, USGS Sweet Home Quadrangle.

McDowell Creek and the park bearing the same name derives its title from James McDowell, an early native of this area. General Irvin McDowell, veteran of the Mexican War, the Civil War Battle of Bull Run and the Nez Perce War, whose name graces several Oregon landmarks is not the inspiration for this piece of geography (although maybe James was a descendent of the General).

This spot is a perfect example of a waterfall which seems rather inconsequential when reviewing its "specifications" but which offers more pleasure

and romance than many which would appear on the cover of a slick publication. While Royal Terrace and Majestic certainly deserve such reverence, this one's just for fun! Spend a day in its cool atmosphere, wet your tired feet, steal a kiss, watch the kids play, or just be a kid yourself. It's that kind of place.

Decompression

With lives of internet, CDs, TV
It takes a while to decompress
And find the real world in the woods
Where life displays its truth and beauty.

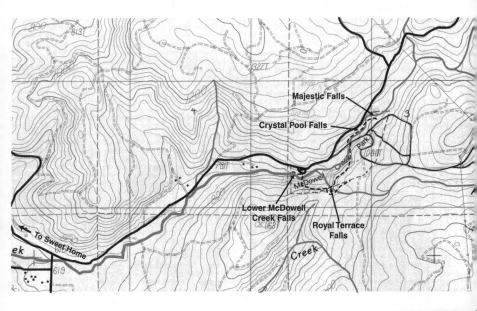

93   **Royal Terrace Falls**
A Unique and Charming Three Tiered Falls

Height: 119'   **Difficulty:** 2 to bridge; 6 to 9 to top   **Romance:** 7

Type: Contact Plunge, Curtain Plunge, Curtain Plunge.

Description: Royal Terrace Falls is well named. Fall Creek drops over the top of the cliff in a wide, though thin, curtain, drops to a large shelf from which it drops again, forming a wide curtain in front of a deep space suitable for a walk-behind (if you could get there), and repeats the plan for the bottom tier. There's even a perfectly round foot-wide hole in the lip of the middle tier through which water drops. You will love this falls.

Distance/Time From Portland: 95 miles, 1 hour and 31 minutes.

Directions to Parking/Trailhead: Follow directions to Lower McDowell Creek Falls.

Distance/Time From Parking: 9 minutes.

Directions From Parking: Walk to the footbridge visible from the primary parking area; cross the bridge and follow the trail for 9 minutes to the bridge at the bottom of the falls.

Distance/Time From Other Landmark: 9 minutes from Lower McDowell Creek Falls (#92); 8 minutes to Crystal Pool (#94).

Elevation Change: less than 50 feet to bridge at the bottom of the falls; 170 to the top of the falls.

Restroom: At the primary parking area.

Picnic Area: At all three parking areas.

View & Kissing Spots: The view from the bridge at the bottom of the falls is ideal. At the right of the falls, a frighteningly steep (and badly deteriorated but soon to be rebuilt) rock staircase with wooden handrails leads you upward to several viewpoints, including a small platform at the very top and to a bridge and trail above the falls. Several wonderful places for views, photos, and kisses!

Accessibility to the Physically Challenged: Difficult but perhaps possible to the bridge at the bottom of the falls. The falls is visible from a spot on the road beyond the Lower McDowell Creek Falls parking area, depending upon the amount of foliage in the way which in turn varies with the time of year.

Hazards: Extreme danger along unprotected, slippery view areas near very high vertical cliffs at the side of the falls.

Information: On Fall Creek (tributary of McDowell Creek), in McDowell Creek Falls County Park, Linn County, Oregon, USGS Sweet Home Quadrangle.

We particularly liked the very old, small and simple wooden sign nailed to a tree high above the left (east) side of the bridge at the bottom of the falls which simply says "Royal Terrace Falls 119 feet". It's one more excellent example of the care and effort exerted by someone long ago to make our visit more enjoyable.

This is the kind of imaginative falls design that landscape architects would love to create. Unfortunately for them, Royal Terrace was designed by a far more creative landscape architect!

Note that there is a trail at the top of the falls which crosses the creek on a small footbridge and continues steeply uphill for some distance to the top of the ridge and along it heading east.

Although we probably should have followed it to its end, we didn't. Sorry!

See detailed map at falls #92, Lower McDowell Creek Falls.

Metaphors

Like love in bloom and long remembered
Or childish glee and wizened smile
Or carefree dance and stately grace.
The waterfall descends in metaphors.
Some find a smile, some find a symphony.

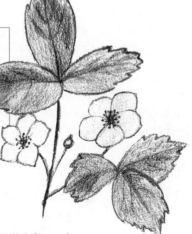

Wild Strawberry

94 Crystal Pool
A Lovely Falls Feeding a Beautiful Clear Pool

Height: 20' **Difficulty:** 4 **Romance:** 5

Type: Spreading Contact Plunge.

Description: In deep woods, McDowell Creek runs wide until it is squeezed to a few feet in width between massive boulders and rock outcrops through which it pushes and falls into a wide, placid pool. Relatively easy access from the trail to the pool makes it a fantastic place to cool off on a hot Summer day.

Distance/Time From Portland: 95 miles, 1 hour and 31 minutes.

Directions to Parking/Trailhead: Follow directions to Lower McDowell Creek Falls.

Distance/Time From Parking: 17 minutes.

Distance/Time From Other Landmark: 8 minutes from Royal Terrace Falls (#93); 10 minutes to the lower viewpoint for Majestic Falls (#95).

Directions From Parking: Follow directions to Royal Terrace Falls then continue upstream on the trail; cross the road to the obvious trailhead on the north side of the road; continue a short distance until you see Crystal Pool. There is a path which leads to streamside downstream from the pool and falls. **Alternative #1:** Park at the small parking area along the road where the trail reaches the road just before the bridge; take the trail on the north side directly to Crystal Pool. **Alternative #2:** Follow the alternative directions listed under Majestic Falls to its large, woodsy parking lot; visit Majestic Falls then take the trail downstream to Crystal Pool.

Elevation Change: Less than 50 feet.

Restroom: At parking at trailhead near Lower McDowell Creek Falls.

Picnic Area: At the parking areas.

View & Kissing Spots: Streamside near the falls and on the trail approaching it.

Accessibility to the Physically Challenged: Not accessible due to the narrow and uneven trail.

Hazards: Only thorns and very cold water.

Information: On McDowell Creek, in McDowell Creek Falls County Park, Linn County, Oregon, USGS Sweet Home Quadrangle.

See detailed map at falls #92, Lower McDowell Creek Falls.

**Anemone
(Wind Flower)**

Transition

My heart was sick, my head was low.
No pill would help nor work of man.
How sad my life, where could I go?
Was life to be a joyless span?

Why did I go, I did not choose
To change my thoughts from where they'd
  been
But as I walked, I seem to lose
Myself inside the forest glen.

As water poured from high above
The flowers bloomed, the light grew bright
The birds began to sing of love
My life had changed, I was alright.

My fears and pains were on the shelf
With one deep breath I let them go.
My thoughts were now outside myself
My soul had joined the water's flow.

I visit waterfalls each week.
I've found the world, I've found release.
I am the falls, the woods, the creek.
I've found my place. I am at peace.

## 95

Majestic Falls
A Well Named Falls, Powerful and Majestic

Height: 55'   **Difficulty:** 4   **Romance:** 6

Type: Wide Contact Plunge.

Description: McDowell Creek runs across a relatively flat shelf of rock until it reaches edge of a cliff, from which it blasts into a narrow bowl.

Distance/Time From Portland: 95 miles, 1 hour and 31 minutes.

Directions to Parking/Trailhead: Follow directions to Lower McDowell Creek Falls.

Distance/Time From Parking: 27 minutes from the parking at Lower McDowell Creek Falls; 5 minutes from the parking at Majestic Falls.

Distance/Time From Other Landmark: 10 minutes from Crystal Pool (#94).

Directions From Parking: Follow directions to Royal Terrace Falls then head upstream on the McDowell Creek trail; pass Crystal Pool and continue on the trail until you reach the amazing "boardwalk" which leads you across the creek to the lower viewpoint of Majestic Falls. Take the stairs to the top of the cliff where you will find another wonderful viewing platform from which to see the falls from its top. **Alternative:** Drive from the main parking area near Lower McDowell Creek Falls east to the first left turn past the McDowell Creek bridge; drive north on this rustic but well maintained road a short distance to a very large gravel parking area set in the forest. Two trails (one on either end of the parking lot) lead downhill to the excellent viewing area at the top of the falls.

Elevation Change: Less than 50 feet.

Restroom: At the parking area at Lower McDowell Creek Falls.

Picnic Area: At the parking areas.

View & Kissing Spots: From the top of the falls, on the upper and lower viewing platforms, and along the creek downstream of the falls.

Accessibility to the Physically Challenged: One of the paths from the parking lot above the falls should be relatively accessible although gravel and sloped. Once you get to it, the upper viewing platform is a very good one and quite accessible. Unfortunately, the long flight of wooden stairs to the lower viewpoint are a significant barrier to reaching it.

Hazards: Sliding on the slippery trail, rocks, or wooden stairs.

Information: On McDowell Creek, in McDowell Creek Falls County Park, Linn County, Oregon, USGS Sweet Home Quadrangle.

What a monumental and well executed project the wooden viewing platform, stairs down to the base of the falls, lower viewing platform, and the stairs, boardwalk, and bridge to the far side of the stream. Linn County deserves

Tiger Lily

praise for their efforts. Hopefully, they will soon extend their work to some of the still crumbling areas of the park.

See detailed map at falls #92, Lower McDowell Creek Falls.

Time and the Falls

Time plays tricks with us
When ere we watch the falls.
It's ever changing, ever new
Yet timeless, here ten thousand years.

No matter how long we watch
Or squint or blink our eyes
Or take our photos super speed
Infinitely the falls keeps changing.

Each season, month or week
The water's flow, the rocks, and moss
Is new and different than the time
We visited before.

As children once we found delight
To play before its plunge
A lifetime later here we are
As if no time has passed.

When first man found this spot
And even long before
This water fell just as right now
And will when we're long gone.

So strange a waterfall can change each
second, month, and year
And bring such joy to humans past as now
To teach each age of time and love
And be here till our kind is gone.

## 96

Lower Soda Falls

A Very Tall Skinny Plunge Along a Crack in the Cliff

Height: 175'   Difficulty: 5   Romance: 5

Type: 3 narrow contact plunge tiers.

Description: Soda Creek's modest flow comes over the edge of a very tall vertical cliff and follows the course of a very narrow vertical crack which takes it to the bottom of the cliff, bouncing twice on the way.

Distance/Time From Portland: 105 miles, 1 hour and 43 minutes.

Directions to Parking/Trailhead: Take Interstate 5 south to the route #34/Corvallis/Lebanon exit; drive east on route 34 to Lebanon where it joins route #20; drive southeast on route 20 for about 7 miles (to about 5 miles from Sweet Home); turn left on Fairview Road and then left on the first intersecting road and very shortly turn right (east) on McDowell Creek Road (hopefully, there will be signs for the park); drive east for a little over 6 miles to the park. which will be on your left. There is ample paved parking in the park.

Distance/Time From Parking: .6 miles, 30 minutes.

Distance/Time From Other Landmark: Visit the mineral springs on an accessible walkway just downstream of the Soda Falls trailhead, which you can enter from the parking lot.

Directions From Parking: Walk to the right from the parking near the entrance on the road toward the "Group Camping" area. Look for the sign marked "Soda Falls" on the left side of the road near the creek. Walk upstream along the creek, crossing several romantic footbridges, until you see the falls. Hike to the end of the trail (just before the falls). To reach the head-on viewpoint, carefully climb up the rocks next to the trail and pick your way to a large flattened rock directly in front of the falls.

Elevation Change: 460 feet.

Restroom: At the parking area and at other places within the park, modern.

Picnic Area: At the campground.

View & Kissing Spots: At the falls and on the footbridges along the trail.

Accessibility to the Physically Challenged: Not accessible.

Hazards: Care must be taken on the rocks and cliffs at the falls viewpoint.

Information: On Soda Creek (tributary of South Santiam River), in Cascadia State Park, Linn County, Oregon, USGS Cascadia Quadrangle; listed in USGS Geographic Names Information System.

Upper Soda Falls is currently inaccessible. In 1895, a health resort was founded at the mouth of Soda Creek by a Mr. Geisendorfer to take advantage of the soda mineral springs along Soda Creek. The area was once called Lower Soda Springs. Something resembling a town had a post office here once upon a time. It was called Lowersoda, Lower Soda, and Cascadia, depending upon when and where you look! There isn't much evidence of habitation remaining. This property was purchased in the 1940's by the State of Oregon to become Cascadia State Park. Cascadia State Park is a well maintained and really wonderful place to camp, picnic, and explore. You will love it!

Another interesting waterfall, 25 foot Rainbow Falls, can be found about two miles south of the Cascadia Park on Dobbins Creek.

For other nearby scenic adventures, visit the covered bridge crossing the South Santiam River just a couple of miles west of the park. Watch for signs (or a glimpse of the bridge from the road). The "Indian Caves" a few miles east of Cascadia is also worth a "look see".

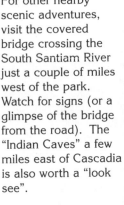

Connections

A waterfall connects us
To time and nature's creativity
To art and love and beauty
Forever there yet always changing
Which brings both smiles and tears
To every eye with every tongue,
Hearts meeting universally.

Mid Willamette Valley & Cascades

97   Sahalie Falls
A Memorable, Fun Falls with a Huge Flow in a Narrow Space

Height: 150'   **Difficulty:** 1   **Romance:** 7

Type: Twin: Arched Plunges.

Description: Sahalie has a huge, powerful flow which is squeezed through two narrow channels to blast into a beautiful circular punch bowl. The entire setting is enhanced by really excellent and convenient yet rustic trails, guard rails, and viewing platforms of logs and stone.

Distance/Time From Portland: 138 miles, 2 hours and 20 minutes via Route 22.

Directions to Parking/Trailhead: Take Interstate 5 for 46 miles south to Exit 253, Route 22, in Salem; drive 83 miles east on Route 22 to the junction with Route 20; turn right onto Route 20 and drive 4 miles to the junction with Route 126, turn left onto Route 126 and drive approximately 5 miles to the well marked Sahalie Falls parking area on your right. Alternatively, one could travel east from the Albany area on Route 20 or from Eugene on Route 126. Sahalie Falls has its own good parking area or you can visit both Sahalie and Koosah from either parking area and hike between them.

Distance/Time From Parking: Less than .1 miles and 5 minutes.

Distance/Time From Other Landmark: 32 miles, 30 minutes from Whispering Falls (#80); .3 miles, 15 minutes downstream to Koosah Falls (#98).

Directions From Parking: Take wooden steps to large wooden railed viewing platform; turn right and hike for a few minutes to the top of the falls; back-tracking to the original viewpoint, a short hike to the left leads to a small, rock wall protected viewpoint. Note that continuing down this trail will take you to Koosah Falls.

Elevation Change: 30 feet.

Restroom: At the parking lot.; primitive but accessible to the physically challenged.

Picnic Area: Excellent facilities within park.

View & Kissing Spots: At platform viewpoints, trailside, and top of falls.

Accessibility to the Physically Challenged: Relatively accessible. Trail from Sahalie to Koosah is inaccessible due to stairs.

Hazards: Very high, steep cliffs offer the aggressively foolhardy the opportunity to experience the very cold, very deep, very swift water below. Be careful!

Information: On McKenzie River, Linn County, USGS Three Fingered Jack Quadrangle; listed in USGS Geographic Names Information System.

This is the highest falls on the McKenzie River. Note that there is another falls with nearly the same name, Sahale, near Mount Hood. The two names are variants of the same Chinook word meaning "High". As described more fully under Koosah Falls, Sahalie Falls was known as Upper Falls before the Clear Lake Recreation Area was developed.

This falls was featured in the Disney movie "Homeward Bound".

A dip and/or shower may be had at the base of the falls by braving the slippery, unimproved trail to the bottom.

Sahalie Falls

Koosah Falls

Come with Me
Come my friend along with me
We'll run away, escape, we'll flee.

Come my love alone with me
We'll speak of life and love and glee.

Come my child and skip with me
We'll hide behind each rock and tree.

Come my parent stroll with me
We'll bare our souls, for once be free.

Mid Willamette Valley & Cascades

Koosah Falls
A Mighty Wall of Water Plunging into a Bowl

Height: 120'   **Difficulty:** 1   **Romance:** 6

Type: Wide Curtain Plunge.

Description: A Powerful, wide curtain of water drops over a shelf of rock, then falls into a large, clear pool surrounded by a bowl of sheer cliffs.

Distance/Time From Portland: 140 miles, 2 hours and 25 minutes via Route 22.

Directions to Parking/Trailhead: Follow directions to Sahalie Falls; continue driving past Sahalie Falls for .5 miles to a paved road just after you cross a small bridge after road #850; follow this road to a well marked and designed viewpoint entrance area with rock walls and a large explanatory display. Koosah Falls has its own good parking area or you can visit both Koosah and Sahalie from either parking area and hiking between.

Distance/Time From Parking: 5 minutes (or 20 minutes via riverside trail from Sahalie Falls parking lot).

Distance/Time From Other Landmark: .3 miles, 15 minutes upstream to Sahalie Falls (#97)

Directions From Parking: Follow well marked trail to excellent viewpoint.

Elevation Change: 40 feet.

Restroom: At Sahalie Falls parking lot; primitive.

Picnic Area: Within park around falls.

View & Kissing Spots: At beautifully developed viewpoints and trails near falls.

Accessibility to the Physically Challenged: Relatively accessible. Trail from Koosah to Sahalie is inaccessible due to stairs.

Hazards: Very high, steep cliffs offer the aggressively foolhardy the opportunity to experience the very cold, very deep, very swift water below. Be careful!

Information: On McKenzie River, Linn County, USGS Three Fingered Jack Quadrangle; listed in USGS Geographic Names Information System.

Chocolate Lily

Koosah is a derivative of the Chinook word for "sky". It was once known as "Middle Falls" because it was between Sahalie Falls upstream and Tamolitch Falls (now "extinct" because its water has been usurped by a dam forming Carmen Reservoir and an aqueduct leaving a dry streambed. The usually dry remains of 60 foot Tamolitch Falls is approximately two miles downstream from Carmen Reservoir and may be reached going upstream or downstream by a relatively good trail.

For those wishing a longer, more comprehensive hike, the trail which links Koosah Falls and Sahalie Falls crosses the stream approximately a half mile above Sahalie, runs downstream on the other side of the river (offering a number of different and interesting views of the river and the two waterfalls), and meets the original trail at the lake a half mile downstream from Koosah. Thus, you can make the complete circuit starting from the lake or from either falls. Your loop can include Carmen Reservoir, a manmade lake, on the downstream end. It's a beautiful hike.

See detailed map at falls #97, Sahalie Falls.

A Drop of Rain

From vapor in Pacific skies
Condensing formed a cloud
I fell as rain toward Mount Hood
To lush green forest flanks.

From hemlock needle high above
I dripped to join my friends
Then slowly oozed past moss and fern
To reach a tiny seep.

We gamboled over roots and stones
To gush and grow in strength.
Now rushing faster ever joyful
We splashed and hurried down.

So soon we reached the cliff you see
And launched ourselves in space
To fly as spray to wet your face
Or plunge into the pool.

I've come so far from cloud to you
My journey's not yet run.
I'll flow along to reach the sea
And do it all again.

99   Salt Creek Falls
A Huge, Beautiful Plunge—One of Oregon's Tallest

Height: 286'   **Difficulty:** 0 to cliffside, 3 to lower viewpoint   **Romance:** 8

Type: Wide Contact Plunge.

Description: For some distance, Salt Creek quietly runs along a smooth, flat layer of rock until suddenly it reaches a sheer cliff over which it drops 286 feet roaring into a huge bowl. The force of its mighty plunge fills the entire area with spray.

Distance/Time From Portland: 170 miles, 2 hours and 50 minutes.

Directions to Parking/Trailhead: Drive south on Interstate 5 to just south of Eugene to State Route 58 (exit 188 Oakridge, Klamath Falls); drive east through Oakridge and on toward Willamette Pass, about 60 miles; right after driving through the tunnel, turn right into Salt Creek Falls State Park. Excellent, paved parking near the falls.

Distance/Time From Parking: Cliffside views are immediately available; the entire trip from parking to lower viewpoint is about .25 miles, 15 minutes.

Distance/Time From Other Landmark: 1.3 miles to Diamond Creek Falls (#100).

Directions From Parking: The log railings of the overlooks near the falls are visible from the parking area. Once you have reached it, walk downstream along the cliffside overlook from somewhat above the falls to well beyond it. By continuing along the cliffside, you will eventually reach a well marked trail with log hand rails which takes you downhill by a couple of switchbacks to a point nearer the base of the falls.

Elevation Change: 0 to cliffside; 200 feet to lower viewpoint.

Restroom: At parking lot, modern.

Picnic Area: An excellent, scenic picnic area is near parking lot.

View & Kissing Spots: At many cliffside spots, along the trail to the lower viewpoint and especially at the lower viewpoint.

Accessibility to the Physically Challenged: Fully accessible upper area including excellent, safe viewpoints.

Hazards: Do not horse around upstream from the falls or next to the cliffside. Despite well engineered railings and other safety precautions, the terminally foolish could ignore the obvious dangers. Note that the approximately 3,500 foot elevation and mountain terrain make this area resemble a ski area in the Winter. Consider weather conditions, capabilities and preparation of your car and clothing, and your expectations before heading for this area.

Information: On Salt Creek, Lane County, Oregon, USGS Diamond Peak Quadrangle; listed in USGS Geographic Names Information System.

The falls were first seen by Europeans in 1887 when shown to Frank S. Warner, a nearby settler, by Charles Tufti, a Native American who was staying with the Warners. Salt Creek has had its name since pioneer days because of its numerous salt springs which were used by deer and humans as sources for the important nutrient. Some descriptions of Salt Creek Falls state that a rock at the top creates a visible letter "S" in the water. We have

never seen anything of the sort!

The park at the falls is very complete and well maintained with trails, camping, picnicking, modern restrooms, and a large informational kiosk.

Although Salt Creek Falls and Diamond Creek Falls are a long distance from Portland and not really in Northwest Oregon, they are such beautiful and significant attractions that we were sure everyone would be very glad they made the trip to see them. Besides, we love them and...it's our book!

Waterfalls Are Poets

Waterfalls are poets who write their
rhymes in drops and spray
Their wordless verse to touch our hearts
As if by some pre-human Shakespeare
Whose poem entwines amidst our DNA.

100   Diamond Creek Falls

A Big, Powerful, Spreading Slide (A Giant Ramona)

Height: 90'   **Difficulty:** 5   **Romance:** 7

Type: Wide Spreading Slide.

Description: Diamond Creek slides down an angled cliff-face punctuated by breaks in its surface to create a widening white froth of spray.

Distance/Time From Portland: 170 miles, 2 hours and 50 minutes.

Directions to Parking/Trailhead: Follow the directions to Salt Creek Falls.

Distance/Time From Parking: 1.3 miles, 65 minutes.

Distance/Time From Other Landmark: 1.3 miles from Salt Creek Falls (#99), .8 miles to Lower Falls Creek Falls.

Directions From Parking: A paved trail leads from the parking lot to a wooden footbridge which crosses Salt Creek. You can also walk upstream along the cliffside from Salt Creek Falls to the bridge. This is the trailhead. Follow this trail, marked periodically with blue diamonds to show the way, past numerous viewpoints until you reach the Diamond Creek Falls sign which marks the trail down to the streamside, and across a bridge to the right side of the base of the falls. The upper viewpoint is only a very short distance uphill beyond this fork. From its viewing platform, you can see the left side of the falls from above. Visit them both!

Elevation Change: 200 feet.

Restroom: At parking lot, modern.

Picnic Area: An excellent, scenic picnic area is near parking lot.

View & Kissing Spots: At trailside viewpoints, at base of falls, at upper viewpoint—several very different and very exciting views of this wonderful falls.

Accessibility to the Physically Challenged: Not accessible due to the narrow, uneven, unpaved trail.

Hazards: Care should be taken near unguarded cliffside areas all along the trail. Winter snow may make this hike impractical and more dangerous if not totally impossible.

Information: On Diamond Creek, Lane County, Oregon, USGS Diamond Peak Quadrangle.

Lower Diamond Creek Falls, a much taller falls, is barely visible through the obscuring trees from clifftop viewpoints along the trail. Be careful! There is no good vantage point from which to see it, but there are plenty of dangerous places from which to fall while trying!

Further upstream from Diamond Creek Falls, you may wish to visit two other significant falls, "Lower Falls Creek Falls" (less than a mile), and "Falls Creek Falls" (a mile more). Look for directions at Salt Creek Falls Campground. Please note that, despite for our frequently mentioned frustration with the repetition of the names "Falls Creek", "Falls Creek Falls", and "Lower Falls", we left these two waterfalls out of the book simply because we had only visited them once under conditions we did not consider representative and we had not fully researched them. In addition, Salt Creek Falls and Diamond Creek Falls are the furthest south of those in the book.

We plan to much more fully document the falls in this area in future volumes. Perhaps you could consider the two we included to be a teaser for things to come or else merely a case of author's license. Please let us know what falls you think we should include in the next book.

Throughout this area, the dominant plant in the forest under story is the wild rhododendron. Look for its beautiful pink blossoms throughout the area in late Spring.

See detailed map at falls #99, Salt Creek Falls.

Oregon Iris

Join the Falls

There are things with which we have a special affinity:
Flowers and babies, sunsets and surf,
Twinkling lights in the distance,
The smell of mother's cooking.

Nothing is as universally attractive as a waterfall.
Every age and nationality, gender, culture, or religion
Stands in awe before the spray
As if awakening long lost memories.

Wildlife

Wildlife is plentiful near waterfalls and the streams around them. To appreciate it, one must be quiet and patient. As a guest in nature's world, you may observe and appreciate the creatures but you mustn't interfere with them. From the lofty eagle to the stately elk to the lowly slug, don't frighten or hurt them. They belong there, not us!

Dead animal warning: If you find a dead animal of any kind, never, ever touch it! It may not be dead, but only very sick and will wake up and hurt you. The big, nasty creature that killed it may be waiting for you for its next dinner. The tiny, nasty germ that killed it may be waiting for you for its next dinner.

If, despite these warnings, you handle a dead animal, wrap it without touching it further, seal it in a bag, and take it with you to a doctor immediately. It will help medical personnel determine whether you need medical attention! This is no joke! Lime disease, the hanta virus, rocky mountain spotted fever, and rabies are life threatening!

Birds

Binoculars and a bird book can increase your enjoyment of birds and other animals.

Migration is different in the Northwest due to the wide variation in climate, elevation, and habitat thanks to the effects of the Pacific Ocean, the Cascade Mountains, and the Columbia River Gorge. Some species simply migrate between elevations, from forest to field, from deciduous woods to evergreen, from small to large bodies of water, or between forest and suburbs. Thus, many birds may be found in different locations in the region at different times of year—even within one waterfall area.

Below is a small portion of the birds in the Northwest. Some are very common, some are the most likely in the areas covered by the book, and others are just favorites!

Great Blue Heron "ardea herodias": A long necked, long beaked, 4 foot, blue to gray wading bird which fishes in shallow water. It flies with deep slow beats with neck folded back and legs trailing and roosts in trees. Landing is an awkward, humorous sight.

Double Crested Cormorant "phalacrocorax auritus": Common on coast, rivers, and lakes, it is easily recognized by its long "S" curved neck and upward slanted beak when swimming and its habit of spreading its wings to dry while perched on pilings.

Canada Goose "branta canadensis": Identified by their "V" shaped flights and their black head and neck with white "chin strap". In Winter, look for large flocks on ponds, foraging in farm fields, and commuting between. Adults mate for life.

California Quail "lophortyx californicus": A delightful, chubby little bird seen in a crowd scurrying across roads. Recognized by its bobbing top-knot which seems to dangle in front of its face. Seen at low altitudes of the Northwest.

Mountain Quail "oreortyx pictus": Less common but similar to its California cousin except for its long straight top-knot which stands nearly straight up.

Blue Grouse "dendragapus obscurus": You may never see a grouse, but you may hear it. In Spring, the male calls his ladies with a loud, deep series of "thumps" with its inflated throat pouch. It sounds like a pile-driver far away, but it's a Blue Grouse.

Ruffed Grouse "bonasa umbrellus": Related to Blue Grouse and equally shy, it makes a rapid beating sound, increasing in speed and pitch, like a steam engine starting up. It also spends Summers in open woods. It Winters in thick mountain forests.

Ring-Necked Pheasant "phasianus colchicus": Called "China Roosters" by old timers because they were first successfully introduced here directly from China. All others in America are descendants of Oregon's. Look for them in clearings or farm fields.

Sparrow Hawk "falco sparverius": A colorful miniature Peregrine with striking "Egyptian" falcon facial markings, this robin-sized bird is seen year round perched on wires and hovering over fields hunting grasshoppers and mice—but not sparrows.

Peregrine Falcon "falco peregrinus": A crow-size hawk with long, pointed wings, distinctive dark "side burns", and the fastest speed of any bird. Peregrines catch pigeons, ducks, and other birds on the wing. Most easily seen in Winter and Spring.

Prairie Falcon "falco mexicanus": Similar in size, speed, and prey but much lighter in color, it is found in the drier open country east of the Cascades.

Red Tailed Hawk "buteo jamaicensis": Abundant year round, this "chicken hawk" is seen perched near roads or soaring. It feeds on rabbits, rodents, snakes (not chickens, lambs, or children) and is identified by a red tail and slight "V" of 4 foot wings.

Osprey "pandion haliaetus": The "fish eagle" is a treat to watch. The black and white color and long slender blunt wings with bent "wrists" is distinctive. They nest in tall trees, on poles, and navigation markers near water. Watch for one flying high above the water, hovering, then hurtling down, folding its wings before hitting the water, then rising with a fish held torpedo-like in its talons. They will scream at you and glare right in your eyes if you get too close—a spooky experience!.

Bald Eagle "haliaeetus leucocephalus": Our national emblem, this very large (nearly seven foot wing span) bird is common along large bodies of fresh and salt water. Look for them perched in trees or flying over water, especially in Winter. Until maturity in the fourth year, they lack the distinctive white head and tail. In flight both Bald and Golden Eagles hold their wings in a very flat, straight line with no "V" angle.

Golden Eagle "aquila chrysaetos": Slightly smaller and lighter in weight than the bald eagle, they are year round residents but rarely seen because they hunt rabbits, rodents, and snakes over barren desert and prairie and nest on remote cliffs. Adults are solid brown with golden neck feathers. Young birds have white in wings and tail.

Turkey Vulture "cathartes aura": A Summer resident soaring effortlessly, watching for carrion. Easily identified by the sharp "V" of its 6 foot wings and its solid black color, it is eagle-size with a turkey-like bald red head. They're so shy that no matter how dead tired you are, they won't feed on you until you're really dead. So, cheer up!

Belted Kingfisher "megaceryle alcyon": A small bright blue/gray bird of streams and marshes that dives head first to snatch fish. Listen for its musical racking call.

Downey Woodpecker "dendrocopos pubescens": A common small woodpecker of deciduous woods, black and white with a tiny spot of red on the top of its head.

Hairy Woodpecker "dendrocopos villosus": Almost identical to the Downey except larger, they're easy to tell apart if they'll just sit together! Note that woodpeckers (except flickers) rarely use their voice. Instead, each species drums distinctively on a resonant branch. They are actually very quiet when tapping for food.

Redheaded Sapsucker (or Red Breasted race of Yellow Bellied Sapsucker) "sphyrapicus varius": A small woodpecker with a bright red head shading into yellow. They drill rows of holes in fruit tree bark to sip oozing sap and eat the attracted bugs.

Red-Shafted Flicker "coloptes cafer": A beautiful bird with "designer pattern" of beige and fine black marks on the back, light underneath with small black spots, broad black "necklace", gray face, bright red whisker pattern, soft brown crown, and it opens a brilliant red lined "cape" when it flies. It feeds on the ground and in trees, is larger than a robin, has a formidable beak, and makes a jungle-like pwip-pwip-pwip...

Pileated Woodpecker "dryocopus pileatus": Crow-size but rarely seen, the largest remaining American woodpecker has a large, bright red crest, a black, white, and red face pattern, and black wings with white patches revealed in flight. You will see the big square holes of its huge chisel beak digging for bugs in dead wood everywhere.

Rufous Hummingbird "selasphorus rufus": A jewel of iridescent green and chinese red which visits flowers tirelessly during warmer months. You'll hear the loud buzz of its wings as it passes you. They arrive with the blooming of the wild red currants.

Scrub Jay "aphelocoma coerulescens": A beautiful uncrested jay with bright blue above, near white below, a large beige area on the back, and attractive light blue horizontal stripes over the eyes. They are noisy robbers and beggars in cities and woods.

Steller's Jay "cyanocitta stelleri": The most beautiful jay, it is uniformly bright dark blue with tiny light blue vertical "eye brows". Beautiful, noisy, territorial beggars!

Gray Jay "perisoreus canadensis": Uncrested with shades of light gray except for a dark patch on the back of its head, Gray Jays live only at high altitudes, such as at Larch Mountain, actively and noisily seeking handouts.

Clark's Nutcracker "nucifraga columbiana": Only seen at high elevations, this large, noisy jay-like bird has a large bill, white face, gray head and body and striking black and white wings and tail. It makes an un-bird-like cracking or rasping sound.

Cedar Waxwing "": A very attractive bird with a striking crest, black eye stripe, yellow edge to the tip of the tail, and beautifully "air brushed" shades of beige overall. They eat fruits and berries. In Summer, they awkwardly catch flying insects on the wing. Their "song" is like a somewhat musical cricket or tree frog.

Crow "corvus brachyrhynchos": The crow is common nearly everywhere, though mostly in open areas at low elevations. It is big, bold, and black and says "caw".

Raven "corvus corax":Larger than a crow but very similar, the raven is distinguished by its loud, deep "gronk" call. Found in lonely locations at higher altitudes.

Black Capped Chickadee "parus atricapillus": A cheerful, friendly, perky little bird with its familiar "chick-a-dee-dee-dee" call. Common year round in brush and trees near trails, it is unmistakable with its black cap and chin, white cheeks and gray back.

Chestnut Backed Chickadee "parus rufescens": Very similar to its cousin but with a striking chestnut back and sides. Both species often hang out together.

White Breasted Nuthatch "sitta carolinensis": At first glance it's a chickadee. They're often seen together. Unlike chickadees, nuthatches are slender, lack the black chin, perch head down and tail up. They prefer deciduous or mixed woods year round.

Red Breasted Nuthatch "sitta canadensis": Preferring evergreen or mixed forests, the red breasted nuthatch is similar to its white breasted cousin but has a striking rosy breast and prominent black stripe through its eye. It is also a resident.

Winter Wren "troglodytes troglodytes": This very brave and friendly small bird of trail-side brush has a barred brown back and barred beige underside, and keeps its tiny tail cocked straight up. Although a resident, it is seen most often in Winter. If heard in Spring, it's cheerful song of rapid, high pitched, clear notes is a delight.

House Wren "troglodytes aedon": Larger than the Winter Wren but only here in warmer months, it is seen in sparse woods and wood margins. It has a lovely bubbling song and very aggressively guards its nest in a hole in a dead tree or birdhouse.

Bewick's Wren "thryomanes bewickii": Like the Winter wren, it is resident west of the Cascades. It is easily identified by its bright white eye stripe, its long white edged tail (rarely cocked up), its plain brown back, and white underside. Its song is also cheerful and melodious. It is most likely seen at field margins and fences but is rather shy.

Bushtit "psaltriparus minimus": This wonderful, gregarious, and friendly bird is nature's "no-see-em"! Little bigger than a humming bird, they move through trees and brush in flocks of twenty to a hundred, continuously chirping and singing to each other while hunting insects, seeds, and berries. You are surrounded by invisible birds so close you could touch one. In a moment, the sounds drift away like smoke, and they're gone—and you didn't see a bird! You may see a tiny, mouse colored bird with a long tail, so unconcerned it might land on your nose if you had a suitable bug on it!

Dipper "cinclus mexicanus": The dipper looks like a long legged, short tailed, drab robin perched on a rock in a creek. Suddenly, it walks off the rock into the rapids and disappears! Moments later it pops up and walks onto another rock. This bird feeds by walking under water in fast flowing streams and nests in mossy cracks behind waterfalls. It even walks straight up waterfalls! Nobody told the dipper what it should look like or how it should behave. In Spring, it even has a lovely wren-like song!

Swainson's Thrush "hylocichla ustulata": A Summer resident of the forest, this drab robin-like bird is rarely seen but identified by its unforgettable truly musical flute-like song which echoes through the forest, a rapid series of repeated rising phrases of pure tones, each in a higher key than the one before. Its sound is a forest Summer!

Hermit Thrush "hylocichla guttata": Similar to Swainson's except for its song, which is a long high note followed by a complicated series of rising and falling phrases.

Robin "turdus migratorius": You'll see these familiar birds year round in open areas. However, they aren't the same birds in all seasons. In Fall, robins migrate south, but the robins which Summer in the far north come to replace them. The process reverses in Spring. "Winter Robins" are lighter and eat berries and fruit instead of worms.

Varied Thrush "ixoreus naevius": Called "Alaska Robin" by natives, it winters in the Northwest. It is Robin-like with a beautiful orange and black pattern on the throat and breast and a striking facial pattern. Its call is a long, loud, beautiful flute-like note.

Warblers: Many species of warblers visit us in warmer months. They eat insects, high in the trees, sing well, and are strikingly colored with yellow makings on virtually all.

Brewers Blackbird "euphagus cyanocephalus": A friendly blackbird, seen at picnic areas. Males are iridescent with white eyes, females brown with brown eyes.

Red Winged Blackbird "agelaius phoeniceus": Seen on marshes, the coal black male is accented by yellow edged red shoulders. Females are a drab, streaked brown.

Oregon Junco "junco oreganus": A common, friendly resident in brush and woods. Despite considerable variations in color between individuals, all have a dark head and neck, pink beak, brown back, beige or pink sides, light belly, and white edged tail.

Song Sparrow "melospiza melodia": A resident, medium size, dark brown sparrow with streaked breast and a dark central chest spot, the Song Sparrow is most notable for its lovely canary-like song from the tops of small trees in sunny areas.

Fox Sparrow "passerella iliaca": Like a large song sparrow, even sharing its chest spot, it prefers to stay close to the ground and loves to scratch around under blackberries and in leaf piles. It is usually only seen in Spring and Summer.

White Crowned Sparrow "zonotrichia leucophrys": A year round resident, they are a large brown sparrow with a light, unstreaked under side and an obvious black and white striped head, who prefer sunny woods and brushy areas and often sing at night.

Yellow Crowned Sparrow "zonotrichia atricapilla": Seen only west of the Cascades in Winter, it is similar to the white crowned except for its yellow and black crown.

Mammals

Although Oregon has lots of big, scary critters, they are rarely seen. If you encounter one, remember: they're not cuddly pets; avoid them; remain calm; do not run; talk softly and back away slowly; never help "lost babies", their mom may object violently!

Note about Footprints: if you see toenails, its not a cat; four toenails, it's a canine; the pad indented at the top and twice at the bottom, a cougar or bob cat; three inches wide or more, a cougar; two inches or less, a bob cat.

Black Bear "urus americanus": So common and wide spread, Oregon hunters have taken 350 yearly for decades with no effect on population. They are often seen in Portland. In 1996, several bears were seen at Silver Falls State Park necessitating their relocation. We have never seen one in years of hiking. At 500 pounds, leave them alone! With poor eyesight but excellent hearing and smell, a soft noise will avoid surprising them. Startled bears act as crazy as startled people—not fun for you!

Cougar "felis concolor" (mountain lion, panther, puma): This shy predator is wide spread and occasionally seen in Portland. Weighing 225 pounds, they hunt deer and other medium size prey, Although a cougar could spoil your hike, you have little chance of seeing one and can scare it with a yell. In recent years, a couple of people (not in Oregon) were attacked and killed while running in wilderness areas, probably triggering the cougar's hunting reflex. More people are killed each year by hunters mistaking them for deer than attacked by cougars in the past 100 years! Moral: Don't look or act like deer! We found wet cougar prints at Sahalie Falls in June, 1996.

Bob Cat "lynx rufus": Looking like a very large house cat, this 13 to 35 pound feline is also very shy and rarely seen, but has a well deserved reputation if molested!

Coyote "canis latrans": You may only hear these very shy 44 pound "scraggly german shepherds" at sundown. Ironically, coyote elimination efforts have enormously increased both their range and their population. If encountered, leave them alone!

Raccoon "procyon lotor": A very common, cute, 45 pound nocturnal omnivore rarely seen while hiking. Leave them alone. They can make mincemeat of you or your dog.

Opossum "didelphis virginiana": Very common and expanding in range nationwide but rarely seen while hiking, this slow 13 pound marsupial has big teeth and can hurt you. They "play possum", another reason not to touch wild animals, alive or dead.

Striped Skunk "mephitis mephitis": Although rarely seen because of nocturnal habits, an encounter with a 12 pound skunk (which can bite and scratch in addition to squirting you with stinging, foul smelling perfume) will make you wish you'd met a bear!

Muskrat "ondatra zibethicus": A 3.5 pound dark brown aquatic rodent with a rat-like tail, living in dens of sticks and mud in ponds, in beaver dens, or in burrows.

Nutria "myocastor coypus": A large Muskrat-like 15 to 20 pound aquatic rodent, which have become pests since being introduced from South America as a source of fur. They dig burrows in banks and earthen dams and are most often seen at dusk.

Beaver "castor canadensis": One of the largest rodents at 30 to 50 pounds lives in small streams by dam building and large ones by digging burrows. Recognizable by their flat tail. Look for gnawed deciduous trees, especially willows, near water.

Mountain Beaver "aplodontia rufa" (also called Boomer): This 2 to 4 pound nocturnal rodent is tailless, eats grass and leaves, holds food with its "hands", and lives alone in deep burrows west of the Cascades. Look for them at Silver Falls State Park.

Pika "ochotona princeps" (also called Rock Rabbit): These six ounce, rat-sized diurnal rodents look like tiny, tailless rabbits with round ears. They live in large colonies in rocky places undisturbed by humans and communicate with distinctive loud chirps.

Marmot: This large, long haired rodent, the west's groundhog or woodchuck, lives in burrows in open and rocky areas at higher elevations. Its loud human-like whistled call may be your only contact with this solitary and shy creature.

Chipmunk: Common and widespread at all elevations and terrains, and often seen at campsites, this small, friendly, ground dweller is a delight. All have stripes on their faces and body and live on the ground rather than in trees like true squirrels.

Golden Mantled Ground Squirrel "spermophilus lateralis": You'll think it's a chipmunk but for its stripeless golden face. They are friendly and charming but found only at high elevations and east of the Cascades, sometimes in company with chipmunks.

California Ground Squirrel "spermophilus beecheyi": A large, gray-brown ground dweller with tiny light spots, common in drier areas along roads, farms, and fences

Douglas Squirrel (Chickaree): Named by naturalist, David Douglas, Native Americans called it "chickaree" for its call. It is the cutest creature in the woods, and the world's smallest true squirrel. Its back is dark brown but its underside is almost orange with a dark line between the two. It eats the cones of evergreens. Look for piles of cone scales under its perches. Chickarees descend huge fir trees in a kind of controlled fall. Their speed, agility and friendly fearlessness make them a real delight to watch.

Gray Squirrel: The common tree-dwelling, medium size squirrel of cities and farms, actually vary in color from light gray to reddish brown. Look in fruit and nut trees.

White Tail Deer "odocoileus virginianus": This deer of eastern U.S. is occasionally seen in the Northwest, especially near the Columbia. Their white tail display, smaller size, smaller ears, and horizontal "stem" antlers distinguishes them from Mule Deer.

Mule Deer: A large, common deer found throughout the Northwest, even in Portland. Its large "mule" ears, black tail, and the male's branched antlers separate them from White Tail Deer. We have come face to face with them when quietly rounding a bend.

Roosevelt Elk: This is the largest elk (or Wapiti) and second only to moose among deer. Over 5 feet at the shoulder and 650 pounds, it's bigger than most horses. With a shaggy neck and chest, a light rump, virtually no tail, and males with 6 foot antlers, Roosevelt Elk are found mostly in the Coast Range. We've seen them in Portland, at Horsetail Falls, the coast, and Jewell Meadows. Bulls can be very aggressive in Fall!

Rocky Mountain Elk: Similar to the Roosevelt Elk but smaller and found from the Cascades eastward. Unfortunately, the two species avoid posing for size comparisons and many elk are crosses due to repopulation attempts. Ask the elk which it is!

Reptiles

There are no poisonous snakes on the west (wet) side of the Cascades. Only the rattle snake is poisonous, and it is found in desert habitats east of the Cascades.

Garter Snake: Beautiful, harmless creatures with stripes, they are found everywhere. They emit an unpleasant smelling fluid when threatened, that causes predators to roll on them. If you handle them, you won't roll on them but your hands may smell bad.

Rattle Snake: Found in dry, desert areas east of the Cascades, they are quite shy and rarely seen. Rattle snakes are an overrated threat. In over 25 years, we've neither seen one nor heard of anyone even being hospitalized of snakebite in the Northwest!

Fish

The Pacific Northwest is famous for fish. Although most native species remain today, their numbers are a tiny fraction of their former abundance. Dams, logging, irrigation, and other human activities have devastated them. Today, sport and commercial fishermen, and Native Americans are left to fight for scraps of a once vast resource.

Trout: Several species of trout are found in cold, fast moving streams and cold lakes in the Northwest. Most common are the rainbow, brook, and brown (and steelhead?).

Steelhead: Rainbow Trout that go to sea and return to spawn, or another species? Lately, the "different species camp" lead. Steelhead migrate like salmon ("anadromous") but do not necessarily die after spawning. A popular Winter/Spring sport fish!

Coho Salmon: A salmon similar in size to steelhead and threatened with extinction. See them at Bonneville and in Multnomah Creek below the lodge at spawning time.

Chinook Salmon: The largest of the salmon. Found in streams throughout the Northwest and viewable at Bonneville. Their numbers are now severely depleted.

Sturgeon: The white sturgeon is either the world's largest freshwater fish or number two. The pioneers left only stories of hauling ashore huge sturgeons weighing tons with teams of horses. Some later photos show 16 foot, 2000 pound fish. Unfortunately, they ate all the big ones! Sturgeons wear a suit of armor, have no bones, suck up food with their huge, extensible mouth, and migrate unpredictably.

Lamprey: Eel-like, the lamprey is an ancient parasitic relative of the shark. They suck blood from fish with their round mouth full of teeth. Like salmon, they are anadromous. Sturgeon eat these ugly three foot critters. At migration, see them at Bonneville holding onto the windows with their mouths to inch their way upstream.

Invertebrates

Slugs: Slugs aren't our state animal! They vary from tiny to six inches long and come in a rainbow of colors, including brick red, bright yellow, green, and black. They fill an important ecological niche and shouldn't be harmed.

Snails: The rainforest so hospitable to slugs is also home to interesting relatives with shells. Look for them along streams and hiding on the forest floor.

Millipedes: The forest floor is the home of thousands of creatures. Millipedes don't have a thousand legs but can be three inches long, shiny black with a yellow spot next to each leg. They are charming and worthy of respect. Do not step on them!

Spiders: Like elsewhere, spiders are common in the Northwest. There are no truly poisonous ones on trails. Spiders are interesting but busy with their own work—eating people isn't a goal! The black widow and the brown recluse are found in houses!

Ticks: Less common than in many parts of the country, these critters spread Lime Disease and Rock Mountain Spotted Fever. Check around collars, pant and sleeve cuffs, in hair, and on pets for quarter inch black creatures with a round flat body clinging to you. If found, remove it by touching it with a hot match or dousing with alcohol. Immediately seek medical attention (and take the tick with you for analysis)!

Crayfish: Like miniature lobsters, these Cajun delicacies hide under rocks and prowl the bottom in virtually every stream and lake in the Northwest. With little meat, crayfish are more fun alive than in a pot. Gourmets may have alternative opinions.

Insects: From fascinating butterflies to giant beetles, the world of the insect can delight you. You will find few bothersome insects in the Northwest.

Mosquitoes: Despite Oregon's reputation for rain, the seasons are damp and cool in the Winter, dry and warm in the Summer. As a result, mosquitoes are less common.

Bees, Wasps, and Yellow Jackets: The half inch yellow jacket is the most likely to be bothersome. It likes dead animals, rotting fruit, and picnics. They are not interested in stinging but get angry if attacked. People who fear them run and swat at them resulting in being stung. Don't attract them and avoid looking or smelling like dead animals or rotting fruit! In other words, avoid perfume or hair spray, don't wear vivid colors or flower prints. They live in holes in the ground. Stay on the trail!

Wild Flowers & Plants

The American Rainforest is unrivaled by all but its tropical counterparts in the diversity, and beauty of its flora. Many species are found nowhere else on Earth. It also boasts most of the largest tree species in the world. Most of them are seen along the trails in this book.

Wildflowers

Rattlesnake Orchid "goodyera oblongifolia": This true orchid of the forest floor has three or four three inch dark green basal leaves with light stripes. In Spring, a thin six inch stem rises from the center with a row of tiny white orchid blossoms.

White Bog Orchid "habenaria dilatata": Found in marshes, this true orchid stands a yard tall with a spike of a couple of dozens of fragrant white flowers at the top.

Lady Slipper "cypripedium montanum": On top of a 30 inch vertical stem with leaves along it, waves a 2 inch orchid blossom with swollen white lip and thin dark petals. This is an amazing Lady Slipper orchid, beautiful, and rare. It dies when picked.

Calypso Orchid "calypso bulbosa": Also called Deer's Head, this wonderful miniature of the classic corsage orchid presents its one inch bright pink blossom with a speckled "lip" on an eight inch stem from a single leaf on the ground. It also dies if picked!

Indian Pipe "monotropa uniflora": A plant without chlorophyll or leaves, the indian pipe looks like a group of white or gray old fashioned clay pipes stuck in the ground.

Pinedrops "pterospora andromedea": A bazaar relative of indian pipe, it is totally bright reddish brown, stands straight up three feet with a shock of ball-like "drops".

Wild Delphinium "delphinium meziesii": Smaller and more delicate than its domesticated cousin, its showy head of blue flowers are delightful. Look for it on sunny trails.

Trillium "trillium ovatum": In March, woods are filled with thick, foot high stems topped by three large heart-shaped leaves and a single large, three petaled pure white flower gradually blushing pink to magenta. If you pick the leaves, it may die.

Avalanche Lily "erythronium montanum": A beautiful white flower with yellow center blooming May to June at high altitudes. Similar to Fawn and Glacier Lilies.

Glacier Lily "erythronium grandiflorum": Blooming in sunny places from March to June, this lily has strap-like light green basal leaves and delicate, nodding, 2 inch bright yellow blossoms with long, narrow, upcurved petals atop a foot high stem.

Fawn Lily "erythronium oregonum": These delicate lilies have two tapering leaves close to the ground from the center of which a thin stalk produces a delicate soft yellow or white downward facing bell of a flower three inches across with pointed petals.

Tiger Lily "lillium columbianum": Like miniature japanese lanterns, the orange blossoms of the wild tiger lily (or leopard lily) dangle from their 4 foot stems during July.

Camas Lily "camassia quamash": A delicate two foot lily with delft blue star-like flowers, found in large patches during June. The bulbs were a Native American staple.

Bead Lily "clintonia uniflora": Two bright green strap leaves are the foundation for a thin six inch stem which holds a large white flower with yellow stamens.

Chocolate Lily "fritillaria lanceolata": An amazing, rare, shy, and unusual lily with thin 10 inch narrow vertical leaves from which a tulip shaped brown flower nods. Wow!

Washington Lily "": Only found south of the Columbia, it stands up to six feet tall, supporting huge trumpet-like white, turning pink flowers. Endangered due to picking.

False Lily of the Valley "maianthemum dilatatum": Not actually Lily of the Valley, its leaves and flowers make its name obvious. Look for blooms in May in moist woods.

Hair Bells "campanula rotundiflolia": This plant is an insignificant clump of green filaments on a cliff. Some "hairs" end in a beautiful one inch by half inch, delft blue bell.

Fairy Bells "disporum hookeri oreganum": This shrub-like lily of the forest has three foot drooping stems of pairs leaves each with a one inch white bell-like flower in April.

Solomon Seal "smilacina racemosa": Long drooping stems of pointed, alternate leaves like fairy bells, end in a very aromatic plume of tiny white flowers late Spring.

Bear Grass "xerophyllum tenax": What a plant! Bear grass looks like miniature pampas grass. In the Spring, a large stalk grows two feet from its center and forms a bulbous head of sweet smelling tiny white flowers. It is abundant at high elevations.

Columbine "aquilegia formosa": Beautiful, complex one inch red-orange and yellow flowers hang like bells and dance in the breeze on a 2 to 3 foot high light green plant.

Lupine "lupine (various)": A widely distributed and greatly varied family, our lupines stand 2 feet high with fuzzy, gray-green, cut leaves and blue snapdragon-like flowers.

Stone Crop "sedum (various)": A "succulent" with fleshy leaves which grows on hot, dry, bare rocks and produces a large spray of bright yellow flowers on a tall stem.

Paintbrush "castilleja miniata": Widely found, in drier areas, it has narrow, 2 inch leaves projecting from a central stalk which grow bright red near its top.

Skunk Cabbage "lysichitum americanum": A harbinger of Spring, it is our giant, smelly daffodil. The spathe (like a giant calla lily) of bright yellow is nearly a foot tall. Its huge, broad, bright green leaves stick out of marshes throughout the region.

Monkey Flower "mimulus (various)": Found near water, all of the varieties have a few yellow snapdragon-like blossoms on short stems of medium green leaves.

Fox Glove "digitalis purpurea": An abundant, introduced plant transitioning from a delight to a weed. Found along roadways, foxglove grows to six feet with fuzzy gray-green leaves and a plume of pink tubular flowers. They contain poisonous "digitalis"!

Penstemon "penstemon (various)": Low growing plants with magenta, blue, purple, or white tube shaped flowers resembling stretched snapdragon—Common on rocks.

Colts Foot "petasites frigidus": One of the first plants in Spring, it is a 2 inch thick, six inch club opening as clusters of white flowers spreading to 12 inch deeply cut leaves.

Vanilla Leaf "achlys triphylla": Another early Spring resident of the forest floor, it sports only its one unique leaf and a shock of tiny white flowers suspended above.

Wild Bleeding Heart "dicentra formosa": A less colorful cousin of the domestic bleeding heart, look for its frilly light green leaves and its pink valentine heart flowers.

Dutchman's Breeches "dicentra cucullaria": A relative of Bleeding Heart, it has white flowers in April which resemble a row of ballooning long underwear on a clothesline.

Western Corydalis "corydalis scouleri": An over 3 foot plant with frilly, green leaves and a shock of pinkish-purple flowers, found in cool areas, like the Oneonta Gorge.

Shooting Star "dodecatheon (various)": A unique short plant of partial sunlight with brightly colored "inside-out flowers" shaped like darts with yellow rings above their black points. Flowers vary up to two inches with colors from white to deep red.

Bunchberry "cornus canadensis": It is a two inch high relative of the dogwood, with four leaves as a setting for a two inch white dogwood bloom leading to red berries.

Rough Wallflower "erysimum asperum": 2-4 feet tall with flat bright orange flowers.

Coast Manroot "marah oreganus": Its 30 foot long vines grow over brush in sunny, moist areas and look like cucumbers. It produces spiny green very astringent fruit.

Shrubs, Small Trees, and Large Weeds

Pacific Rhododendron "rhododendron macrophyllum": This ancestor of many domesticated rhododendrons with its showy pink flower trusses is widely found along roadsides and meadows with enough sunlight and water, especially in the mountains and at the coast.

Snowberry "symphoricarpos albus": One of many native plants now domesticated, it is a small shrub with round, snow white, inedible berries on thin, drooping branches.

Cow Parsnip "heracleum lanatum': Growing six feet with dinner plate-size deeply cut leaves, a giant Queen Ann's Lace-like flower head, and a two inch diameter stem, this perennial carrot on steroids fills the shady damp under-canopy of the rainforest.

Non-flowering Plants

Sword Fern — The envy of houseplants, sword ferns abound in the rainforest. They are evergreen, and healthy year round, with a cluster of two foot dark green fronds.

Deer Fern — Similar to sword fern but much smaller, with lighter green one foot long fronds which are less tapering.

Maidenhair Fern — My favorite! Found in continuously moist, shady places, especially around waterfalls, maidenhair ferns have glossy black leaf stems with broad fronds which are very soft and delicate. Maidenhair ferns are evergreen but very fragile.

Wood Fern — In Spring, light green stalks come out of the ground in shaded places and grow to four feet in height before opening into enormous, multi-branched fronds.

Parsley Fern — A very small curly-leafed fern found on hot, dry, sunny rock slides.

Moss — There are hundreds of varieties of mosses in the rainforest. Some look like miniature palm trees, like thick fern fronds, like dendrites, like fuzz, etc. In the Winter, mosses become so happy, they make the rainforest greener than it is in the Summer.

Mushrooms — The litter of the rainforest floor is home to great numbers of varieties of mushrooms. Because each kind "eats" only its own particular food, you will see different kinds near different kinds of plants. Although many are sought by gourmets, others can make you sick or even kill you! Do not eat wild mushrooms unless you are an expert! Poison mushrooms often taste good and wait days to make you sick!

Lichens — A primitive synergy of algae and fungus, lichens are usually gray and are found in many shapes clinging to rocks and branches, often looking like peeling paint or Spanish Moss (which doesn't live here and isn't moss). An oddity is "chrysothrix candelaris", a bright chartreuse powdery growth on cliffs near waterfalls. Lichen are now believed to contribute up to a third of the nitrogen (fertilizer) to the rainforest!

Liverworts (hepatics) — One of the lowest forms of multi-celled plants, they are found in damp, shaded areas and look like green 2-3 inch prostrate fern leaves.

Trees

Pacific Yew "taxus brevifolia": This endangered multi-trunked tree of the deep forest is virtually a big, dense shrub. It is recognized by dark green inch long flat needles, red peeling bark, and bright red fleshy fruit. It is the source of the cancer drug "taxol".

Western White Pine "pinus monticola": A giant of the Cascades, it grows to 180 feet and 4 foot diameter and has 3 inch light green needles and narrow 10 inch cones!

Sugar Pine "pinus lambertiana": Related to Western White Pine with two foot long cones, it is found in the southern Cascades reaching 200 feet and 5 foot diameter.

Ponderosa Pine "pinus ponderosa": The giant of the dry side of the Cascades, "yellow pine" has long, floppy needles, two-color bark, 180 foot high and 4 foot diameter.

Western Larch "larix occidentalis": One of the only deciduous (loses its leaves in the Fall) needled trees. Spring brings fresh, bright green needles. In Fall. needles turn bright yellow and drop. Up to 150 feet tall and 4 feet in diameter, at high altitudes.

Sitka Spruce "picea sitchensis": The coast giant has scaly gray bark, prickly needles, Douglas fir-like cones with no "tongues", 200 foot height and 6 foot diameter.

Western Hemlock "tsuga heterophylla": Though a giant, hemlock was considered virtually a weed. Its feathery boughs, short flat needles, miniature round cones, and nodding top branch are recognizable. It grows to 175 feet high and 5 foot diameter.

Douglas Fir "pseudotsuga menziesii": The third tallest tree on Earth. Look for deeply furrowed bark and forked "tongue" cones. It reaches 250 feet and 8 foot diameter.

Grand Fir "abies grandis": A stately fir tree with long, flat, light green needles, prefers more temperate and moist areas and grows up to 150 feet tall and 4 feet in diameter.

Pacific Silver Fir "abies amabilis": Another common true fir found in the higher forests of the Northwest and reaches 150 feet tall and 3 feet in diameter.

Noble Fir "abies procera": A popular Christmas tree which is found in mountainous regions and can grow up to 150 feet tall and 5 feet in diameter.

Subalpine Fir "abies lasiocarpa": A narrow-growing silver-blue tree which prefers high mountains up to timber line and grows to 100 feet. Look for its big vertical cones.

Western Red Cedar "thuja plicata": One of the largest tree in the world, this giant likes moist, cool areas. It not only lives for hundreds of years, its remarkable wood contains a chemical which can preserve a fallen log for additional hundreds of years.

Alaska Yellow Cedar "chamaecyparis nootkatensis": Resembling the Western Red Cedar, it lives east side of the Cascades and grows to 100 feet and 3 foot diameter.

Pacific Madrone "arbutus menziesii": A rhododendron-like broad-leaf evergreen with red, peeling to green, smooth bark, growing up to 100 feet tall and 4 feet in diameter.

Black Cottonwood "populus trichocarpa": Found in sunny places where they can get "their feet wet", cottonwoods have heart shaped leaves which are dark green above and silvery below which seem to "sparkle" in the breeze, and they produce "cotton".

Red Alder "alnus rubra": Very common on the wet side of the Cascades, look for its blotchy gray bark, tiny "cones", filbert-like catkins, and elm-like serrated leaves.

Pacific Dogwood "cornus nuttallii": Beautiful white blossoms on a 60 foot tree.

Big Leaf Maple "acer macrophyllum": Largest maple, to 100 feet with 12 inch leaves.

Vine Maple "acer circinatum": Like Japanese maples, these spindly forest residents have lacy leaves that are reddish in Spring and scarlet in Fall and grow to 40 feet.

Garry Oak "quercus garryana": Our only significant native oak is found on sunny, dry hillsides, frequently near poison oak and madrone trees. Garry oaks (also called Pacific white oaks) have large acorns, large oak leaves, and 70 foot height.

Cascara Buckthorn "rhamnus purshiana": A deciduous tree up to 40 feet with bright green, deeply veined leaves from whose bark is extracted an ingredient of laxatives.

To Eat

Blackberries "rubus (various)": Many native and introduced varieties thrive west of the Cascades. If it looks like a blackberry and tastes good, it's a blackberry. Eat!

Salmonberries "rubus spectabilis": A blackberry relative which grows more like upright canes than vines, has insignificant thorns, attractive large dark red blossoms, and luscious large orange blackberry-like fruit. Edible but tastes like weak Koolaid!

Thimble Berries "rubus parviflorus": This widespread rose and blackberry relative has large white "single rose" blossoms, large "maple" leaves, an upright stance, no thorns, and red cap-like fruit with an exquisite strawberry flavor. You'll love them!

Huckleberries, Red: Not a "true" Huckleberry, this widespread shrub of the rainforest has tiny red berries with a bright, thirst quenching citrus flavor. Recognized by its green branches and stems, small round leaves, and tiny translucent round red berries.

Huckleberries, Black "vaccinium membranaceum": Bigger and far more flavorful than their cousin, the blueberry, this is one of the secrets of the rainforest! Found in dappled shade at middle to high elevations, this deciduous shrub can be abundant.

Salal "gaultheria shallon": A common and widespread broad-leaf evergreen with shiny leaves which produces long trusses of tiny vase-shaped white flowers from which large black blueberry-like fruit develop. The berries are reasonably tasty but bland.

Wild Strawberry "fragaria (various)": Another family of berry that thrives all over western Oregon. If the leaves and fruit look like strawberries, eat all you can find!

Oregon Grape "berberis nervosa": The state flower of Oregon has leaves like holly arranged along branchlets but topped by bunches of small ball-like yellow flowers which become small purple fruit. Its edible but very tart fruit will quench your thirst.

Red Currant "ribes sanguineum": A small shrub with drooping clusters of very attractive small bright pink blossoms with white centers, which blooms on sunny slopes in early Spring. Its a favorite of Hummingbirds. The small red fruit are tart but tasty.

Elderberry "sambucus (various)": Several varieties of this tall, spindly shrub are found along roadsides, including red, blue and black. All have clusters of tiny white flowers followed by bunches of tiny fruit at the ends of long branches. Used in jam and wine.

Nootka Rose "rosa (various)": A large variety of wild roses abound. Though most have small white or pink blossoms, some have significant flowers. Look for them along sunny trails. The outside of the "hips" have a delicious citrus/orange flavor.

Wild Ginger "asarum caudatum": Large glossy but hairy heart shaped leaves identify this forest floor dwelling herb. A leaf will refresh your mouth with its ginger flavor.

Miner's Lettuce "montia perfoliata": A small, bright green "weed" of the forest floor with attractive, small, white flowers. Has a tasty lettuce-like flavor in tossed salads.

To Avoid

Stinging Nettle "urtica dioica": A 2 to 8 foot annual plant with three inch triangular serrated leaves and strange worm-like flowers and seeds dangling from its upright stem. It is found in moist, sunny places such as the Latourell Falls trail. It is covered with tiny hairs which, like sea anemones, inject poison into anything touching them. When touched, you immediately feel intense pain and itching. Stay on the trail!

Devils Club "oplopanax horridum": Resembling Cow Parsnip, this deciduous woody plant is one of the most unpleasant anywhere. Nearly every inch of it is covered with long, straight, needle-like thorns. An encounter with devils club is truly memorable!

Poison Oak "rhus divirsiloba" & "rhus radicans": As feedback for nature's "Stay on the Trail" program, poison oak offers slow but long lasting instruction. Shiny bright green (red in Fall) three-part leaves on low shrubs or tall vines in sunnier, drier locations, poison oak exudes an oil which produces an uncomfortable itching rash within hours. Washing immediately after contact may save you.

The Chinook Language

The Chinook are a Native American people who lived along the Columbia River.

Long before the arrival of Europeans, the Columbia was already the great trade route of the Northwest. As today, it linked the coast and lush valleys with the mountains and prairies to the east. The Chinook controlled the area from the "pinch point" of the gorge to the mouth of the river, through which raw materials and manufactured goods were traded as far away as the Atlantic. The extent of this trade was not understood by the newcomers. An early example was the hatchet made at the Mandan village on the Missouri by the blacksmith on the Lewis and Clark expedition which was discovered already in use by the Nez Perce when they arrived in Idaho.

During the salmon migrations, all tribes gathered at Celilo Falls in a "United Nations" of languages and customs, continuing until 1957 when The Dalles Dam flooded it.

Chinook was the "lingua franca" and the source of botanical and geographic names. When members of different tribes conversed, they often spoke Chinook. It became an amalgam of languages including French, English and many Native American ones.

Due to the sense of humor of native peoples, naivete of the newcomers, and their difficulty in spelling and pronouncing native words, this "Chinook Dictionary" should be taken with a dose of salt! Notice below "cow", "heart", "laughter", and "talk".

Examples of the Chinook Language or "Jargon":

arrow	=	kaleetan	friendly people	=	tillicum	sandy	=	polallie
aunt	=	kwolh	friendly spirit	=	tamanawas	sea	=	wecoma
bear	=	itswoot	graceful	=	tokatee	seven	=	sinamox
beaver	=	ee-na	hair (head)	=	yakso	six	=	taghum
berries	=	olallie	hair or grass	=	tipsoo	sky	=	koosah
blanket	=	sisi	half	=	sitkum	small	=	tenas
by and by	=	winapee	heart	=	tumtum	stone	=	calamet
carry (v)	=	lolo	hidden	=	ipsoof	strawberry	=	amato
circle (ring)	=	kweo	high	=	sahalie	swan	=	waluga
crooked	=	kiwa	hole	=	klawhop	sweet	=	camas
cow	=	moosmoos	horse	=	ikiuatan	swift	=	hyak
coyote	=	talapus	land or earth	=	illahe	talk	=	wawa
coyote god	=	speelyai	laughter or fun	=	hehe	three	=	klone
crazy	=	pelton	middle	=	katsuk	tub	=	tamolitch
cup or bowl	=	ooskan	mountain	=	lemili	two	=	mokst
cut off	=	klak	no or none	=	wake	uncle	=	tot
die	=	memaloose	none (little)	=	halo	water	=	chuck
downstream	=	mi-mie	one	=	ikt	water (stream)	=	wah
elk	=	moolack	otter(river)	=	ne-nam-ooks	weed	=	champoeg
evil spirit	=	skookum	oyster	=	hetlo	whale	=	ecoli
far off	=	si-ah	place to sleep	=	ne moosum	wild	=	lemolo
five	=	kwinnum	razor clam	=	ona	wolf	=	leloo
fly (v)	=	kewak	red	=	pilpil	woman	=	kloochman
four	=	lockit	robber	=	klickitat	woodpecker	=	kokostick
friend	=	sikhs	round	=	lo-lo			

By Spring of the Lewis and Clark's stay near Astoria, the sophisticated visitors had traded away most of their valuables, uniforms, and tools, to the hard bargaining Native Americans. When they left, they were so broke that against all their own rules, they stole a canoe and lied to the tribe in order to make their way upstream.

An example of the Northwest Native Americans' sense of humor, especially about their language, is a story we first heard from several members of the Colville tribe, a version of which was later dramatized on the TV show, *Northern Exposure*:

In the 1700s, two Jewish traders visited the Colvilles. During a protracted stay, including offspring, they taught the tribe some English and a lot of Yiddish. Generations later when the first government land surveyors arrived, they urged the tribe to teach them their language. For fun, the Colvilles substituted obscenities and yiddish, all of which the white men memorized and wrote down. The fun came when the surveyors tried using their new knowledge. Thus, when they ate together, one might think he said, "Pass the salt", when he had actually said "Pass the elk droppings" causing the natives to roll on the floor with laughter. The puzzled whites would simple be told, "It was your *accent*"! Somewhere in Washington, D.C. is an amazing dictionary! Of course, this story itself may only be a joke!

Reservations & Info

National Campsite Reservations and
  Information (Natl. Parks & Forests)
  (800) 280-2267
Oregon Bed & Breakfast Guild
  (800)944-6196
Oregon Highway Conditions
  (541) 889-3999
Oregon Lodging Association
  (800) 547-7842
Reservations Northwest (for state parks
  in Oregon & Washington)
  (800) 452-5687
Reservations Northwest Information
  (for fishing, attractions, hiking, etc.)
  (800) 233-0321
Snow/Avalanche Information—Oregon
  (503) 808-2400
Snow/Avalanche Info—Washington
  (206) 526-6677
Trail Info—Nature of the Northwest
  Portland, OR 97232
  (503) 872-2750
Washington Highway Conditions
  (888) 766-4636

For More Info

Albany Visitors Association
  Albany, OR 97321
  (541) 928-0911; (800) 526-2256
Astoria/Warrenton Area Cmbr. of Comm.
  Astoria, OR 97103
  (503) 325-6311; (800) 875-6807
Audubon Society
  Portland, OR 97210
  (503) 292-6855
Barlow Ranger District
  Dufur, OR 97021
  (541) 467-2291
Bear Springs Ranger District
  Maupin, OR 97037
  (541) 328-6211
Blue River Ranger District
  Blue River, OR 97413
  (541) 822-3317
Bonneville Dam Visitor Center
  Cascade Locks, OR 97014-0150
  (503) 374-8820
Clackamas Ranger District (Ripplebrook)
  Estacada, OR 97023
  (503) 630-4256
Columbia Gorge Ranger District
  Troutdale, OR 97060
  (503) 622-3191
Columbia River Gorge Natl. Scenic Area
  Hood River, OR 97301
  (541) 386-2333
Columbia River Gorge Visitors Assn.
  The Dalles, OR 97058
  (800) 984-6743

Detroit Ranger District
  Mill City, OR 97360
  (503) 854-3366
Eugene Convn. & Visitors Assn. Lane Co.
  Eugene, OR 97440
  (541) 484-5307; (800) 547-5445
Estacada/Clackamas River Chamber
  Estacada, OR 97023
  (503) 630-3483
Estacada Ranger District
  Estacada, OR 97023
  (503) 630-6861
Gifford Pinchot National Forest
  Vancouver, WA 98682
  (360) 891-5000
Hood River County Chamber of Comm.
  Hood River, OR 97031
  (541) 386-2000; (800) 366-3530
Hood River Ranger District
  Mt. Hood-Parkdale, OR 97041
  (541) 352-6002; Portland: 666-0701
Lowell Ranger District
  Lowell, OR 97452
  (541) 937-2129
Marine Park Visitor Center
  Cascade Locks, OR 97014
  (503) 374-8427
McKenzie Ranger District
  McKenzie Bridge, OR 97413
  (541) 822-3381
Mt. Adams Ranger District
  Trout Lake, WA 98650
  (509) 395-3400
Mt. Hood Information Center
  Welches, OR 97067
  (503) 622-7674
Mt. Hood National Forest
  Sandy, OR 97055
  (503) 668-1700
Mt. St. Helens Natl. Volcanic Monument
  Amboy, WA 98601
  (360) 247-3900
Mt. St. Helens Visitor Center
  Castle Rock, WA 98611
  (360) 274-2100
Multnomah Falls Information Center
  Troutdale, OR 97060
  (503) 695-2376
Nature Conservancy
  Portland, OR 97210
  (503) 228-9561
Nature of the Northwest Info Center
  Portland, OR 97232
  (503) 872-2750
North Santiam Cmbr. of Comm. Info Cntr.
  Mill City, OR 97360
  (503) 897-2865
Oakridge Ranger District
  Westfir, OR 97492
  (541) 782-2291
Oregon Outdoors Association
  (800) 747-9552

Reference   **Page 247**

Oregon Parks & Recreation Commission
Salem, OR 97310
(503) 731-3411; (800) 452-5687

Oregon Tourism Commission
Salem, OR 97310
(800) 547-7842

Packwood Ranger District
Packwood, WA 98361
(360) 494-0600

Port of Cascade Locks Visitors Center
Cascade Locks OR 97014
(541) 374-8619

Portland Visitors Center
Portland, OR 97209
(503) 275-9750; 228-9411

Randle Ranger District
Randle, WA 98377
(360) 497-1100

Rigdon Ranger District
Oakridge, OR 97463
(541) 782-2283

Salem Convention & Visitors Association
Salem, OR 97301
(503) 581-4325; (800) 874-7012

Sandy Chamber of Commerce
Sandy, OR 97055
(503) 668-4006

Silverton Area Chamber of Commerce
Silverton, OR 97381
(503) 873-5615

Skamania County Chamber of Comm.
Stevenson, WA 98648
(509) 427-8911

Sweet Home Chamber of Commerce
Sweet Home, OR 97386
(541) 367-6186

Sweet Home Ranger District
Sweet Home, OR 97386
(541) 367-5168

Tillamook Chamber of Commerce
Tillamook, OR 97141
(503) 842-7525

Vista House Crown Point State Park
Corbett, OR 97019
(503) 695-2230

Washington County Visitors Association
Beaverton, OR 97005
(503) 644-5555; (800) 537-3149

Willamette National Forest
Eugene, OR 97401
(541) 465-6521

Wind River Ranger District
Carson, WA 98610
(509) 427-3200

Zigzag Ranger District
Zigzag, OR 97049
(503) 622-3191

Zigzag Visitor Center
Welches, OR 97067
(503) 622-5741

Emergency Numbers

For true Emergencies, always dial 911 regardless of your location.
It is toll-free even from pay phones. For non-emergency problems, call the appropriate number below:

AAA (American Automobile Association)
(800) 222-4357

Benton County Sheriff
Corvallis, Oregon
(541) 757-6911

Clackamas County Sheriff
Oregon City, Oregon
(503) 655-8218

Clark County Sheriff
Vancouver, Washington
(360) 699-2211

Clatsop County Sheriff
Astoria, Oregon
(503) 325-2061

Hood River County (Oregon) Sheriff
Hood River, Oregon
(541) 386-2711

Klickitat County Sheriff
Goldendale, Washington
(509) 773-4547

Lane County Sheriff
Eugene, Oregon
(541) 687-4150

Linn County Sheriff
Albany, Oregon
(541) 967-3911

Marion County Sheriff
Salem, Oregon
(503) 588-5032; (800) 606-4460

Multnomah County Sheriff
Portland, Oregon
(503) 230-2121

Skamania County Sheriff
Stevenson, Washington
(509) 427-9490

Tillamook County Sheriff
Tillamook, Oregon
(541) 842-2561

Wasco County Sheriff
The Dalles, Oregon
(541) 296-5454

Washington County Sheriff
Hillsboro, Oregon
(503) 629-0111

Yamhill County Sheriff
Newberg, Oregon
(503) 538-7302

Index   **Page 251**

Post Script: This drawing is scanned directly from Barbara's little pocket sketch pad in which she makes her preliminary sketches in the field (and often in the rain). One remarkable day, we were whizzing east on Interstate 84 when, as we passed Horsetail Falls, we saw this huge bull elk right in line with the falls. I slammed on my brakes and pulled onto the shoulder where we sat for a few minutes while Barbara sketched the image in her little, beat-up pad. The artist at work! When we arrived at Horsetail Falls, we discovered dozens of excited people trying frantically to find a vantage point from which they too could watch the elk. Incidentally, if you were the poor person driving behind me...I'm sorry that I scared you half to death!

Nature's Monuments

I've never seen the Parthenon
Or toured the gardens of Versailles
But here before this waterfall
I've witnessed wonders greater still.

The pyramids the Pharaohs built
Colossus, lighthouse, or the Minotaur
Are only manmade imitations
Of nature's works right here.

Colophon (how this book was produced): Apple Macintosh II-SI and Apple PowerMac G3 computers, Apple Trinitron color monitors, Microtek E6 scanner, SyQuest 44MB and 1.5GB cartridge drives, Adobe Photoshop, Adobe Illustrator, Quark XPress. All design, typesetting, scanning, etc. performed by the authors and publishers. Waterfall drawings were done at 9"x12" size, then scanned into Photoshop, adjusted and imported at reduced size into the Quark Document. The completed Quark file with its included graphics files (totaling more than 600MB) was output to film at 3,000dpi on a PostScript™ imagesetter and printed in the United States with metal plates on a sheet fed offset press on high quality recycled paper. The cover art is two oil paintings by Barbara which were photographed by Garry with a Nikon 35mm camera. The photos were scanned, adjusted, and composited in a Quark file like the main portion of the book.